CONTENTS

D1368376

Back to Basics

Part 1: *Chris Graham gets to the heart of the matter, with a look at engine basics.*

Whether you own a Ferrari 550, a Ford Mondeo 1.8i 16v or a Reliant Robin three-wheeler, your car's heart is its engine – a muscular structure packed with valves, pipes and fluids that all work in harmony to breath life into the machine. Engines may seem impossibly complicated nowadays but strip away all the bolt-on goodies and modern electronic control systems, and you're left with a basic design, which has altered little in the past 60 years.

In its simplest form, the internal combustion engine is a device used to burn fuel and convert the energy produced into a useful and controllable mechanical action. Modern petrol engines rely on a clever operating sequence called the four-stroke cycle – the Microsoft Office of the automotive world! This system governs the way the engine's internals operate, and ensures that it will continue to run while there is fuel to be burnt.

Trying to describe how an engine works is rather like attempting to explain why the earth orbits the sun – there are simple bits, complicated bits and a good deal in between. Combustion is perhaps the key moment in the four-stroke cycle, because it's this that generates the output power. Fuel and air are mixed in carefully controlled proportions (normally around 15:1) and drawn into the cylinder by a partial vacuum created as the piston drops. This movement is controlled by the crankshaft, which works rather like the pedals on a bicycle. The piston's up and down, or reciprocating, action is produced by the rotation of the crankshaft. Most engines nowadays have at least four pistons, all of which are

Modern engines look daunting, but innards are much the same as ever.

TOP: Crankshaft converts reciprocating into rotary motion.
MIDDLE: Connecting rods link pistons with crankshaft.
BOTTOM: Valves allow fuel mixture in and spent gas out of cylinder.

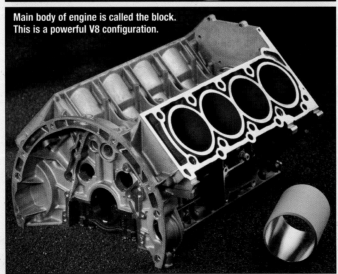

Main body of engine is called the block. This is a powerful **V8** configuration.

joined to the single crankshaft by con rods. The crankshaft itself is designed so that the pistons are raised and lowered in a precise sequence and we'll look at this in more detail later in the series.

The pistons move up and down within finely machined cylinder bores, and it's the total volume of these which gives an engine its capacity, measured in cubic centimetres or, more commonly these days, litres. Screwed into the top of each cylinder is the spark plug, which is essentially nothing more than a hefty electrode used to spark the fuel/air mixture into life. On either side of the spark plug are the cylinder valves – sometimes two, sometimes more. These carefully controlled, spindly mushroom-like components are used to regulate the flow of mixture into and out of the cylinder and, therefore, perform a crucial role in the whole process.

One of the keys to a petrol engine's success lies in its ability to compress the fuel/air mixture efficiently. Squeezing the mixture into a small space causes its temperature to rise, making it more readily combustible. It's the piston's job to provide this compression as it rises up the cylinder and, to do this, it must form a gas-tight seal with the cylinder wall. This is ensured thanks to a number of sprung metal rings that sit in machined grooves around the piston, neatly filling any gap that may exist. Once the piston reaches the top of its upward stroke, a position known as 'top dead centre' (TDC), compression will be at its maximum and the mixture is then ready for ignition.

The spark, supplied to the plug via the car's ignition system, sets the mixture on fire and the rate at which it burns is another important factor. For the best results, it must be a controlled burn rather than a violent and potentially damaging explosion. The great increase in pressure caused by the burning mixture forces the piston back down the cylinder to create what's known as the power stroke. This burst of force is channeled down the con rod, into the crankshaft and out of the engine to the gearbox, after which it's transmitted to the driven wheels.

Of course, as with everything else in life, good timing is vital if an engine is to perform well. Even the simplest of motors is a wonder to behold when it's running sweetly. We've already mentioned that the piston creates the compression necessary for combustion but it can't do this without the co-operation of the valves. The effective control of these cylinder entry and exit points is essential for efficient running. Even slight discrepancies in their timing can wreak havoc with performance. If, for example, the inlet valve fails to close as the piston rises, then compression will be lost and the prospects for combustion scuppered. Likewise, if the exhaust valve opens a fraction too early, then unburnt mixture will leak out with the same result.

Clearly, then, the valves have to be precisely timed in relation to the movement of the pistons, to guarantee smooth and powerful running. This is achieved by linking their operation directly to the rotation of the crankshaft. The valves themselves are controlled by the camshaft, which is, essentially, a straight piece of metal rod with a number of oval-shaped lobes

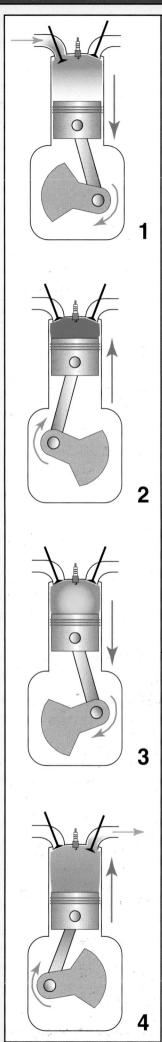

1

2

3

4

Four-stroke cycle

To understand the four-stroke cycle you must break it down into its constituent parts. These are illustrated in the diagram and, working from the top, consist of:
1. **Induction**
2. **Compression**
3. **Power**
4. **Exhaust**
or, more graphically, suck, squeeze, bang and blow!

On the induction stroke, the piston drops and the inlet valve is opened by the camshaft allowing the combustion mixture from the inlet manifold to fill the low-pressure area inside the cylinder. The amount of mixture drawn in depends on variables including; valve size and lift, air filter type and inlet manifold design.

The compression stroke involves the piston moving back up the cylinder, once the inlet valve has been closed, to force the mixture into the combustion chamber immediately under the spark plug at the top of the cylinder.

The power stroke begins when the high voltage spark from the plug ignites the compressed mixture and the rapid increase in temperature and pressure forces the piston back down towards the bottom of the cylinder.

The exhaust stroke concludes the cycle as the piston returns back up the cylinder, once the exhaust valve has been opened, to expel the spent gas.

spaced along its length. These act on the tops of the valve stems to open and close the valves as the camshaft is rotated. It's an ingeniously simple solution to a complex timing problem, and the camshaft's speed of rotation is governed by a notched rubber-

timing belt that links it positively to the crankshaft. Toothed drive gears on the ends of both shafts – the one on the camshaft normally has twice as many teeth as that on the crankshaft – allow the two to be perfectly synchronised.

One other important function of the timing belt is to provide drive for the distributor. This is the component that sorts out exactly when voltage pulses are sent to each spark plug and, as you can imagine, the correct timing of this is absolutely fundamental as well. So, in many ways, the humble timing belt is the unsung hero of the motorcar as it links and synchronises the three primary control functions of the engine.

Unfortunately, the belt's image becomes decidedly less heroic when it fails, and the engine is thrown into destructive disarray. Breakage can be caused by a number of factors – stone and debris damage, oil contamination – but perhaps most common among these is neglect. The belt is a service item, which needs to be replaced at regular intervals, (refer to this month's Technical Topic) and owners ignore this task at their peril.

An additional consequence of the internal combustion process, apart from the power produced, is the generation of excessive amounts of heat. Unfortunately, this is essentially wasted energy that's lost to the environment via the exhaust and the engine's cooling system. In fact, it might surprise you to learn that just about 50% of the energy put into an engine is lost in this way, so understanding and controlling 'thermal efficiency' is an important area for research. At a practical level, though, temperature is a bit of a double-edged sword. Left to its' own devices, any engine will quickly overheat and become seriously damaged if an effective cooling system isn't used. On the other hand, overall running

The fuel/air mixture burns in a very controlled and progressive manner inside the cylinder, as this sequence illustrates.

temperatures need to be kept high (ideally about 120°C) to maximise operational efficiency and minimise nasty exhaust emissions. Warm-up times should be minimal too, to reduce mechanical wear and toxic gas production. So, in a nutshell, an engine should run at a constantly high but very carefully controlled temperature, and it should reach this in the shortest possible time.

The most effective way to keep engine temperatures in check remains the cooling effect of water. Heat, having been transferred to the liquid as it's pumped around the engine, is then dissipated to atmosphere via the radiator. But water isn't the only coolant used in a modern engine; oil plays a vital role too. Actually, just about 40% of engine cooling is undertaken by the lubrication system as it works to smooth the motor's running and minimise mechanical wear and tear. On a modern engine, only about a third of the total oil volume is being pumped around the engine on lubrication/cooling duties at any one time. The rest sits in the sump, found at the bottom of the engine, and enjoys the cooling effect of airflow as the car moves. In cases where this natural 'wind chill' is insufficient as a cooling device, designers fit specific oil coolers.

TECHNICAL TOPIC: *Cambelt swap*

We've already mentioned the importance of changing the cambelt at the manufacturers' recommended interval, to avoid the disastrous damage caused when a tired belt eventually gives up the ghost, as it inevitably will. Tackling this job yourself is a viable proposition on simpler applications, but the prospects do become increasingly remote the larger and more specialised the engine becomes.

So, to provide some expert guidance on the basics involved in a typical swap, we enlisted the help of automobile engineering lecturer Eddie Smith at the Colchester Institute, together with a couple of his young students and a willing 1991 Ford Sierra 2.0-litre.

1 The cambelt is hidden behind a protective cover at the front of the engine, and gaining access to it involves stripping away the radiator, its cooling fan and the V-belt from the alternator drive by slackening its slide (inspect the belt for signs of wear and cracking). The coolant will have to be drained and we advise that this is done with the engine cool to avoid the risk of burns. Remove the crankshaft pulley also.

2 The viscous fan coupling is secured with a left-hand thread and requires an impact to release it. Ford produce a special tool for this job although the college has made its own which, with the help of a hammer, worked just as well. When replacing the fan never over-tighten the securing bolt otherwise it'll be nigh on impossible to get off next time!

3 Once the timing cover has been removed it's important to make sure the engine is set at TDC, by turning the crankshaft pulley bolt so that the mark on the pulley rim lines up with that on the block flange.

4 Ensuring that the engine is set at TDC and firing on number one cylinder is an important operation because, once the belt's off, you need a point of reference so that the new one goes on correctly. Double-check this using the mark on the distributor body. The rotor arm should be point towards this notch, indicating that it's at No.1 cylinder's firing point.

5 Plus, there will normally be a timing mark to check on the camshaft's timing wheel.

6 Removing the cambelt is then simply a matter of loosening its tensioning wheel and lifting it clear. Once it's off make a careful inspection for signs of oil contamination. The belt should be completely dry and if you find signs of oil spray then this is bad news because the leak – most likely from one of the seals or valve cover gasket, at the front of the engine – will have to be put right. Oil is one of the most effective killers of cambelts so be sure there are no leaks before fitting a replacement.

7 Also take time to assess the condition of the idler wheel, which tensions the cambelt, by rotating it by hand. If you detect any 'notchiness' then this will indicate bearing failure. Again, wear here must be put right before fitting the new belt otherwise its service life will become unpredictable.

8 When fitting a new belt it is important to adopt the correct method. First feed it in around the crankshaft pulley and then, keeping the belt tensioned as you work, fit it round the auxiliary drive wheel and then up on to the camshaft drive-wheel, maintaining the tension as you work. If all is well, the belt's teeth should mesh perfectly with the camshaft's wheel. With the belt correctly routed, temporarily secure the tensioner and check the belt tension by hand using the twist method. If, at the midway point on the drive side, you can comfortably twist more than 90°, then the tension is too low. If alternatively it's hard to get much beyond 45°, then it's too tight.

9 The professional approach to assessing the tightness is to use a belt-tensioning gauge. However, before making your final check, rotate the engine, using a spanner or socket on the crankshaft pulley nut, through 720°. Having done this, check the timing marks once again to make sure that the engine is still at TDC, and that nothing was knocked out of alignment during the fitting stage. If it has been, you must remove the belt, correct the alignment and try again.

10 Once all is positioned to your satisfaction, set the tension using a suitable lever while you lock the tension wheel into place. Make one final tension check before beginning the re-assembly.

TOP TIPS

● Some modern engines are fitted with 'stretch bolts' securing the crank pulley. These are not reusable and will not re-tighten correctly if you try.

● The torque of the crank pulley securing bolt is very important. It is essential to get this accurately set, using a torque wrench.

● Always check ignition timing once a new belt has been fitted. Slight variations in manufacturing tolerances can result in alterations sufficient to cause significant engine performance variations.

TOOLKIT BUILDER:
Socket set

One of the most important things to buy when putting together your first toolkit is a socket set. The choice is enormous, as is price variation, but there are a number of commonsense pointers which you should bear in mind before parting with your cash.

As a general rule it makes sense to buy the cheapest comprehensive set you can find. This may sound like a recipe for disaster but it's not. Unless you're going to give the sockets serious amounts of use, a cheap and cheerful box full will be fine. In reality, most DIYers find that they only use a handful of items out of the set anyway so it makes sense, once you have discovered which these are, simply to replace the bargain basement originals with something more expensive.

One of the most fundamental choices to be made concerns drive size. The common automotive options are ¼in, ⅜in and ½in, but you might need to buy bigger if you're into heavy-duty work on military vehicles or classic commercials. The choice between the main three largely depends on the type of work you do most. While a ½in drive set will certainly provide the necessary brawn for dealing with most automotive jobs, it can lack subtlety with more fiddly tasks. By and large, ½in sockets are much chunkier, so access can sometimes be a problem.

You can buy converters, which allow smaller-drive sockets to be used with larger-drive ratchets and bars, but, the danger with this approach is that overloading the socket may become a serious risk, particularly if you're working with budget-priced kit.

The only practical guide a buyer has about manufacturing quality tends to be the price, which isn't really a lot of help as this can vary so dramatically! Strength is linked directly to the quality of the steel alloy used by the manufacturer, but nobody is

going to tell you about that either. In terms of finish, the three basic options are; plated, non-coated and 'industrial'. Plating, unless it's of the highest standard, is likely to crack and peel off, which is irritating and even unpleasant as the slivers can be sharp. The non-coated variety look more classy and professional and their 'naked' finish leaves nothing to the imagination in terms of quality of finish/casting etc. The dark-coloured 'industrial' products may look grim but they will work just as well and are far less attractive to thieves!.

I mentioned at the start that buying a big set was a good idea and, generally, it is. However, take a bit of time to consider what's actually in the set before

you splash that cash. Remember, unless you are working on much older vehicles, there is little point in shelling out for a shiny row of Imperial sockets. Likewise, Whitworth applications went out with the ark so, unless you're into classic British motorcycles or industrial plant, forget these too.

Another point of interest is that most sockets will either have a six or a 12-point design – relating to the number of sides you can see inside the socket's rim. Most manufacturers nowadays produce 12-point sockets as these are thought to be generally easier and quicker to locate. But they are not necessarily better. A six-pointer will be far better at dealing with a rounded-off nut, and it'll usually be a good deal stronger too because the turning load is being spread over a larger surface area.

A more modern alternative is the 'flank-drive' socket that is designed with semi-circular lugs, which grip on to the faces of the nut, rather than its corners.

Socket sets need not be in their first flush of youth – older sets like this one perform just as well as something brand new from the motorist discount store. Note the breaker-bar in this box – a handy yet under-used component as many prefer the convenience of using the ratchet instead. The most commonly used sockets for general-purpose vehicle work nowadays are 13mm, 17mm and 19mm.

Size does matter with socket sets! This neat ¼in system is great for fiddly, limited-access work.

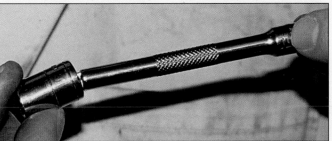
A clever and relatively recent arrival is the 'wobble bar' fitting which allows the socket to articulate while maintaining a positive and secure drive.

Next Month
The cylinder head.

Expert assistance
Colchester Institute has a large Automobile Engineering Centre which provides part-time (one day per week) and full-time courses in automobile engineering, body repair and welding. For more information contact:
Dave Roberts
Head of Centre for Automobile Engineering, Colchester Institute, Sheepen Road, Colchester, CO3 3LL.

One simple and practical test of quality is the ease with which the sockets can be fitted to and removed from the drive.

Cheap ratchets will have a very limited service life, so it makes sense to invest in something more expensive which will hopefully last longer.

Six-point (left) versus 12-point – you're balancing usability against effectiveness and strength.

Remember that you can always buy one-off sockets for specialist jobs. Boot fairs and secondhand shops can provide rich pickings.

Back to Basics

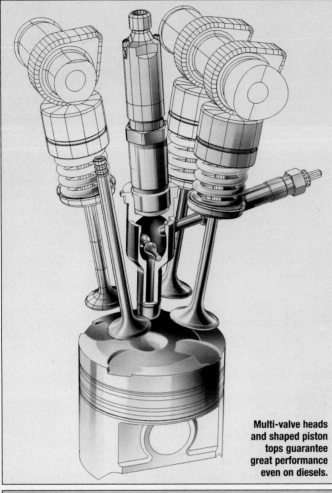

Multi-valve heads and shaped piston tops guarantee great performance even on diesels.

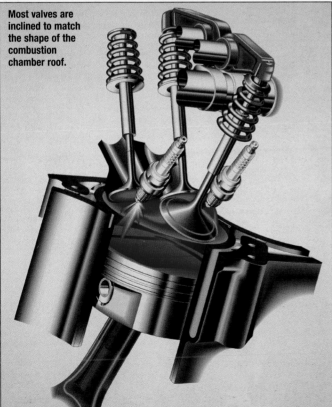

Most valves are inclined to match the shape of the combustion chamber roof.

Part 2:
Chris Graham investigates the intricacies of the cylinder head and its function.

We've all played with balloons at birthday parties I'm sure and, with young eyes, wondered at their ability to spin off upwards as the air inside is released slowly but noisily. Of course, it's the controlled way in which the pressurised air is let out – through the crude nozzle – that causes the balloon to fly. While releasing it more quickly, by bursting the balloon, creates a sudden, erratic movement and an exciting bang, all control is lost. An internal combustion engine manages air pressure in rather the same way, although the end result is different, and even more exciting!

Pressure management is a vital function for any petrol engine, in fact, the whole operating process hinges on it. Unless the pistons are able to compress the fuel/air mixture inside the cylinders sufficiently, the spark from the plug will not cause combustion, and the engine won't run. Apart from the piston's fit inside the bore, it's the job of the cylinder head to ensure that pressure is maintained. The head, often referred to as the 'top end', is an extremely influential component on any engine, and is arguably the most technically complex in terms of its function.

Normally cast as a single piece of either iron or aluminium alloy, the precisely-engineered cylinder head is bolted on to the engine's block to form an air- and liquid-tight seal. Aluminium alloy is the more modern alternative because it's lighter and offers superior heat conductivity which is great for cooling. The head accommodates the inlet and exhaust valves plus their operating mechanisms (rockers), the camshaft which drives and times valve operation, and the spark plugs. The casting is drilled with an often intricate system of passages used to supply water and oil for cooling and lubrication, and a gasket is sandwiched between the head and the block to help guarantee a complete seal. Head gaskets used to be made from thin sheets of asbestos with copper coverings but, nowadays, stainless steel is preferred, and is often supplied pre-coated with a sealing compound. The inlet and exhaust manifolds are bolted on to either side of the head are ferry fuel/air mixture and waste gases to and from the combustion chambers.

The degree of compression achieved by the piston is another important factor which has a direct bearing on an engine's efficiency, and it's always expressed as a ratio, for example 10:1. This is calculated by comparing two fundamental volumes. The first is the total volume of the cylinder when the piston is at the bottom of its stroke – known as bottom dead centre (bdc). The second occurs at the other extreme, when the piston reaches top dead centre (tdc). At this point it can rise no further, and the space left above it is known as the clearance volume (refer to Diagram 1). This is obviously much smaller than the total volume, and it's the relationship between these two which is expressed as the compression ratio. Generally speaking, the higher the compression ratio, the more powerful the engine.

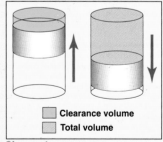

☐ Clearance volume
☐ Total volume

Diagram 1

We saw last month how it's the inlet and exhaust valves which orchestrate gas movement within the cylinder. Their precisely-controlled opening and closing is what guarantees mixture supply, spent gas disposal and adequate compression to ensure combustion. To achieve the necessary air-tight seal, each valve is very carefully

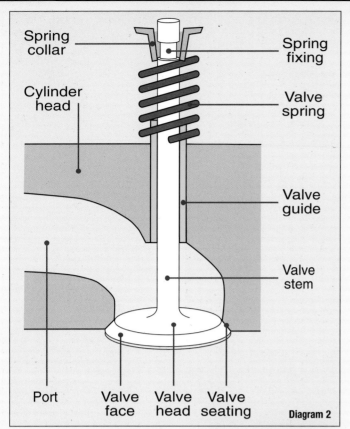

Spring collar
Spring fixing
Cylinder head
Valve spring
Valve guide
Valve stem
Port
Valve face
Valve head
Valve seating

Diagram 2

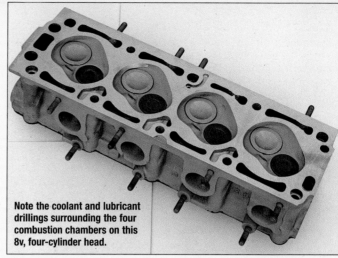

Note the coolant and lubricant drillings surrounding the four combustion chambers on this 8v, four-cylinder head.

shaped, with a 'face' machined around the circumference of its head to an angle which matches the seating where it rests when closed (refer to Diagram 2). The type used on modern engine applications is called the poppet valve which, although an old design that began life inside steam engines, has proved itself the best option for automotive applications.

Poppet valves have a large circular but predominantly flat head, and a long, thin stem which extends from the centre of one side. As well as the accuracy of their machining, it's the valve's alignment which helps ensure complete sealing when closed. To guarantee this the valve stems slide up and down inside close-fitting and perfectly-aligned guides, which are usually separate inserts pressed into the head. Unfortunately, this

Tuning experts like Bill Blydenstein appreciate the importance of combustion chamber and valve design when maximising thermal and volumetric efficiency.

level of precision only lasts until prolonged use starts to wear the components. Valve faces and seats become mis-shapen with time and the 100% gas seal is inevitably lost. Once this happens compression is reduced through leakage, and overall engine performance deteriorates. The valve stems wear too, which apart from allowing engine oil down past the valve and into the combustion chamber to be blown out of the exhaust as nasty blue smoke, puts extra strain on the valve head, accelerating wear there too.

Each valve has its own spring which, together with some assistance from the pressure within the cylinder, ensures that it remains tightly closed when necessary. Valve opening is controlled by the camshaft which spins in well lubricated bearings, and does a neat job of converting rotary motion into an up and down, reciprocating action. The camshaft, which is normally made from chilled-cast iron, features a number of eccentrics or cams that, as they rotate, act on the tops of the valve stems, via cam followers or tappets. The number of eccentrics matches the number of valves in the engine – modern 16v engines typically have two camshafts – and, in this way, the valves are operated in the correct sequence. As each cam is

rotated, no force is exerted on the valve stem as the base circle passes (refer to Diagram 3). The action only begins at the joint between the base circle and the opening flank, and continues to the tip of the cam's nose, at which point the valve will be fully open. Continued rotation allows the valve to close. Varying the profile of the eccentric alters the speed and duration of valve opening and fiddling with these dimensions has been the preserve of engine tuners since the year dot!

Of course, everything we've covered so far becomes meaningless without effective combustion. If the fuel/air mixture fails to burn properly then the engine will not run or, if it does, its power output will be worse than useless. An efficient burn is the key to everything really, but the trouble is that there are a great many factors which affect the likelihood of this happening, and most relate to the cylinder head and the components immediately connected with it.

At the core of the whole business is the combustion chamber, which is the space left above the top of the piston when it's at tdc. The shape of this is important and a number of different approaches have been tried over the years. But it's generally regarded now that a domed or hemispherical chamber provides the best

The condition of a cylinder head provides a very good indicator of how an engine has been maintained. The oily mess on the left is typical of an engine that's not enjoyed frequent lubricant changes.

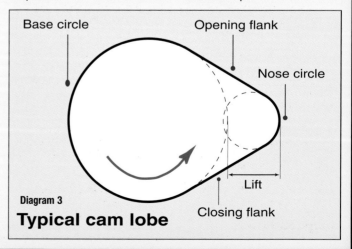

Base circle
Opening flank
Nose circle
Lift
Closing flank

Diagram 3
Typical cam lobe

TECHNICAL TOPIC: *Head Gasket Swap*

In practical terms a cylinder head is only as good as the gasket which sits between it and the engine block. Although the face of the head and the top of the block are carefully manufactured to exacting standards, the presence of a gasket is still necessary to ensure a 100% gas- and liquid-tight joint.

Failure of the gasket is a serious business which must be put right sooner rather than later, before lasting damage is done. If your engine's getting on a bit and has started consuming significant amounts of coolant or oil, but there are no obvious leaks to be seen, then the chances are that the gasket has blown and needs to be changed.

So, to advise and guide us on the correct procedure, plus some of the potential pitfalls of this important job, we consulted automobile engineering lecturer Eddie Smith at the Colchester Institute.

1 When tackling a head gasket replacement the first job is to remove the rocker cover. There is no specific sequence in which the bolts should be undone.

2 As you lift the cover clear, try to make sure the gasket comes away with it in one piece but, if it breaks, watch for any pieces that may fall off and drop down on to the head. This gasket should be replaced as a matter of course.

3 The cylinder head is secured to the block by a number of large bolts. Each should have its tightness 'broken' using a large torque wrench or a sway bar. Resist the temptation to use a ratchet because this will almost certainly overload it. Breaking the tightness means turning the bolt through the initial quarter of a turn. Bolts should be undone in the opposite order to the tightening sequence, which will always be detailed in the owner's manual. While loosening is not as important as tightening, it's good practice to follow the correct sequence anyway, to avoid the risk of distorting the head. Never attempt any work on the head if the engine is warm, particularly if it's made of aluminium alloy. This Ford head is secured with stretch bolts which are not designed to be used twice so replacements must be bought.

4 As you try to lift the head clear, bear in mind that it may be partially stuck down by carbon deposits, making it difficult to move. Often it will also be located with a couple of short dowels which can make things even more awkward. The best way to break the seal is to rock the head by hand. Never try to lever it clear because this will almost certainly damage the soft metal casting. Also, before you lift it clear, make sure you have somewhere clean and flat to put it down afterwards. Never place the removed head face down the bench because you might damage a protruding valve head.

5 With the head resting on its side, take time to inspect the condition of its face before you remove the gasket. There will be lots of clues here about the performance of the engine and its state of wear. Look closely for breaches in the 'fire-ring' on the gasket. If all is well this should be a shiny and uninterrupted strip around the circumference of the combustion chamber aperture. Problems are highlighted by blackened sections. Breaches near waterways normally indicate coolant loss although, if this is happening, the water which enters the combustion chamber steams everything spotlessly clean – obviously not the case here!

6 These sticky black deposits suggest that oil has been leaking in past the gasket to be burnt in the combustion chamber. While an over-rich mixture will create a dark, sooty coating, the shininess evident here indicates oil. Other possibilities are that the oil is finding its way up past worn piston rings, or down past worn valve guides.

7 Of course, the oil won't always be drawn in towards the combustion chamber. Sometimes it will blow outwards through the gasket, but this is normally much easier to spot as it's clearly visible trickling down the outside of the engine block.

8 Remove the old gasket and try to get it off in one piece so that you can check it for signs of damage on the reverse side. Then you must prepare the head with careful cleaning and scraping as necessary. Use a solvent-based cleaning product – aerosol brake cleaner is ideal – to produce a smooth finish for the new gasket.

9 While the head is off, check for the presence of wear ridges on the thrust side of the cylinder bores using your fingernail. This provides another simple indicator about the engine's overall condition. Unworn engines should have no ridge here.

10 Finally, before offering up the new gasket, use and air line to ensure that the cylinder bores and casting drillings are cleared of loose debris and oil. For safety's sake, it's best to wear a pair of goggles for this high pressure cleaning job.

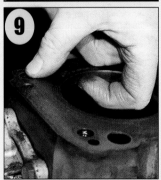

ESSENTIAL FITTING TIPS

- Always read gasket fitting instructions carefully
- Be sure you know whether gasket requires additional sealant or not
- Fit it the right way up – many marked with 'Top' or 'Oben' (German)
- Align head carefully before lowering on to new gasket, to avoid pinching
- Check owners manual to see if head bolts to be fitted dry or lubricated
- Tighten bolts in correct sequence and progressively to exactly the right torque – follow manual instructions to the letter!

results. The fundamental requirements are that sufficient air/fuel mixture is allowed to enter the cylinder as the piston drops away on its induction stroke, and that as much of the fuel present is actually burnt to produce usable energy after compression has taken place. Both of these aspects can be measured, and are classified as volumetric and thermal efficiencies, respectively.

Volumetric efficiency is surprisingly low on most engines, despite the latest computer-aided design techniques. The number of obstructions which hinder air movement into the engine – air filter, restrictive ducting, inlet manifold shape, inlet valve etc. – is sufficient to

Expert assistance

Colchester Institute has a large Automobile Engineering Centre which provides part-time (one day per week) and full-time courses in automobile engineering, body repair and welding. For more information contact:
Dave Roberts
Head of Centre for Automobile Engineering, Colchester Institute, Sheepen Road, Colchester, CO3 3LL.

ensure that the space available within the cylinder is never filled to capacity at the end of the induction stroke. One of the most obvious ways to help the fuel/air mixture enter is by fitting a large diameter inlet valve. However, the ultimate size of this is limited by the space available and the neatest and most volumetrically-

efficient solution is to up the anti by fitting four valves per cylinder (two inlet and two exhaust). For the best effect these are inclined at an angle of about 45°, and positioned in pairs on either side of the centrally placed spark plug in the hemispherically shaped roof of the combustion chamber.

Finally, thermal efficiency is a more complex issue that relates to the efficiency with which the fuel is burnt, and the amount of heat produced. Heat lost to the surroundings is wasted energy, so it's important that this is minimised. Consequently, it makes sense to keep the combustion chamber small in surface area. It's also important that the compression ratio

should be as high as is reasonably possible, to ensure effective combustion and a quick, powerful burn. Another factor affecting the quality of combustion is how well the fuel and air are mixed. To help ensure this, modern combustion chambers are designed so that the mix is swirled as it enters. Also, many modern pistons used in 16v engines feature a domed top surface which, as compression takes place, enhances the mixing action thanks to a sort of eddying phenomenon know as squish.

Next Month
Crank, rods and sump.

TOOLKIT BUILDER:
Spanners

Spanners come in a variety of designs, sizes and prices. In fact, you can pay virtually whatever you like for these versatile tools – everything from the ludicrously cheap to the ridiculously expensive. Most of us will fall somewhere in between, particularly with the first tools we buy.

As with sockets, much of the price of spanners is determined by the style of their finish. The flashy stuff features polished chrome which looks great and, if it's of good quality, stays looking great. However, cheaper attempts at this sort of shiny coating can prove problematic, being prone to unsightly chipping as they age. At the other end of the glamour scale there is the moody industrial finish which, while perhaps dull to many peoples' taste, will stay in your tool box for years because nobody will ever be tempted to lift them!

Spanners tend to be a personal thing, and many professional mechanics will stick with their faithful favourites for years. Consequently, it's not that common to come across quality gear in secondhand sales or 'car boots'. So, unless you're very lucky, you're going to have to buy your spanners new and your first choice must centre on type.

Basically you have two fundamental options. Either you go for the most traditional open-ended design, or you choose the ring spanner route, which is basically like a socket on a stick! Of course, as with most things these days, there is a 'best of both worlds' option called the combination spanner, which

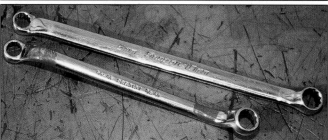
Traditional open-ended spanners are probably still the best option in skilled hands, although ring-end spanners do provide better grip for initial loosening.

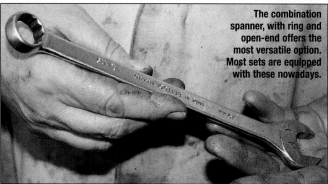
The combination spanner, with ring and open-end offers the most versatile option. Most sets are equipped with these nowadays.

Watch out for spanners which are too long, particularly with the smaller sizes. You'd be surprised how easy it is to snap a fixing with a long-handled tool, simply because of the extra leverage.

features an open end and a ring end at either end of the same shaft. Most budget-priced sets available in motorist discount stores contain a selection of combination spanners, with the bigger one offering a smattering of sockets too.

In absolute performance terms ring spanners are probably the better bet because they are more effective in the

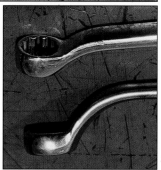
Ring spanners are made with varying degrees of head crank. This is another factor worth considering. Many professionals find it easier to work with a shallower angle..

way they work. Compared to an open-ended spanner, the ring design spreads the load much more evenly around the fixing being worked, so you're far less likely to cause any damage. However, it's worth noting that once you've cracked the tightness, an open-ended spanner is then probably the quickest option simply because, with practice, it's the easiest and fastest tool to manoeuvre on and off the fixing.

While the more extensive spanner sets may appear to offer great value for money, remember that there will be quite a number in the box that, because of their oddball size, you'll never need in a month of Sundays. The really useful sizes are 10, 11, 13, 17 and 19mm for most everyday types of automotive job. The larger two are particularly appropriate for working on gearbox, suspension and steering fixings on a great many common vehicles. So you may think it worthwhile to buy a cheap and cheerful set and then replace the most commonly used sizes with higher quality kit bought individually.

Manufacturing quality is a bit of a grey are with spanners. There are perhaps 50 suppliers in the UK and it's unlikely that you'll get anything meaningful out of any of them in terms of the materials used etc. So the only guides to quality are the price and any guarantee that may be offered. But one thing is for sure and that's that there are few things more irritating than a cheap spanner which stretches, becomes burred or even breaks at the merest sniff of a tight bolt.

Those with deeper pockets might like to consider ratcheting spanners as a more luxuriously convenient option. In the early days these labour-saving tools were large and clumsy affairs but nowadays superior design and manufacturing standards means they are much smaller and more manageable.

LASER®
Hand Tools

Put a **spanner** in the **Works**

Laser Tools leads the market with its new and innovative automotive tools.

The range covers all essential tools for the workshop and there is a vast array of vehicle-specific tools for service and maintenance.

A particular strength is timing tools, available for most makes of engine. They come with a full application list and back up support service.

Anyone seeking the right tool for a job can make the search simple by logging on to Laser's comprehensive application directory **www.tool-point.co.uk** it is an invaluable source of information.

Back to Basics

Part 3:
Chris Graham gets heavy and delves into the engine's powerhouse with a look at pistons, conrods and crankshafts

In the same way that the complexities of the human body are contained and supported by skin and bone, so the internal workings of a car's engine rely on the block casting to keep everything in place and functioning correctly. The real powerhouse of any engine is contained within the block, where you find the pistons, their connecting rods and the crankshaft. The intricacies of the cylinder head and its delicate valve assemblies are all very well, but these would count for nothing if the power of combustion was not effectively harnessed and transmitted to the driven wheels, via the gearbox. This is the job of the engine's heavyweight components, and it's these we're concentrating on this month.

Modern engine blocks are made from a single and often very complicated casting which forms the main body of the unit. The shape of the casting is determined by the number of cylinders needed in the engine and, in road cars, this varies from the simplest eco-friendly three-cylinder unit right up to biggest, fire-breathing V12. Most saloons, though, make use of a straightforward four-cylinder

configuration utilising a 'monoblock' construction. The basic metal casting contains the cylinder bores surrounded by a drilled water jacket for cooling, mountings for the crankshaft and the provision to bolt on an oil sump underneath.

Lubricant from the sump is drawn up into the engine and circulated, by the oil pump, to feed the main bearing points on the camshaft and crankshaft, the cylinder bores, and anywhere else where metal-to-metal

contact requires oiling. Having circled the engine, and done its fair share cooling in the process, the oil returns to the sump via the main filter which removes any nasties, and is itself cooled before starting off around the engine once again.

Internal engine wear is a big problem with all engines and is usually what causes eventual failure given enough time. Metal surfaces that scrape, rub and grind together as the motor operates inevitably damage

themselves through friction. Then, once the surfaces become scratched and scored, so the process accelerates. Oil is obviously the primary weapon used to fight mechanical wear, but any lubricant's effectiveness is determined by its condition which, in turn, relates to its age. Failure to change the engine oil at regular intervals spells disaster for the internal workings of an engine. Old lubricant is of little use to man nor beast, so be warned.

One of the key areas for potential wear is in the cylinder bores. The up and down action of the pistons is very aggressive and so effective lubrication here is essential. To help fight the problem, engine designers fit the bores with hard cylindrical liners, usually made from top quality cast iron, which are far more resistant to wear than the softer iron used for the main body of the block. The other big advantage of cylinder liners is that, if the worst comes to the worst and wear becomes excessive, they can be re-bored to recreate a perfect surface again, or even replaced.

At the absolute heart of any engine is the crankshaft, and this is one of those components which becomes more complicated the more you look at it. Fundamentally it provides the link between the pistons and the gearbox, transferring the energy from combustion into a rotary motion that can be fed, eventually, to the car's driving wheels. Essentially the crankshaft is a hefty metal rod that is held in place at three or more fixed points along its length. At these points, known as the journals, the shaft is supported in precisely engineered and well-lubricated metal bearings that allow it to rotate at whatever speed is necessary while, at the same time, maintaining its correct alignment.

TECHNICAL TOPIC: *Piston Removal*

Nowadays many drivers regard their cars as disposable items. Most people drive company vehicles that rarely run for longer than three ye[ars] and so, for a high proportion of motorists, engine wear is a thing of the past. The rest, however, still have to contend with problems associa[ted] with mechanical aging although, it must be said that progress with lubricant technology and engine manufacturing standards have impro[ved] the situation no end. Nevertheless, poor maintenance coupled with unsympathetic use can still reduce an engine to that proverbial 'bag of nails'. Motors that rattle, have low oil pressure, poor compression and belch oily blue smoke from the exhaust are not uncommon.

If you're unfortunate enough to own such an engine, but you're keen to put it right, then there really is no alternative but to have a good poke about inside. Stripping the bottom end and removing one or more of the pistons for inspection is the only way to get things sorted. While this may sound a complicated and advanced job, it's not actually as daunting as you might imagine, assuming you have a workshop manual and don't run a V12 Jaguar!

Handy Hints

- When replacing rings remember to stagger the gaps to prevent loss of compression.
- Always keep ring gaps away from the thrust side of the pisto[n]
- Never use a spray lubricant to oil the ring pack prior to re-fitting. These products are too thin, and will drain away.
- Don't forget to liberally lubricate the big end shell bearing and the crank journal during re-assembly.

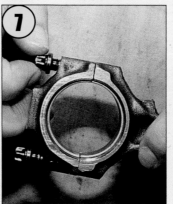

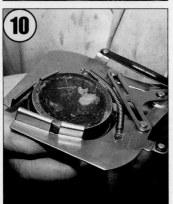

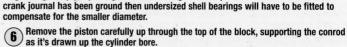

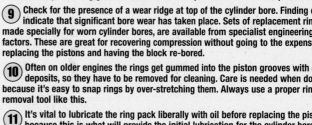

① Having drained the oil (best done with it warm) and removed the sump and its gasket, the first job is to loosen the big end bolts which, in this example, are Torx headed. In most cases it's not recommended that you re-use big end bolts because their performance is so vital. Check with your manual.

② Lift the end cap clear together with the lower half of the shell bearing. If you are removing more than one piston, be careful to keep the end caps clearly identified because it is vital they are replaced on to the same conrod during re-assembly.

③ Shell bearings are easy to assess in terms of wear. If you spot signs of bad surface scoring, or the white metal coating has been worn away to reveal the copper backing, then replacement will be necessary. Note the oilway drillings.

④ Shell bearings are stamped with identification marks on the reverse side. This must be checked when ordering replacements, to make sure the new parts are correct. Even slight variations in size can spell disaster.

⑤ With the cap out of the way you are able to assess the condition of the crankshaft journal. Once again, you are looking for signs of scoring on the polished metal surface. If the damage is severe on the crankshaft then it will need to be sent away for re-grinding. Simply replacing the shell bearings will not provide a solution. Once the crank journal has been ground then undersized shell bearings will have to be fitted to compensate for the smaller diameter.

⑥ Remove the piston carefully up through the top of the block, supporting the conrod as it's drawn up the cylinder bore.

⑦ It is very important to keep the cap and rod together as a matched pair. The best advice is to bolt them back together as soon as you can, then there can't be any doubt in the future, regardless of how long it is before you re-assemble the engine again.

⑧ Check the piston itself for discolouration and score marks on the skirt. Worn pistons, which are losing compression ('blow by') around the rings, will often show coloured lacquer deposits down the sides. Assess the condition of the piston rings. An engine that has over-heated can cause the rings to lose their springiness. They can also snap or may just be worn. Use feeler blades to measure the ring gaps to test for this. The piston ring groove clearance will be quoted in the workshop manual.

⑨ Check for the presence of a wear ridge at top of the cylinder bore. Finding one will indicate that significant bore wear has taken place. Sets of replacement rings, made specially for worn cylinder bores, are available from specialist engineering factors. These are great for recovering compression without going to the expense of replacing the pistons and having the block re-bored.

⑩ Often on older engines the rings get gummed into the piston grooves with carbon deposits, so they have to be removed for cleaning. Care is needed when doing this because it's easy to snap rings by over-stretching them. Always use a proper ring removal tool like this.

⑪ It's vital to lubricate the ring pack liberally with oil before replacing the piston because this is what will provide the initial lubrication for the cylinder bore on start-up. Use a good quality gear oil or something similar which is thick and won't drain away down the bore.

⑫ To replace the piston, complete with rings, you'll need a correctly-sized ring clamp. Never hit the crown of the piston hard when replacing it. Use the handle of a light hammer to provide a series of gentle impacts so that the piston is eased in.

⑬ Be sure that the cap and the conrod are both round the right way before you bolt them together. Tighten in two stages, first to finger tight and then to the correct torque setting.

⑭ It's good practice to turn the engine after torquing down each end cap to make sure it rotates freely.

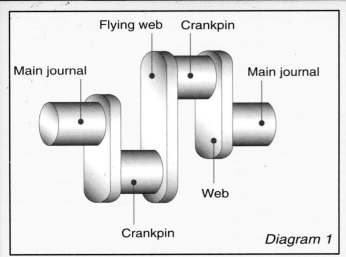

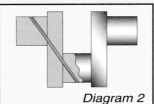

Diagram 1

Flying web · Crankpin · Main journal · Main journal · Web · Crankpin

The journals and the crank pins on the crankshaft are carefully polished during manufacture to help guarantee smooth running. But, in addition to this, they run within specially made bearings which are manufactured from metal alloy that is both soft and smooth. These 'shell bearings' take the form of paired semi-circular strips that fit closely together to encase the shaft.

The crankshaft is linked to the pistons by connecting rods. These steel castings feature, quite logically, a top end which is connected to the piston via a gudgeon pin, and a bottom end that is bolted to the crank pin. To help resist the tremendous forces exerted by combustion, the 'conrod' is usually shaped in the form of an 'H', when viewed in cross-section. In most cases the bottom end is split to simplify piston fitting and removal. The high tensile steel bolts used to secure the bottom end cap can be removed to detach the conrod from the crankshaft, allowing the piston and rod to be removed from the engine.

Pistons themselves come in many and varied designs but the basic principles of all remain the

A piston and its con rod with end cap and shell bearings in place. The piston pivots on top of the rod thanks to its gudgeon pin mounting.

In between the journals, the main shaft features a number of offsets, known as crank pins, and it's these that are used to connect with the pistons. Imagine a Swiss roll that's sliced in the middle, with two cuts about an inch apart. Sliding the centre section to one side then creates the type of staggered effect on which the crankshaft is based. It works along the same lines as the pedals on a bicycle. The number of crank pins needed is determined by the number of pistons used in the engine, and each is supported by a pair of webs (see **Diagram 1**). The shape of these webs varies from engine to engine, although most nowadays are flared out into a sort of bell shape, when viewed in cross-section. This is done specifically to add extra weight to the crankshaft and help balance it during rotation. Without this added mass, the crankshaft would vibrate horribly, and probably snap, as it spun.

Additional 'rotary calming' is provided by the flywheel, which is a solid metal disc normally bolted directly on to the rear end of the crankshaft. The effort needed to set the flywheel spinning smoothes out engine acceleration and deceleration, to make the unit much easier to control for everyday driving.

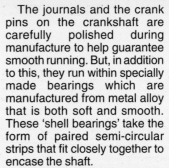

Diagram 2

Lightening the flywheel gives an engine greater responsiveness to the throttle but, at the same time, makes it harder to drive smoothly. Anyone who has heard a modern Formula 1 car's engine being revved in the pits before a race, will appreciate how a super-light flywheel allows the engine to pick up and loose revs almost instantly.

The fact that the crankshaft has to be capable of spinning at up to 6,500rpm in most modern engines means that lubrication becomes a vital factor if wear to the journal and crank pin faces is to be avoided. To ensure a good supply of oil, the crankshaft is drilled with holes which run between the main journals, diagonally through the webs, to the centre of the crank pins (see **Diagram 2**). Oil is supplied under pressure to a groove in the bearing around the main journal. As the shaft rotates, lubricant is carried down the drilling to the surface of the crank pin, where it's used to minimise wear rates.

same. To allow smooth movement within the cylinder, the piston has to be slightly smaller in diameter than the bore. So to ensure a gas-tight seal between the piston and the cylinder wall, and to prevent excessive amounts of lubricating oil reaching the combustion chamber above, the piston is fitted with a number of sprung rings. These run in

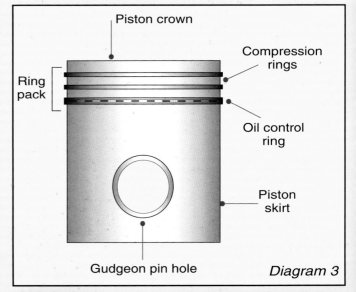

Piston crown · Compression rings · Ring pack · Oil control ring · Piston skirt · Gudgeon pin hole

Diagram 3

Note the oil drillings on the bearing faces of this crankshaft. Also notice how the webs are shaped to help balance the shaft as it rotates.

Avoid this at all costs! When fitting compression rings always ensure that the gaps are not lined up like this otherwise there'll be a distinct lack of compression!

Expert assistance

Colchester Institute has a large Automobile Engineering Centre which provides part-time (one day per week) and full-time courses in automobile engineering, body repair and welding.
For more information contact: **Dave Roberts**
Head of Centre for Automobile Engineering, Colchester Institute, Sheepen Road, Colchester, CO3 3LL.

machined grooves around the top half of the piston, in what's known as the 'ring belt', and are normally made from cast iron (see **Diagram 3**). Most will be straightforward compression rings, but one is of a more complex design and is called the 'oil control' or 'scraper' ring. This is designed to collect excess oil from the cylinder wall on the downward stroke of the piston, and to make sure that this lubricant then drains back to the sump below, through specially drilled holes in the ring groove.

Due to the fact that, for most of the crankshaft's rotary cycle, the conrod is actually working at an angle to the vertical centre line of the cylinder bore, the piston gets pushed against the side of the bore. This is particularly apparent on the combustion stroke, when the full force of the mixture's explosive burn propels the piston rapidly downwards. This 'side thrust' is countered by the piston's 'skirt' but, inevitably, wear takes place and affects the piston, its rings and the cylinder bore as the engine ages.

Next Month
Cooling Systems

TOOLKIT BUILDER:
Pliers & grips

The old adage about extra hands making light work rings very true when applied to DIY vehicle mechanics assuming, of course, that the hands are controlled by more than just a couple of brain cells. Pliers and grips can form a sort of halfway house, providing a useful extension of your own hands, with the added advantage that they never answer back!

They can be used for turning, gripping, pulling and, in some guises, cutting too. But, as with most hand tools these days, the choice available is bewildering. Pliers are available in all shapes and sizes and prices vary accordingly. So what we've done here is cut through the hype to provide an informed shopping list for those of you just starting out.

Most people regard standard, square-nosed pliers as a toolbox essential and I suppose they are. They are great for general gripping and pulling duties but you might be surprised at how infrequently you actually use them. Prices can range from just a few pounds right up to £30 but our advice is that, unless you have a specific regular use for a pair of standard pliers, don't spend too much.

Of course, quality does vary and is almost always linked directly to price. But, unless you are a tool snob, or you have heavy use in mind, 'cheap and cheerful' should be good enough for most occasions. After all, what's the point in spending a fortune on such a utility item? Just for the record, though, the quality of pliers is determined by a number of factors including the type of the steel used to make them and the accuracy of the machined finish. A practical guide can be the number of serrations included at the tip of the jaws – the more there are the better. Budget-priced tools will tend to be made from softer metal which, with time and use, will wear and distort. In the worst cases the ends of the jaws can deform to such an extent that they don't meet at all, meaning that it becomes impossible to grip anything effectively with the tips.

Handle design can be another important factor, with a definite effect on the tool's ease of use. Plushy, non-slip plastic handle covers are certainly more comfortable to use than bare metal handles.

A variation on the standard pliers theme is the long-nosed type which, in reality, is the sort of tool that may seem like a good idea when you're staring at it in the shop. However, once home it's not unusual to find that you rarely need them for routine maintenance duties. Of course, they can be indispensable on those odd occasions when a nut drops down just out of reach, or you need to grab hold of a tiny wire or pin in a confined space. But ask yourself how often this happens and then whether or not you really need a pair as part of your starter kit.

A pair of Mole grips, on the other hand, is of far more general-purpose use. These are extremely useful and come in a range of sizes and styles. Some can be clamped to the bench and used like a vice, while others are small enough to be useful in the tightest of spaces. Mole grips feature what's called an 'over centre' action which is a simple lever mechanism that allows them to be locked shut. What's more, the width of the jaw spacing can be adjusted to suit a variety of job sizes. Once again, you can spend a little or a lot on Mole grips but, in practice, there is little difference between the two extremes unless you are working the tool hard.

But perhaps the most versatile tool of all in the pliers family is the adjustable gap wrench, often called 'pump pliers'. These are extremely useful around the motor car for all manner of holding, gripping and pulling jobs. We'd have no hesitation in recommending that you buy a small and a medium set to cover most eventualities. The larger sizes, preferred by plumbers, have fewer useful applications on vehicles.

In terms of buying tips, the same sorts of rule apply. Look at the number and accuracy of the serrations and watch for overall finish and handle coverings. You'll also find a number of pivot designs, some better than others. Most well-known brands these days feature non-slip jaws which are by far the safest to use. Older and cheaper styles, which simply rely on the pivot nestling in a groove, tend to be less satisfactory, particularly once they start to wear.

Finally, although most standard pliers will offer a limited cutting facility for dealing with wire, we think it's far better to get yourself a proper pair of side cutters. You'll find these brilliant for cutting metal cables, split pins on wheel bearings, welding rod, electrical cables, wire and plastic cable ties. The cheapest around will work okay for a short while but will quickly become blunt. Better then to invest £20 or so in a good pair that will be well made and feature top-quality and accurately machined blades.

Good quality pump pliers like these are the real unsung heroes of most modern tool kits. They are versatile, easy to use and extremely effective.

Long-nose pliers have limited applications in general use, but there are those occasions when nothing else will do!

Standard pliers are good for general pulling, twisting and pinching duties, but you probably won't use them as often as you might imagine.

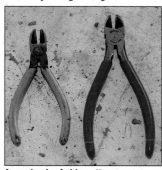

A good pair of side cutters are a really useful addition to any tool kit.

It's worth buying a couple of pairs of Mole grips too. Their clamping action is always handy.

Back to Basics

Back to Basics

Part 4:
Chris Graham investigates how and why engines keep their cool.

As far as temperature is concerned, modern engines work on a knife-edge. Ever-tightening exhaust emission legislation means that they must operate efficiently to minimise the production of carbon monoxide, nitrogen dioxide and a lung-full of other nasties. But it may surprise you to learn that operating temperature is one of the key factors governing exhaust efficiency, and that it's the often neglected cooling system that battles tirelessly to keep this in check.

The internal combustion engine produces a lot of heat. Temperatures inside the combustion chambers of a motor being driven at speed on the motorway can reach an eye-popping 2,000°C, and even the exhaust gases leave the cylinder at around 800°C. Quite obviously, such heat would destroy an engine in seconds if left unchecked. No metal could withstand these temperatures without distorting or melting, and seizure would be assured. So the effective and rapid dispersal of this excessive heat is vital and, basically, there are two ways of achieving this – one relies on heat transfer to the

Whatever car you drive maintaining its cooling system correctly should be high on your list of maintenance priorities.

surrounding air while the other utilises the excellent heat-absorbing properties of a water-based solution.

Air-cooled engines really are a thing of the past when it comes to powering cars. Nowadays you'll find this dated technology limited to use on lawn mowers, chain saws and mopeds. The motor industry, as a whole, has moved to water cooling as the preferred option, for a number of fundamental reasons. For a start, liquid-based systems are much more effective when working at the extremes – they promote faster warm-up from cold and are better able to deal with really hot weather running.

To work well, the air-cooled approach requires lots of space around the engine and its cylinders and, while this was fine with designs from the 1960s and '70s, it's no longer practical on today's tightly packaged engine layouts. So, despite the reliability and low maintenance advantages of air cooling, the practical need to minimise engine dimensions and maximise temperature control meant that water cooling won the day.

Controlling an engine's operating temperature has a direct bearing on how efficiently

the unit works, both in terms of mechanical wear rates and exhaust emissions. For the best performance, and to ensure the clean and thorough burning of all the fuel, cylinder head temperature must be maintained at about 250-300°C. Anything above this starts to increase the risk of heat distortion and will also begin to burn off the vital lubricant layer which coats the cylinder bores and pistons.

Both of these unfortunate

consequences significantly increase the likelihood of mechanical wear. But over-heating also causes a loss of power because it affects the density of the air entering the engine. As temperatures rise air becomes progressively less able to carry fuel in suspension, and so performance falls away. It can also promote an undesirable condition called 'detonation', which occurs when the fuel/air mixture is burned too fast inside the combustion chamber. The higher than normal temperatures cause the mixture to ignite fully ahead of schedule, as the piston is still travelling up towards the top of its stroke (TDC). This

The pressure cap on top of this expansion tank doubles as the system's safety valve. As the coolant heats up and expands the pressure builds. If levels get too high then a simple valve inside the cap allows the excess to escape.

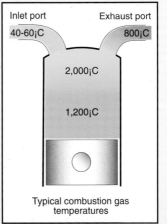

Inlet port	Exhaust port
40-60°C	800°C

2,000°C

1,200°C

Typical combustion gas temperatures

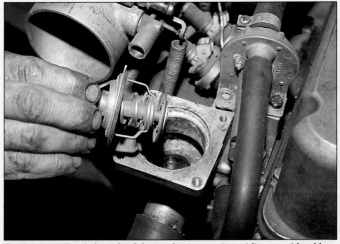

The thermostat's role in maintaining engine temperature at its correct level is a vital one. Most modern units rely on a wax core which melts and solidifies as engine temperature varies. The expansion and contraction operates a valve which determines whether or not the coolant is allowed to flow through the radiator.

Radiators are good at cooling because they have a large surface area through which to lose the heat from the coolant. Each of these tiny metal fins helps transfer heat from the coolant to the atmosphere.

results in an explosive impact on the piston's crown and generates a characteristic metallic 'pinking' sound.

But, there are additional subtleties to the modern cooling system, which are perhaps less obvious. For a start, precise control of coolant flow ensures that modern engines warm up very quickly from cold, thus minimising mechanical wear and emissions. An engine is least efficient when cold, so it's vital to get it up to normal operating temperature as rapidly as possible. Low temperatures mean that the lubricating oil remains thick and less able to flow easily where it should and, also that combustion efficiency is low making exhaust impurity levels high.

In addition, when an engine is being used under winter conditions, an effective cooling system will prevent it from running too cold. This may sound like a contradiction in terms but it's an important point.

You see, a 'cool' engine increases the tendency for the fuel vapour to condense on the inside of the cylinder bores, which dilutes the lubricant film and washes it away down into the sump. The same thing can also happened with water vapour (a natural by-product of the combustion process). Instead of remaining in suspension and being blown harmlessly out through the exhaust, it too condenses out on the cylinder bores, leading to the formation of sludge in the sump and less efficient lubrication around the engine.

Fortunately, water is just about ideal for cooling engines because it has all the right properties. Primary among these is its ability to absorb high amounts of heat energy before changing its physical state.

However, it has its disadvantages too. For a start it freezes at 0°C, expanding disastrously as it does so. It also boils at 100°C at which point it alters state into a vapour and can be lost to the atmosphere. Finally, and perhaps most seriously, it actively promotes metal corrosion and so provides a constant threat to the inside of the engine that it's cooling.

Luckily, these problems can be overcome. The corrosion risk is tackled by the addition of rust inhibitors, while the danger of cracking caused by ice formation is dealt with by the use of anti-freeze agents (ethylene glycol). The boiling point problem is slightly more involved but was solved by a clever manipulation of a natural property.

The temperature at which water boils relates directly to the atmospheric pressure being exerted on it. Increasing the pressure raises the boiling point, allowing the liquid to be heated to a higher temperature before it starts to vapourise. Lifting the pressure by 1 bar (about 14psi)

increases the boiling point by an impressive 20°C. This is the principal behind the pressure cooker, and explains why food can be cooked more quickly when sealed into one of these units.

So how is all this clever science actually put into practice? Well, cooling systems are essentially very simple, and rely for their success on good circulation and correct additive concentrations. The coolant solution is pushed around the engine, through a series of pipes and water jackets which surround the hottest parts of the motor, by a mechanical pump that's driven by a belt from the engine. The coolant is circulated continuously all the time the engine is running, although its route can be varied by the thermostat. This important component is located between the engine and the radiator, and acts as a straightforward, heat-triggered switch.

Put simply, the radiator is constructed from small pipes which are trimmed with hundreds of thin metal fins. These form a honeycomb-like affair, allowing air to pass through from front to back, cooling as it goes. Coolant solution, which has been heated during its journey around the engine, enters the radiator through the top hose. It passes along the folded pipe and the heat it's carrying is dissipated out through the walls of the tube and into the metal fins, from where it's lost to the atmosphere. The cooled solution leaves the radiator through the bottom hose, and sets off around the engine to repeat the process.

A large fan, placed immediately behind the radiator, is used to supplement air throughput and assist the cooling process when conditions demand it. On older vehicles this fan was continuously powered by a rubber belt but, nowadays,

Water pumps like this one on a Ford Sierra, used to be driven by the fan belt. The more modern approach is to utilise the toothed cambelt as a more reliable power source.

Nowadays all radiator cooling fans are electrically operated. Triggered by a heat-sensitive switch, they work to draw air through the radiator's core to enhance the cooling effect when temperatures are high.

this power-sapping option has been dropped in favour of a more efficient electric motor governed by a heat-sensitive switch sited inside the radiator.

The thermostat's function is to control whether or not the coolant is allowed to flow around the radiator, and this is determined by temperature. When in the 'closed' position, the thermostat effectively blocks the top hose and the coolant is forced to bypass the radiator and flow straight back into the engine. This happens when temperatures are low and this setting is intended to minimise engine warm-up time. But, the thermostat may also close when the 'wind chill' effect of high speed motoring in the winter causes coolant temperature in the radiator to drop below 80-90°C, thus protecting the engine from running too cold.

As I mentioned earlier, modern cooling systems are run under pressure which effectively delays the boiling point of water to well over the normal 100°C. The necessary pressurisation occurs automatically because

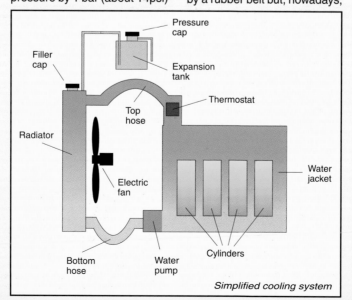

Pressure cap
Filler cap
Expansion tank
Thermostat
Top hose
Radiator
Water jacket
Electric fan
Bottom hose
Water pump
Cylinders

Simplified cooling system

TECHNICAL TOPIC: *Coolant flush*

Whatever car you've got, you ignore the maintenance and condition of its engine cooling system at your peril. Problems can be singularly disastrous, and nowadays it might take just one 'boil-up' to put the motor beyond economic repair. Of course, part of the problem is that most of us are spoilt nowadays, because we drive efficient, modern cars which rarely seem to get terribly hot at all. It's a far cry from the 1960s and '70s when overheating in summer traffic jams was a regular part of the driving experience.

The trouble is that modern systems run on much finer tolerances than ever before. Consequently, problems are triggered with a good deal less provocation, and things go wrong very quickly. Also, at the other extreme, damage can take place at a slow rate too, if antifreeze concentrations are allowed to fall away. The danger with this type of problem is that the damage occurs gradually and with no outward sign of trouble. The increasing use of 'soft' alloy components means that engines are becoming more and more vulnerable to internal attack and, to prevent this, coolant with the appropriate levels of corrosion inhibitors must be used.

So, bearing all these worrying facts in mind, we thought it would make sense to get right back to basics and feature coolant replacement as the 'technical topic' this month.

(1) The first job is to ditch the engine's existing coolant. If you've just bought the car or are servicing it yourself for the first time then this should be one of your first jobs. Make sure the engine is cool and, having placed a sufficiently large collection tray under the vehicle, disconnect the radiator's bottom hose.

(2) The Environmental Protection Act dictates that it's now an offence to tip used coolant down the drain – antifreeze residues are very toxic. Instead, you must bottle-up the liquid and take it to your local council tip where you will be advised on how best to deal with it.

(3) Once you're drained away the old coolant it's a good idea to 'back flush' the system. This simply means running a supply of water up through the radiator from bottom to top – it helps dislodge dirt and sediment which might remain if you simply flushed from top to bottom, in the normal direction of flow. If working on the radiator in situ then, having disconnected the top hose, use a rag bung to help seal the hose pipe into the bottom of the radiator.

(4) It's actually much easier to do a thorough back-flushing job if you remove the radiator from the car which, in most cases, isn't a terribly complicated job. As before, make sure that you catch the overflow to prevent any contaminants leaking away into the earth.

(5) One of the most common causes of engine overheating is fan failure, and this can be caused by a number of things. Most basic of all is a fault with the motor that drives the fan. A simple test for checking if this unit is operational involves bridging the motor's two supply wires. Momentarily touching them together should fire the fan into life. The fan is designed to cut in and out as the temperature of the engine varies but if this important switching action fails then overheating can result. The control switch, normally located inside the radiator, is another potential weak point in the system. The most practical way to check this is to allow the engine to warm up then leave it to idle and note whether or not the fan cuts in (you'll hear it easily) as the temperature continues to build. If the gauge inside the car gets appreciably beyond the 'normal' sector of the scale and the fan still hasn't started, then assume there is a problem and switch off.

(6) It's very important to make sure that you mix water and your chosen coolant solution in the correct ratio. Refer to the owners manual for the concentration required. Resist the temptation to add a bit more antifreeze for good luck because this can actually do harm and hinder the overall effect of the coolant.

(7) Refill the system having re-connected all hoses carefully. Use a proper pouring jug like this, or an old watering can, so that it's easy to avoid spillages. Make sure the interior heater is on it's hottest setting.

(8) Warm up the engine without refitting the pressure cap until you feel the top hose heating up, indicating that the thermostat has opened. It's important that the new coolant circulates completely around the system and that any air pockets are removed. Switch on the heater inside the car and check that it blows hot air, proving that hot coolant is flowing through the heater matrix behind the dashboard. Re-fit the pressure cap and allow the engine to warm further until the fan cuts in. Switch off and allow everything to cool down. Check the coolant level once the fluid is cold, and top up as necessary.

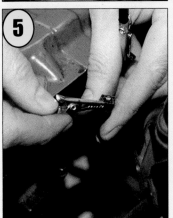

Handy Hints

● Buy the best, branded coolant solution you can afford.
● To be accurate, always check coolant levels when cold.
● Never open the pressure cap on a hot engine.
● Change coolant every two years. It degrades with time, forming mild acid which attacks metal.
● An engine which runs cold on the move, but warms when you stop, could indicate a failed thermostat.

Expert assistance

Colchester Institute has a large Automobile Engineering Centre which provides part-time (one day per week) and full-time courses in automobile engineering, body repair and welding.
For more information contact: **Dave Roberts**
Head of Centre for Automobile Engineering, Colchester Institute, Sheepen Road, Colchester, CO3 3LL.

the system is sealed.

However, as with a pressure cooker, to prevent pressure building too high, the system is fitted with a safety release valve usually fitted in the pressure cap on top of the expansion tank. Boiling coolant is bad news for a number of reasons, not least because the steam produced causes a loss of fluid, and can create hot-spot generating air locks in the system.

Therefore, the correct function of the pressure cap is vital. In fact, this cap actually incorporates two valves, the first of which allows excess pressure out as the coolant expands with heat. The second, working in the opposite direction, ensures that the pressure can be equalised as the engine cools, to prevent the creation of a vacuum which could collapse and possibly damage the rubber hoses.

But don't imagine that preventing the engine from overheating is the coolant system's only job. It may be the most obviously thought of, but tackling the risk of freezing in winter and keeping a check on internal engine corrosion are both also vital functions. Modern engines require coolant additive levels to be maintained

accurately all year round. No more is it a case of simply topping up with a drop or two of good old antifreeze in October, to see you through the winter months. The concentration of coolant solution within the system has become a vital factor in recent years.

Modern engines, that utilise aluminium alloy heads and blocks, require permanent protection from correct amounts of the recommended solution. The danger, of course, is that any damage being done by failure to maintain the coolant correctly, is undetectable by the day-to-day motorist. You may be wrecking the inside of your car's engine without even realising it.

A number of manufacturers now recommend that coolant solutions are mixed 50/50 with water for their latest engines, to guarantee adequate protection of the 'soft' metal components.

Vigilant maintenance and dealership servicing should be enough to avoid problems, but trouble can strike if leaks occur and the system is simply topped up with water alone.

Next Month
Ignition systems

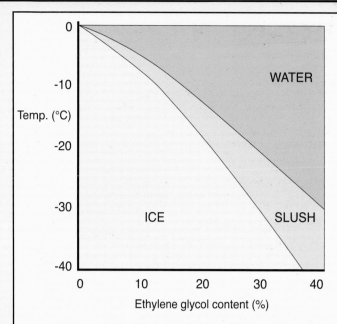

It isn't just when water turns to ice that it can cause damage to your engine's coolant system. On its way to freezing solid, it passes through a dangerous 'slushy' stage during which it expands and, because it also thickens, becomes unable to flow properly. The problem with this is that it can cause partial blockages sufficient to inhibit coolant circulation, leading to overheating. Adding antifreeze not only lowers the freezing point of water but also delays the onset of the 'slushing' stage, as the graph illustrates.

In the UK it's generally accepted by vehicle manufacturers that a good quality, ethylene glycol-based antifreeze product should be maintained in the cooling system at a concentration of 25%. This will ensure protection from ice damage down to -25°C but, perhaps more importantly, will also lower the slush threshold to about -12°C.

TOOLKIT BUILDER:
Coolant testers

Some would say that a coolant tester is an obscure piece of gear which has no place in a starter toolkit. Others might not even know what it is! The reality, as I hope you all now appreciate, is that it's probably one of the most important pieces of kit you could ever hope to buy. After all, the information it provides can literally mean the difference between life and death for your engine.

As we've already mentioned, the amount of coolant solution that you mix with the water that's pumped around the hot bits on your car, is a vital factor. To work effectively, and provide complete protection from both low temperatures and corrosion, it must be present in the correct concentration, and this must be maintained at all times. Those motorists who still regard antifreeze as a product

that you bung in when the leaves begin to drop and the first frost starts nipping at their trunnions, are living in the past.

The coolant tester is the only weapon we have in the armoury to help fight the war against weak coolant. It's a simple hydrometer which works by measuring the specific gravity of the solution to determine the proportion of ethylene glycol (the antifreeze agent) present. Water and antifreeze have different specific gravities and so when the two are mixed it is possible to work out the relative concentrations by checking the overall value. Thankfully, the coolant tester does all the calculating work for you, and couldn't be simpler to use.

There isn't much choice on the market and all versions rely on the user being able to note the position of a small float, which bobs around in a coolant sample, against a printed scale.

The more sophisticated, 'professional' models incorporate a thermometer so that coolant temperature can be added to the equation to produce a more accurate result. The most basic, DIY-types offer less subtlety but

can be used to pretty good effect with a little care and attention.

Buying a tester can be a bit of a struggle and, during the research for this feature, I was actually told in a popular motorist discount store that they were out of season! What a perfect example of the ignorance which, even today, still surrounds the use and maintenance of coolant solutions.

In reality, of course, the regular use of these simple tools should be encouraged by all. Checks are easy and quick to make and, with the cheapest testers costing about £5, there really is no excuse for not using one.

Such a tool is doubly important if your car suffers from even the slightest coolant leak. The big danger in these cases is that the owner tops up the system every now and again with plain water, forgetting that the coolant concentration is being progressively weakened with each addition. So go on, do yourself and your engine a favour and take the time and trouble to check your coolant condition regularly. Your bank manager will thank you in the long term!

A cheap and cheerful coolant tester like this is easy to use and reasonably accurate.

Professional versions (left) cost more and include a coolant temperature facility which boosts accuracy.

Back to Basics

Part 5:
Chris Graham roots out the shocking truth about modern ignition systems

A modern car's ignition system is not something to be trifled with, let's be quite clear about that. There are major safety issues to be considered and I would advise anyone who is not completely confident about what they're doing, to leave well alone. If you think that getting a shock from a 240V three-pin domestic power socket is a nasty business then think again. Getting it wrong and taking a jolt from a state-of-the-art automotive system could send 80,000+ volts shuddering through your body – that's enough to deal the old ticker a terminal blow. So do yourself a favour and don't dabble!

Having said that, no self-respecting vehicle engineering series would be complete without an episode on ignition. It's a fascinating and fundamental aspect of the motor car and, as such, every motoring enthusiast can benefit from a greater practical understanding of its subtleties. It's also an aspect which has developed in leaps and bounds, particularly in the past 20 years. Although the basic principles remain just about the same, the methods used to achieve them have changed radically. Nowadays ignition control is very high-tech. Computers dominate and the top-spec systems are perfectly capable of regulating themselves, on a second-by-second basis, to ensure that engine efficiency and performance remain at the highest levels.

The fundamental purpose of the ignition system really is twofold. At its core is the necessity to produce a spark that is sufficiently powerful to ignite the compressed fuel/air mixture inside the combustion chamber. But, irrespective of its

power, the presence of this spark is absolutely useless unless it is timed correctly. It must be encouraged to jump between the spark plug's electrodes at just the right moment, so that it catches the mixture at the ideal degree of compression and effective combustion is assured. Timing of the spark is the ignition system's other primary function.

All ignition systems, be they on a Morris Marina or a Vauxhall Vectra, are essentially the same in that they share the same fundamental components. Put most simply, a battery is used to provide a 12-volt supply which is converted into a high voltage charge by the coil. This is then dispatched to the spark plugs,

Be a bright spark

Fitting the correct spark plug is a very important factor nowadays on modern engines. All modern plugs are designed with a specific resistance, and the whole ignition system is balanced around this. Fitting an inappropriately specified plug will upset the balance of the entire ignition circuit, and can even induce engine mis-fires.

Modern coils now bolt directly on to the individual spark plugs, giving fantastic control potential and the ultimate ignition performance.

often via the distributor, where it straddles the gap and ignites the fuel/air mixture.

This electrical 'conversion' from low to high voltage is a key stage in the process and is a complicated aspect to explain in a couple of brief paragraphs. Those of you who can remember messing around with magnets and iron filings in the school physics lab will have an advantage here! Basically, the process relies on the interaction between a magnetic field and a coil of wire – an effect first discovered by that clever Mr Faraday. Known as electromagnetic induction, the principle centres on the fact that a magnetic field can be used to generate an electrical current in

a separate coil of wire, if the two are placed close together. It is actually the interference between the magnetic field and the coil, which generates the electro-magnetic force (emf). I know it's a hard concept to grasp, and it only gets worse when you discover that, for some obscure and deeply scientific reason, the most significant emf is actually produced the instant the magnetic field is switched off!

So, in a conventional automotive coil, the primary winding carries the 12V supply from the battery, and is wound around an iron core which becomes magnetised when the current flows.

Cutting the battery voltage cancels the magnetic effect and the electrical interference that results induces a current in the nearby secondary coil, which is made of much finer and more tightly-wound wire. The number of turns in the secondary coil has a direct bearing on the emf voltage produced – the more there are the greater the current. This is how a mere 12 volts is neatly converted into the scary 50,000 volts needed to feed a modern system. Although it takes considerably less voltage than this to get a spark to jump across the plug gap under normal conditions, put the whole thing under pressure, as it is in the combustion chamber, and the voltage requirement sky-rockets.

As you can imagine, the accuracy of the coil switching action is very important. It has to be linked to the rotation of the engine so that the sparks produced can be sent to the relevant spark plugs at the correct point in the combustion cycle. For this the system relies on another vital component, the distributor.

For many years the job of switching the coil fell upon the tiny and essentially unreliable contact points. A cam-operated, sprung-steel lever with a contact at the tip, was buried deep inside the distributor, and took its drive from a gear linked directly to the camshaft. It was opened and closed – making and breaking the circuit to fire the coil – at a rate equal to the engine's speed of rotation.

Getting the sparks to the correct plug, at the right time, was the job of the rotor arm, found higher up in the distributor body, just under the cap. The distributor cap is fitted with high tension

Simplified points-based ignition system

1. Distributor
2. Condenser
3. Contact breaker arm operated by cam
4. Ignition coil
5. Ignition switch
6. Battery
7. Spark plug

Vacuum advance units, like this rusty example, are a thing of the past now. Timing adjustments are all controlled electronically nowadays.

A conventional distributor cap with rotor arm beneath. Note the central king lead and the other HT leads on this four-cylinder application.

(HT) leads which run directly to the plugs. These have terminals within the cap and, as the rotor arm spins, it makes contact with each in turn, delivering the spark as it goes. The rotor arm is mounted on a central spindle and spins thanks to the same gear drive from the camshaft.

This basic system worked reasonably well for many years, until the combined effects of the 1970s fuel crisis, a growing awareness for pollution and engine efficiency, plus an increasing need to boost reliability and lengthen service intervals, heralded the beginning of change. It was decided that the contact points were just about the weakest link in the whole system. Although simple, their moving-part construction wore out quickly and detrimentally affected engine performance as it did so (increasing fuel consumption and reducing performance). The challenge was to devise another way of switching the coil on and off – a method that would be more reliable and have fewer moving parts to wear out or break. The solution was to ditch the contact points completely and switch to electronic control.

So-called 'electronic ignition' started to appear in the mid-1980s. It began in fits and starts with a number of aftermarket bolt-on systems, some of which worked, others which didn't. But the manufacturers soon caught on. At the heart of the revolution was a smart little switching device called a pulse generator. This was linked to a transistor-based amplifier unit and, between the two of them, they worked to control coil switching. Pulse generators came in various forms, but all were still timed according to the engine's speed of rotation.

The practical approach varied from manufacturer to manufacturer. Some opted to fit the component inside the distributor body, exactly where the points had been before, so that it could retain the direct link with the camshaft. Others chose a more direct method, preferring to work from the crankshaft, and placed their pulse generators so they were governed by the rotation of the flywheel.

Pulse generators come in three types – inductive, Hall and optical. The least successful of these was probably the optical version, which relied on a photo-transistor that measured the on/off action of an LED. While essentially a good idea, this technology never really caught on and its most notable application was on the Nissan 200ZX. The other two proved far more popular, and now share the modern market in more or less equal proportions. Both the inductive and the Hall type operate using variations on the emf theme – yes, more head-scratching I'm afraid! The inductive unit employs and iron rotor (reluctor) which is spun at engine speed in front of a permanent magnet with electrical coil winding. The interaction between the two generates a small emf in the winding, and this is used to trigger the coil via the amplifier.

The Hall-type pulse generator works in a slightly different way, and relies on a strange electrical effect first discovered by Sir Edward Hall way back in 1879. This unit is build around a small semi-conductor chip which is fed with battery voltage. The weird part is that when the chip is exposed to a magnetic field, it generates a small, separate current, known as a Hall voltage. The flow of this is controlled

directly by the presence of the magnetic field, and so a permanent magnet is used, in conjunction with a rotating vane, to switch the Hall voltage. As with the inductive type, the output voltage is again fed to an amplifier unit which does the final switching of the coil.

As time passed the process of eliminating the weakest link continued with the demise of the mechanically-controlled advance mechanism. This was a unit found sticking out of the side of the distributor, and was used to vary ignition timing. As we've seen in earlier episodes of this series, successful combustion relies on the mixture being ignited at the correct moment. Maximum compression occurs just after the piston reaches tdc but, because it takes time for the flame front to spread throughout the fuel/air mixture, allowance must be made for the burn time. Consequently, the spark has to be timed to occur just before tdc. However, as the engine spins faster, the crankshaft turns further during the short space of time it takes the mixture to burn. So, to keep pace and retain sufficient time for combustion, the ignition point has to be brought forward, or advanced. The opposite occurs as the engine slows, but this adjustment to ignition timing is called retardation.

All ignition advance mechanisms rely on centrifugal weights and rubber diaphragms for their operation, the latter being subjected to varying degrees of vacuum from the inlet manifold. But both approaches suffered with inherent weaknesses, and the decision was taken to drop the device

altogether. In its place the designers, once again, went for electronics. They upgraded the specifications of the amplifier unit, added sensors to monitor engine load and speed, then sat back feeling very pleased with themselves. The new system proved very successful although was somewhat of a halfway house because, before long, the amplifier unit had been combined with the then separate fuel injection control unit, to create a single electronic control unit (ECU) which managed all engine functions.

Simplified electronic ignition system

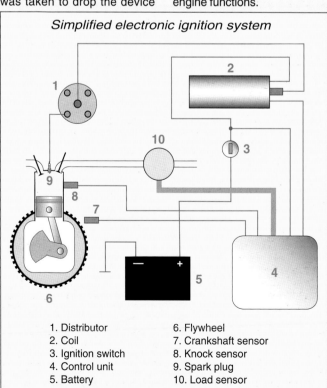

1. Distributor
2. Coil
3. Ignition switch
4. Control unit
5. Battery
6. Flywheel
7. Crankshaft sensor
8. Knock sensor
9. Spark plug
10. Load sensor

TECHNICAL TOPIC: *Checking out a non-runner*

Although cars that refuse to start are less common now than they were 20 years ago, there are still plenty of vehicles around that suffer in this irritating way. Often the problem relates to the ignition system but putting it right can be a tricky and expensive business if you don't know what you're doing.

Lot's of enthusiasts are wary of vehicle electrics and, on balance, that's probably a good thing. As we've already seen, modern systems are both complicated and potentially dangerous for the inexperienced DIY mechanic. However, if you're dealing with an older vehicle and fancy having a crack at some basic fault-finding, there is still plenty you can try in complete safety.

The first point to realise is that when you're dealing with vehicle electrics it's essential to adopt a methodical approach. Never simply dive in on a whim, just because you think you know what the problem is, or because a mate has told you what went wrong on his car. Effective diagnostics must always follow a logical route through the system. Checks must be made systematically to avoid missing a vital clue and drawing the wrong conclusion.

The picture sequence here details a sensible way to tackle an engine which is refusing to start, although it's cranking well and there is evidently fuel getting through. The checks begin with the spark plugs and work progressively back through the system.

1 The first thing to check for is whether or not there is a spark reaching the plugs. Ideally we would recommend the use of a plug spark tester for this check, particularly on newer vehicles. This is a device which fits between the plug and its lead, and enables the spark to be seen easily and safely while the engine is running. In this case though, on an older engine, the careful use of insulated pliers is acceptable. Hold the end of the lead about 6mm from a good earth point on the engine, and away from any flammable substances! Check each plug in turn.

2 When using this 'manual' method of checking for a spark through the plug lead, be sure that you have exposed the tip of the metal connector by gently easing back the rubber boot. If you do not do this the spark may not show and you'll be none the wiser.

3 If there is no spark reaching one or more of the plugs then you must take a step back and check the distributor. Unclip the cap and carry out a visual inspection inside. Check that the centre electrode hasn't been worn away and assess the general condition of the plug lead terminals around it. These should be clean and dry. Any sign of yellowish discolouration, corrosive pitting or excessive wear spells trouble. Also, carefully inspect the cap itself for any signs of cracking. These only need to be hairline to allow electrical charge to leak away to earth.

4 If the cap is okay then transfer your attention to the rotor arm, looking for any signs of wear at all on the centre contact or the electrode at the tip. If you have any doubts about either the cap or the rotor arm, the two should be replaced as a pair. Often people will leave the original arm in place despite fitting a new cap. This is bad practice. As a final check, get a friend to crank the engine as you watch to make sure the rotor arm actually turns. It's not unheard of for distributor drives to sheer.

5 Continuing the process, assuming you've found no problem with the distributor, involves checking its power supply. This arrives down what's called the 'king lead', which is a push fit on to the cap's centre contact tower. Having removed it and exposed the metal contact inside the boot, use insulated pliers as before to check for a spark against a good earth.

6 No supply down the king lead tends to suggest there's a problem with the coil, assuming the lead itself isn't at fault. You'll need to check the coil with a voltmeter – set on a 20-volt scale – and measure the voltage reading between the 'minus' terminal and a good earth point (on the '-' battery terminal is ideal). You are looking for battery voltage here of 10-12 volts with the engine being cranked. Then switch to the coil's positive terminal and test it in the same way and, if all is well then you should find battery voltage here also. If you get a reading on the supply side (+), but not on the output side, then there is an open circuit within the coil and the component will need to be replaced. To check a coil in this way you must leave the wires connected, so use a piece of thin wire fed into the connector as a contact point.

7 The correct voltage in and out of the coil indicates that all is well here, so your final port of call is the coil's switching device which, in this case, is a pulse generator inside the distributor. This is relatively easy to check thanks to its convenient three-pin connector socket on the side of the distributor. Inside here you'll find '+', '-' and earth connectors. With the ignition switched on, the supply pin (+) should be carrying battery voltage, there should be 4-8V at the '-' terminal and a good earth reading at the third pin. The 4-8V value is actually being supplied by the amplifier unit so, if this is missing the fault probably lies with that.

8 As a final check, make sure all the earth points you can find in and around the engine bay are clean, dry and tightly secured.

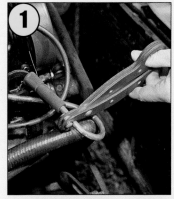

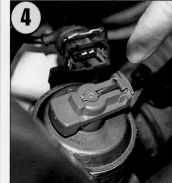

Handy Hints
- Renew HT leads every two to three years.
- Take care when probing electrical sockets to avoid damaging the delicate contact pins.
- Be careful when removing HT leads, always pull boot and not lead itself.
- Always make sure you fit the correct spark plugs, matched for resistance.
- Avoid fiddling with modern ignition systems and, if in ANY doubt, call in the professionals.

Expert assistance

Colchester Institute has a large Automobile Engineering Centre which provides part-time (one day per week) and full-time courses in automobile engineering, body repair and welding.
For more information contact: **Dave Roberts**
Head of Centre for Automobile Engineering, Colchester Institute, Sheepen Road, Colchester, CO3 3LL.

But the development story doesn't end here. There was still one potentially weak moving part left to deal with, and that was the rotor arm inside the bulky distributor. Superseding this meant devising a new way of distributing the current to the individual plugs, which was quite a significant problem. Then some bright spark came up with the idea of adapting the standard coil so that it became double-ended, producing usable voltage outputs from both ends of its secondary winding, instead of just one. Each output was then directed to a pair of spark plugs, so that a single unit could supply ignition for a four-cylinder engine. Obviously, only one of the two plugs was actually using the spark for ignition purposes – the other being fired on its exhaust stroke. For this reason the system is popularly known as 'wasted spark' ignition.

But, of course, designers being designers, the search for ultimate ignition efficiency continued a pace, and attention turned to the poor, unsuspecting HT lead. This apparently straightforward cable can be the source of a great many niggling faults and, as such, is yet another weak point in the system.

Eliminating the lead could only mean one thing, and that was mounting the coil directly on top of the spark plug, which is exactly what has happened. Many engines now feature miniaturised coils that sit, one per cylinder, bolted directly on top of the plugs. This is perhaps the ultimate ignition set-up because it opens up almost infinite amounts of control. Supported by advanced engine management software, this latest refinement allows for high levels of control which virtually guarantee efficient running under all conditions.

State-of-the-art systems are now able, for example, to prevent an individual plug becoming contaminated by firing them at anything up to 200 times a second to burn off unwanted coatings. They can also vary the sparking rate at will to suit the conditions – particularly handy to up this during initial start-up in cold weather. Individual cylinders can be tweaked if detonation is detected, which is a tremendous advantage. In the old days the whole system was retarded which, of course, reduced efficiency and performance levels as well.

Finally, as an added subtlety, large engines are now able to switch off pairs of cylinders when the car is running at high speed on light throttle settings, simply to save fuel!

So there you have it, ignition in a nutshell. Next time you have to start your car on a wet and cold morning, just thank your lucky stars that the modern systems are so well controlled, and spare a thought for the hard-working spark plugs in your engine – they could be the next component to be eliminated.

High voltage!

Successive refinements of ignition systems have systematically increased the voltage levels which whiz around a car's engine. In the old days a conventional coil, running with a contact points system, would generate about 20,000 volts. The arrival of the pulse generator pushed output to around 35,000V, and this was upped again following the demise of the mechanical advance mechanism, when it leaped to 50,000V.

The advent of 'wasted spark' systems brought with it an increase to 75,000V or so, while the newest coil-per-plug set-ups can throw out over 150,000V. Over the years this increase in power has enabled the spark to jump an ever-larger plug gap – an essential factor for combustion efficiency, particularly on modern lean-burn engines.

Next Month
Fuelling systems

TOOLKIT BUILDER:
Multimeters

If you're at all serious about doing any electronics work on your car then you're definitely going to need to buy yourself a multimeter. Regrettably, engine management technology has moved so fast in recent years, that all but the most high-spec multimeter is excluded from meaningful diagnostic testing on modern systems. However, these versatile tools still have a place on older machinery, so adding one to your toolkit can make a lot of sense it you're an enthusiastic amateur.

The good news is that you don't have to spend a fortune to get a thoroughly usable, basic tool. Don't worry too much about the big brand names either, unless you're a real anorak! Modern manufacturing standards mean that the extra

money spent on expensive gear is simply buying enhanced functionality, rather than greater accuracy.

At the bottom of the scale you can lash out between £15-35 for an entry level tool that will happily provide you with accurate resistance, voltage (AC and DC) and low current (below 10 amps) readings. For £50-80 you'll get a mid-ranger that will probably add the ability to measure engine rpm and dwell angles, while top-spec machines, at £100+, provide the ability to monitor temperatures, pulse widths and frequencies. The latter really are professional-type operations and, before being tempted into buying a bells and whistles machine, you should ask yourself what you really want to do with it.

Our advice is certainly to go for a meter with an LCD digital display. The more old fashioned analogue versions, with a scale and needle, are still available at the cheaper end of the market, but really aren't worth bothering about. Needle readings are

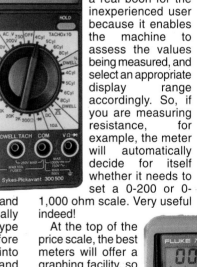

nowhere near precise enough for dealing with electrically-fast modern applications. Another reason for spending a little more cash is to secure a very useful feature called 'auto ranging'. This can be a real boon for the inexperienced user because it enables the machine to assess the values being measured, and select an appropriate display range accordingly. So, if you are measuring resistance, for example, the meter will automatically decide for itself whether it needs to set a 0-200 or 0-1,000 ohm scale. Very useful indeed!

At the top of the price scale, the best meters will offer a graphing facility, so that readings can be plotted and assessed – particularly useful when measuring potentiometer outputs where even the tiniest glitch can cause a serious drivability problem. But, once again, ask yourself how often you would use such a feature, and whether having it warrants the extra expense?

Finally a word about instructions. Terrible! This describes the pathetic offerings from most manufacturers producing equipment at the lower end of the price scale. Part of the problem is that most assume a fairly high level of knowledge in the reader, so beginners tend to be left high and dry very quickly. This is a great shame because there is a lot to be learned and understood about the correct use of a multimeter.

Not only do you need the knowledge to be effective with the machine, but it also helps when avoiding the many possible pitfalls. Basic mistakes such as connecting a meter that's set for an 'ohms' reading, across the battery terminals, will destroy the unit in a trice.

Although higher quality machines have internal protection against this, the more affordable units don't. Resistance and amp readings are potentially the most risky and can, in some cases, even damage the circuit being tested! It can be a technical minefield and I'd certainly advise seeking out a quality reference source on the subject, if you're really interested in using a meter properly.

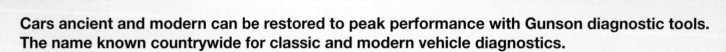

Back to Basics

Fuel pressure is an important factor with any fuel injection system, new or old. The difficulty of measuring it varies from system to system, and is rarely a DIY job anyway.

Engine fuelling is one of the most subtle and complex aspects of the modern motor car. We no longer live in an age when fuel consumption is an irrelevance and smoking exhausts are a regular occurrence. Modern vehicle engines operate within tightly controlled parameters, and development money has been poured at an ever-increasing rate into the quest for ultimate fuel efficiency.

The realisation that the motor car was a significant world polluter resulted in a raft of exhaust emission legislation – emanating from America – which really put the cat among the pigeons as far as the vehicle producers were concerned. All of a sudden they were faced with having to make their engines run efficiently, and they didn't relish the prospect because it involved spending lots of cash.

Under ideal conditions, the burning of petrol vapour in air produces heat, water, carbon dioxide and nitrogen. The heat is used to power the engine but the other products of combustion are dumped into the atmosphere through the exhaust pipe. However, achieving these 'ideal' conditions is not that easy. The

Injection in a nutshell

Modern petrol injection has reached an advanced stage of development thanks to the need for minimal exhaust emissions. Car manufacturers have been forced to fit the best available technology, even to their entry-level models, to ensure that the ever-tightening legislation is met.

Most modern systems include basic components including: an electronic in-tank fuel pump, a fuel filter, an injector rail on which the fuel injectors are mounted, a fuel pressure regulator. The latter is needed to control the pressure at which the fuel is being injected, which varies constantly due to engine loading. Excess fuel is piped back to the tank.

System control comes via the car's main electronic control module (ECM), which makes its mixture calculations based on inputs from a number of important sensors around the engine.

key factor is the ratio between the air and the fuel vapour. For the most efficient burn the two must be mixed in a 14.7:1 proportion of air to fuel vapour. Now, while this may sound a particularly unlikely sort of mixture ratio, it is a vitally important one in this context. You see, the slightest deviation either way – producing a richer or leaner air/fuel mixture – has a drastic effect on combustion

efficiency, engine performance and exhaust gas quality.

As our understanding of pollution issues has developed, it's become apparent that much that's found in exhaust gas is bad news for the environment. Particular nasties include carbon monoxide and nitrogen oxides, and even good old CO_2 has been linked with global warming. Controlling these undesirables means mastering

the combustion process and this, in turn, necessitates accurate metering of both air and fuel into the engine. As exhaust gas emission legislation appeared on the horizon it quickly became apparent that conventional carburettor-equipped engines were never going to meet the required standards. So the race was on to boost combustion efficiency and the solution to the problem was fuel injection.

The basic idea was to provide an effective way of accurately matching fuel delivery to the amount of air being sucked into the engine. But, in addition, the arrival of the fuel injector itself guaranteed much better atomisation of the fuel – another vital factor for ensuring combustion efficiency and minimising unwanted exhaust emissions. Of course, fuel injection had been widely and successfully used in aircraft and on diesel applications for many years before it was adopted for the automotive petrol engine. But, despite this, the earliest attempts weren't terribly impressive. One of the first cars to be equipped with fuel injection in the UK was the Triumph TR6, which used a Lucas system. Unfortunately, it wasn't a success and proved so problematic that many owners opted to have it removed and replaced by conventional carburettors!

The real breakthrough came when Bosch stepped in with its now famous K-Jetronic system in the mid-1970s. It took a year or two for this to gain acceptance but, by the end of the decade, it was being fitted on most German cars and many others were destined to follow. The secret of K-Jetronic's success lay in its reliable performance. It was a well-designed and

Measuring the amount of air entering the engine is a vital function if an accurate fuel/air combustion mixture is to be maintained. Methods of monitoring vary and this air flow meter is just one solution.

This indirect, multi-point fuel injection system utlises a fuel rail which links all four injectors, supplying them with fuel from the tank.

The fuel regulator is an important component in many systems, as it varies pressure on the supply side to match the ever changing demand and ensure that appropriate quantities are fed to the injectors.

Catalytic converters, which clean up the exhaust gases leaving a car's engine, are very sensitive to unburnt fuel. Their presence on all cars now is one of the primary reasons why modern injection systems have to be so efficient and reliable.

Simplified electronic fuel injection system

1. Fuel filter
2. Electric fuel pump
3. Fuel tank
4. Fuel regulator
5. Main injector
6. Cold start injector
7. Throttle pos. switch
8. Air temp. sensor
9. Extra air valve
10. MAP sensor
11. Thermo switch
12. Coolant temp. sensor
13. Distributor
14. ECM
15. Fuel pump relay
16. Main relay
17. Ignition switch
18. Battery

Coolant flow

affordable 'mechanical' system which proved little short of revolutionary in terms of the performance advantages it offered. At the heart of the system was a component called the fuel distributor which was responsible for measuring the quantity of air flow into the engine and then calculating the amount of fuel which needed to be added to achieve the desired 14.7:1 mixture ratio.

K-Jetronic worked on a 'continuous injection' basis, meaning that once the engine was running, the injectors operated constantly. However, they were not electronically switched but, instead, were opened purely by the pressure of the fuel in the system. A hefty pump was used to jack pressures up to around the 70psi mark. The 'continuous' action meant that there was no need to time injection to the engine in any way, thus simplifying the control side of the operation. Admittedly, by today's high standards, this ground-breaker wasn't the most efficient system but, when compared to the carburettor based set-ups which it replaced, it was little short of marvellous. Engines suddenly became more responsive, more economical and more reliable, so everyone was happy.

Adjustments to the mixture, necessitated by changes in engine loading and speed, were made simply by varying the fuel supply rate. The distributor unit controlled this in response to a hinged flap located in the main air induction trunking. This swung according the amount of air passing it and so at idle, with a relatively low air intake rate, fuel supply was reduced to a minimum. But with the engine responding to hard acceleration, and with air rushing in to meet demand, the supply rate was upped to ensure enough fuel was injected.

The success of the K-Jetronic fuel injection system is best illustrated by the fact that it remained current well into the mid-1980s. Unfortunately what killed it was the arrival of the catalytic converter – it simply wasn't efficient enough to be used with this exhaust gas-scrubbing device. Cats are notoriously sensitive to the presence of unburnt fuel and even small amounts can cause irrepairable damage. To guard against this, and protect the expensive cat, fuelling controls had to be tightened still further and the only way to achieve this was to switch to electronic control.

Bosch had a crack at adapting K-Jetronic by bolting on some additional electronic goodies and christening it KE-Jetronic, but success was limited. It was notably fitted to the Mercedes-Benz 190E and Ford's RS1600 Turbo, but was only ever really a stop-gap until the first truly electronic systems arrived.

Complexity increased significantly with this new breed, and all adopted high specification control systems that acted on inputs from a number of key sensors around the engine. Air intake measurement remained the core priority, but additional information concerning throttle position, coolant temperature, crankshaft position and air temperature was worked into the mixture calculations to help ensure accuracy.

Electronic fuel injection systems vary from application to application. Price is a big factor and, of course, many vehicle manufacturers have done all they can to keep costs to a minimum. In the early days it was generally accepted that vehicles at the cheaper end of the market were equipped with basic injection systems, while those at the top end were more lavishly specified. But as time has passed, and emissions legislation has grown tighter, the car makers have been forced into compliance and so, nowadays, even relatively ordinary vehicles enjoy the benefits top-spec and highly efficient fuel injection systems.

The method used for keeping track of air induction levels varies too. Traditionally the budget-priced systems relied on 'indirect' monitoring, using a sensor which measured the degree of vacuum in the inlet manifold (MAP sensor). As vacuum level is directly linked to the flow rate of the air, it's possible to calculate air volumes and use the information to set injection performance accordingly. However this method is rarely as accurate as measuring the intake air directly, which was the route chosen by the more sophisticated systems. They relied on the inclusion of an air flow meter which, although considerably more expensive than the MAP sensor, produced a far more precise reading. As production processes improved and the cost of air flow meters fell away, many systems came to rely on their performance.

The original designs used a simple flap that was deflected by the incoming air, rather like the device used in the mechanical K-Jetronic set-up. The degree of deflection was measured and used to calculate the mass of the air entering at any time. But this approach had significant weaknesses, with the two most serious drawbacks being potentially slow response times and the propensity for the mechanism to become clogged up and inefficient. A more accurate and reliable solution came with the introduction of the hot wire air flow meter, which relied on the cooling effect of the passing air on a heated titanium wire. The more air which passed, the greater the cooling effect on the wire and so the lower its temperature would become. Relating these temperature fluctuations to the passage of air was a simple matter, and the 'solid state' nature of the hot wire unit made it a cheaper, more reliable and yet extremely accurate performer.

Fuel injection systems can be classified in a number of ways but perhaps the most fundamental of these relates to the actual number of injectors used. The most basic systems, used on small cars like the Vauxhall Corsa and Nissan Micra, were categorised as 'single point'. These, as you

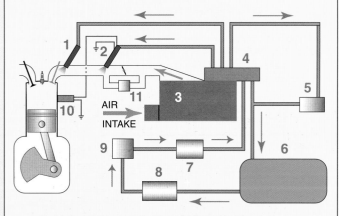

Simplified mechanical fuel injection system

AIR INTAKE

1. Main injector
2. Cold start injector
3. Air flow sensor with flap within
4. Fuel distributor
5. Warm-up regulator
6. Petrol tank
7. Fuel filter
8. Fuel pump (electric)
9. Accumulator
10. Thermo switch\
11. Auxiliary air by-pass

TECHNICAL TOPIC:
Fuel filter swap

The disappointing fact for all enthusiastic DIYers is that, while fuel injection certainly delivered little short of a revolution in terms of engine power outputs and efficiency levels, its arrival also heralded the end of home tinkering. No longer can the amateur mechanic fiddle with the mixture setting on his car, or revel in the prospect of choosing and fitting an uprated carburettor. The complexity of the modern control systems, not to mention the high-tech nature of the components involved, mean that servicing and repair work requires specialist knowledge and equipment.

However, the fuelling system on your car shouldn't be regarded as a completely closed book, because there remain a few worthwhile things that you can do on a Saturday morning, one of the most important of which is changing the fuel filter. While this may sound a boring and straightforward job, it's actually an extremely important one. The humble fuel filter is a vital link in a very important chain. It's effective operation is key to the functioning of the whole injection process and it's a component which is often ignored, particularly on vehicles which are no longer on main dealership service programmes.

The sensitivity and engineering precision of modern fuel injectors means that they are susceptible to damage and blockage from dirt and other debris that may find its way into them from the fuel tank. The only defence against this is the fuel filter, so it's very important for this to be kept in tip-top condition. Consequently, it must be changed regularly and here we've used a mid-1990s Ford Mondeo to illustrate just how it's done.

1 Before doing anything else the fuel system must be de-pressurised. Never forget that pressure is retained within the system at all times, to ensure effective engine starting. So never wade in and start undoing connections before you've taken this precaution otherwise you're sure to squirt fuel everywhere. One of the easiest ways to de-pressurise the system on this car is to disconnect the fuel pump, which is accessed under the rear seat cushion. Simply disconnect the pumps power supply.

2 Alternatively, you can lift the bonnet and remove the fuel pump's control relay or fuse. Either way, the single objective of cutting power to the pump will be achieved.

3 Next crank the engine for a short while. It will probably start and run for a second or two, which is fine. But, because the pump has been disconnected the fuel supply held under pressure in the system will soon be consumed and, thus, the system will be de-pressurised. At this point it will then be safe to proceed with filter removal.

4 Fuel filters are tucked away in differing locations under the vehicle, depending on the design. Consult a workshop manual if you're not sure. In most cases they will be clamped into place with a Jubilee clip-type fastening which will have to be loosened. In this case the clip hooks over a bracket slung from the underside of the vehicle's floorpan.

5 With the filter unit free to move, begin removing the pipe connectors. Take care when doing this as the design of these fixings varies. In some cases they will be a simple push fit while, in others, quick-release locking tabs or similar security devices will be employed. If the filter has not been changed for a long time, disconnection may prove a struggle. Nevertheless, be patient and take care not to damage the end of the pipework.

6 Even though the system has been depressurised, it's likely that you'll still find a small amount of fuel held in the filter. Be prepared for this as the first pipe is separated and have a cloth or small container ready to catch any spillage.

7 Fuel filters are not reversible and so it is very important that the new one is fitted the right way around! In most cases you'll find that the manufacturers make things easy by stamping a clear indicator as to the direction of flow. Obviously, for best results, the arrow must point towards the engine!

8 Once the new filter has been connected and secured into place, you might like to finish the job by giving the Jubilee clip a quick spurt of a long-lasting lubricant such as Duck oil – to help ensure that it's easy to remove next time.

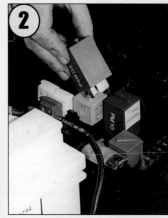

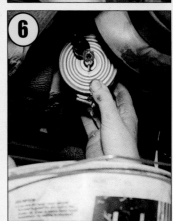

Handy Hints

- Dose your car's fuelling system regularly with one of the quality injector treatments.
- Remember that old-style K-Jetronic injection operates at about 70psi.
- All injection systems remain pressurised even when the engine is not running.
- Ensure your fuel filter is changed according to the service schedule.
- Unfortunately, modern fuel injection systems are NOT DIY-friendly.

might imagine, employ just one injector – normally positioned fairly well back in the inlet manifold, more or less where an old-style carburettor would have been. Fuel vapour was injected into the air stream travelling through the manifold, and drawn into the cylinders for combustion. Unfortunately, while very affordable, the single point approach was inherently inefficient and, consequently, is no longer used in modern car production.

The alternative, and generally preferable option in terms of performance, was the multi-point system, which gave individual cylinders their own fuel injector. These were placed much closer to the inlet valves and provided

significantly improved efficiency. All major manufacturers now use variations on the multi-point theme.

Most of the latest electronic injection systems operate on an intermittent or pulsed basis. This means that instead of the injectors working continuously, as with K-Jetronic, they are opened and closed electronically which adds control and flexibility to the whole fuelling process. The 'intermittent' systems can be sub-divided into 'group' and 'sequential' versions. The former opens and closes all injectors at once, while the latter controls them in an order appropriate to the engine's firing sequence. The earliest systems all worked on the group control principle

and this ran well into the 1990s. But the added refinement of the sequential approach boosted efficiency further, and so most manufacturers have switched to this now.

Two further refinements relate to the specific placement of the injectors, in relation to the cylinders. So called 'indirect' fuel injection was the traditional approach, utilising injectors placed upstream of the cylinders, somewhere in the inlet manifold. The more modern 'direct' injection option places the injectors right on top of the cylinders, so that the fuel is squirted down just where it's needed, directly into the combustion chambers. Up until quite recently, virtually all automotive petrol engines relied on indirect injection simply because it was cheaper to manufacture and easier to engineer.

Direct injection systems have to work in a harsh environment

and at a much higher pressure because the injector is battling against the compression inside the cylinder. Consequently, a bigger and better fuel pump, more sturdy injectors and top quality pipework is essential, all of which drives up the cost. Nevertheless, the system works really well. Injecting the fuel straight into the top of the cylinder ensures that it mixes more completely with the incoming air than when it's added in the manifold. Mitsubishi was the first manufacturer to introduce widely available direct injection technology with its GDI range of petrol engines. This system has proved very successful over the past couple of years and it seems that the likes of Bosch are working hard to develop their own versions for more widespread use.

Next Month
Engine management basics

TOOLKIT BUILDER:
Screwdrivers

The humble screwdriver is available in many different types and styles these days, and buying the right sorts is important for those establishing a first-time tool kit.

There are four basic head types which you're likely to need for everyday maintenance jobs – flat, cross-head, Posidrive and Torx – although much depends on the age of your vehicle. In the past five years the trend has swung markedly in favour of Posidrive and the newer star-shaped Torx fastenings, but on older cars cross-head (Philips) and conventional flat blade designs will be more appropriate.

As a starting point we would recommend you buy a couple of each sort to give you a basic working kit to cover most common eventualities. Most screwdriver sizes are classified by a simple number scale, with 'one' being the smallest. Anything much bigger than size three is probably going to be too large for general automotive applications. Flat screwdrivers are not classified in this way, but are sized by blade tip width – 3.2mm small, 5mm medium, 8mm large. So, for starters pick size two and three flat heads, and one and two for both the cross-head and Posidrive types. Torx drivers are a slightly different kettle of fish, and are classified on a different number scale which relates specifically to the size of the fastening being dealt with. Normally, they are sold in sets.

Apart from the head diameter, the length of the screwdriver blade is an important consideration. Ideally, for most work you should be

looking for a four to five-inch blade. This means that the tool will be manageable but still able to generate a useful amount of purchase. It's also worth adding one or two 'stubbies' to your kit. These have very short blades and are designed for use when access is limited. You may occasionally need a longer blade length, particularly for getting at deeply recessed screws used for securing dashboards etc, but it's perhaps best to buy these on a 'need-one-now' basis. At the bottom end of the size scale you'll find the Jewellers'-type screwdriver, with tiny heads. These can be useful for stripping components such as ECMs, wiper motors or radios.

As far as price is concerned, as with most hand tools, the variations can be enormous. By and large though, the more you pay the better the tool. Metal quality is a key factor and, quite honestly, the sort of screwdrivers you might find in a £1 shop will normally be worse than useless. The relative softness of the metal used means that their heads will bend and distort at the merest whiff of exertion. Better quality screwdrivers will offer a superior standard of finish. They are sure to

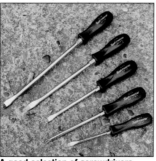
A good selection of screwdrivers provide an important part of any tool kit. Note that some of these feature the 'captive nut' arrangement at the handle-end of their blades – a good sign of quality.

be more accurately shaped, and will work more effectively under all conditions, reducing the risk of slippage.

As a guide you should expect to pay about £8-12 for a good standard screwdriver (whatever its head type) with a five-inch blade. A top quality example will cost anything from £20 up while, at the other end of the scale, anything costing less than £5 really isn't worth considering. If you're serious about your toolkit, then it's certainly worth regarding screwdriver purchase as an investment.

If you're working on a really limited budget which, let's face it, many of us are nowadays, you might also like to consider one of the now widely available multi-purpose tools. These are supplied with a number of driver bits, stored in the handle, and often feature a ratcheting action for easy one-handed operation. Some people may regard these as a bit amateurish but those produced by the well-known and respected manufactures are serious pieces of kit. Good ones can represent great value for money but, as always, cheap ones should be avoided.

At a practical level, it's important to make sure that you are actually using the right size of driver for the screw being tackled. It may sound an obvious point but you'd be surprised how many people get it wrong – even some professionals who should know better! Failing in this respect is likely to cause the tool to slip but, perhaps more importantly, will also greatly increase the risk of damaging the screw you're trying to deal with. So, if ever you're not sure about which size to use, take a few seconds to make certain by gently testing a couple of alternatives.

Another all too common, but

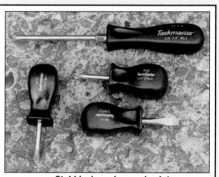
Stubbies' can be an absolute godsend when space is limited

Multi-piece screwdriver kits like this, with a ratchet action and magnetised shaft, give flexibility, convenience and can save you money too.

generally inadvisable practice, is to use screwdrivers as convenient levers or chisels. In the main they are not designed for the purpose and should never be used as such. Whacking a standard will normally achieve little apart from splitting the handle. There are exceptions though. The so-called 'pound-through' screwdriver is made specifically to be hit, and features an extended blade which runs right up through the handle and ends in a tempting impact cap on the top.

Finally, if you're operating at the luxury end of the market then one useful refinement worth seeking out is the inclusion of a 'captive' nut-arrangement at the handle-end of the blade. This enables a spanner to be used to assist with the most stubborn screws, greatly increasing the amount of leverage that can be exerted.

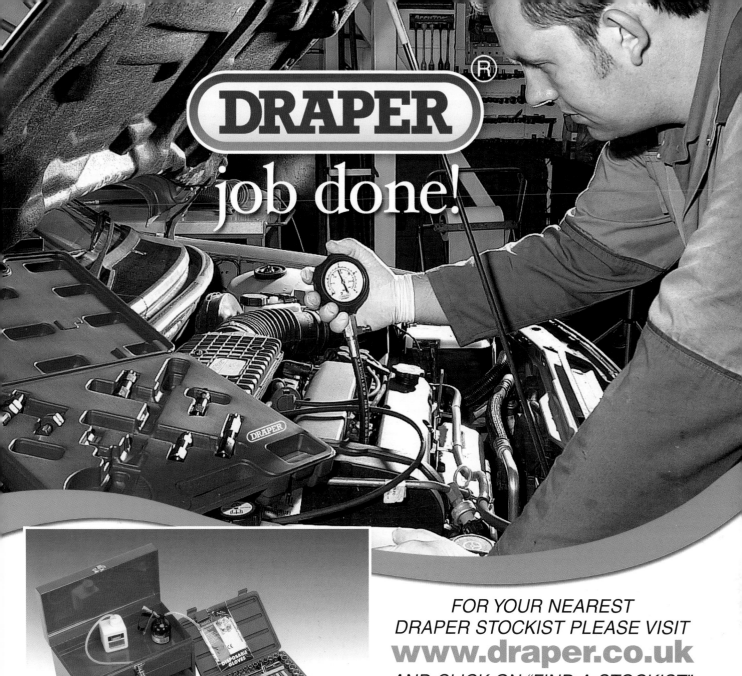

Back to Basics

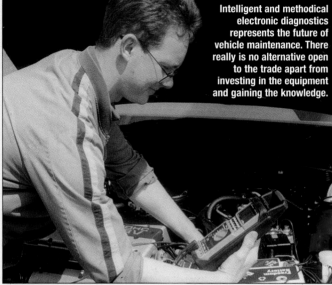

Intelligent and methodical electronic diagnostics represents the future of vehicle maintenance. There really is no alternative open to the trade apart from investing in the equipment and gaining the knowledge.

There's no doubt that computers are pretty wonderful things. What's more they're getting more wonderful by the week. I'm typing this on a new iMac – a personal computer which continues Apple Macintosh's groundbreaking tradition in a most spectacular way. An infinitely adjustable and perfectly flat, biscuit-thin LCD screen is linked to a domed base unit by a single, beautifully engineered, chrome-plated tubular arm. The dome is just 11 inches in diameter at its base, and about six inches high, yet it contains everything normally found in those ugly grey plastic towers which clutter office desks across the world.

I mention all this simply because it illustrates perfectly just how the changing face of computer technology allows designers ever more freedom. The computer revolution has impacted on virtually every aspect of modern life including, of course, the automotive industry. The cars of today are technological masterpieces which rely progressively more on high-tech electronics to keep them going. Whether or not this turns out to be a good thing remains to be seen. Personally, I have my doubts. I certainly believe that there will be serious maintenance issues to be faced in years to come, when owners and the motor trade are forced to grapple with the array of niggling problems thrown up by temperamental and ageing vehicle electronics.

The term 'engine management' is actually outdated already, because in most cases so much more than just the engine on a modern vehicle is controlled by computer. Transmission, brakes, climate control, vehicle stability, security

and in-car entertainment are all often plumbed into the vehicle's central processing units. Cars such as the latest BMW 7 Series have no ignition key or gear lever because they've been engineered out of the equation.

The driver uses a screen in the car to navigate through the various control options. Another example is Renault's new Laguna, which utilises a credit

It's all just Greek to me! Well, this may look complicated but this is one of the simplest ECMs around, taken from an early Bosch LE3 engine management system fitted to a MkII Vauxhall Astra.

card-like 'key' to activate security and engine.

But this is all a far cry from how the engine management revolution began way back in the early 1980s. The whole movement was driven by the need to force down exhaust emissions so that car engines could be brought into line with environmental legislation. Once it was established that common exhaust constituents such as carbon monoxide, benzene, lead, oxides of nitrogen and carbon dioxide, were potentially serious sources of pollution, action was taken to reduce them.

Old-fashioned, carburettor-controlled engines were simply incapable of running at the required levels of efficiency. The only way to regulate fuelling and ignition timing effectively, thus ensuring efficient combustion and minimal exhaust pollution, was by switching to electronic control. The adoption of fuel injection heralded the demise of the carburettor, and brought the

internal combustion engine into a new age of efficiency. Modern electronic control modules (ECMs) regulate virtually everything on today's cars. They do this by keeping close tabs on all the key activities going on around the vehicle, thanks to electronic inputs from a complicated array of sensors. These measure everything from engine speed and load, to coolant temperature and exhaust gas make-up (Lambda).

The ECM is able to make judgements about what it 'sees' because it's cleverly pre-programmed during manufacture with a database of operating parameters relating to all the most important operating functions. These detail upper and lower tolerances in each case, so that the ECM is able to check that the signals it's receiving fall within the recommended operating range. But as soon as an output breaches its range limit – for whatever reason – the ECM recognises the deviation and a fault code (in the form of a two or three-digit number) is logged within its memory.

What's really interesting though is that modern ECMs are capable of a limited degree of intelligent 'thought'. They can adapt and learn to adjust when some sensors alter their output, as gradual engine wear starts to have an effect, for example. Also, if a sensor completely fails – as a good number eventually do – the ECM has the brains to take over by substituting the missing inputs with a set from its own memory.

This enables the engine to continue running in what's known as 'default' or 'limp home' mode. While this normally results in reduced performance levels, often combined with increased fuel consumption and exhaust emissions, the main thing is that the engine continues to operate without damaging itself.

In most cases nowadays, any stored fault codes will trigger an engine management warning light somewhere on the dashboard. Illumination of this indicates that some degree of problem exists within the system, and that further investigation is required. It's the exploration, analysis and rectification of these faults which make up the specialised and exacting process known as 'electronic diagnostics'. Many experts within the industry

Despite the complexity and state-of-the-art nature of modern vehicle electronics, faults with the fuel injectors or spark plugs can still bring the whole system to it's high-tech knees.

It takes little more than a dirty block connector like this, on a Fiat Brava, to induce faulty electrical contacts and throw overall engine control into chaos.

Designers continue to drop clangers, despite CAD assistance. The ECM on this VW Polo is tucked away under a flexible plastic panel at the base of the screen. Once the panel gets cracked or is badly refitted, water off the screen showers the ECM to cause all sorts of mayhem.

consider that this specialised business represents the real future of vehicle maintenance.

The rapid increase in engine management system complexity has led to a correspondingly sudden rise in the number of problems afflicting most modern vehicles. Design and component quality varies enormously across the industry. However, it's probably true to say that the majority of faults are still caused by nothing more complicated than interference from dirt and water.

Most of the components used nowadays, including the majority of ECMs, are pretty reliable and premature, component-related failure is comparatively rare. Unfortunately, though, the connectors used to link up the various engine management components with the vehicle's central wiring loom remain the Achilles heal.

Despite the manufacturers' best efforts at designing tamper-proof, sealed connectors, problems do still arise, particularly after they have been disturbed. Every system, be it fitted to a Mercedes-Benz S Class or a Ford Ka, relies on the integrity of its electrical connectors for successful and reliable operation. Even relatively minor plug connector corrosion can be sufficient to inhibit an electrical contact, throwing the whole system into operational disarray. Voltage output levels are very finely controlled in many cases and so it only takes a slight deviation from the norm to throw up a major gremlin. Modern ECMs are extremely sensitive to voltage fluctuations and will shut themselves down at the first whiff of trouble, at which point the engine stops.

In the past few years the industry has struggled to standardise certain aspects of engine management technology. The powers that be thought it would be sensible to devise a universal socket into which diagnostic equipment could be plugged to simplify testing procedures – the result was

imaginatively-named J1962 socket. This development originated in California, which suffers with an astonishing 30 million cars that choke its sunny freeways. Los Angeles is one of the most heavily polluted cities in the world, and officials there are getting serious about sorting out the problem. Such is the concern that there are already tester-toting officials with the power to stop vehicles and carry out spur of the moment 'interrogations'. But it's not the drivers being questioned, it's the engine management system, via the 16-pin onboard diagnostic (OBD) socket!

Here in Europe things are not quite at that stage yet, although what starts in America tends to happen here eventually. While some manufacturers have been slow to introduce 'official' OBD sockets, the hotch-potch of system operating software poses a much more practical problem for repairers. A wide

This basic code reader from Gunson is ideal for the DIY enthusiast who wants to interrogate a car's fault code memory.

variety is used across the industry here and, to date, I am not aware of one single piece of diagnostic equipment which can be used to deal with every system likely to be encountered. Herein lies the problem for independent workshops who, if they are working on a variety of vehicle marques, need to make a significant investment in equipment to survive.

Modern engine management systems are a closed book to all those without the correct diagnostic equipment. Everything is controlled electronically and the days of Saturday morning tinkering are sadly long gone. Unless you have the appropriate piece of diagnostic hardware in your toolbox, and the expertise to use it properly, you wont even be able to adjust the tickover on your car.

Of course, the vehicle manufacturers have a vested interest in keeping system access as difficult as possible, because it helps ensure that owners remain locked into the dealership service program – which is how most make their money nowadays. Fortunately, a flourishing industry has sprung up among clever independent equipment producers who delight in the challenge of 'reverse engineering' their way into the vehicle manufacturers' software. This has resulted in a range of hardware becoming available to access even the

most complicated vehicle operating systems.

The good news is that it's now possible to buy everything from a basic code reader which plugs into the diagnostic socket and downloads any stored fault codes found in the system's memory, to full-blown oscilloscope or laptop-based vehicle diagnostic systems which will do everything. Serious users must be prepared to tackle both major and minor faults with air conditioning, automatic transmissions, security systems and all manner of engine-related problems. Often, it's the minor, niggly complaints which are the hardest to deal with. Intermittent faults can be an absolute nightmare to track down, calling for the best available equipment combined with great experience and expertise. Unfortunately, the bad news is that the ability to deal effectively with complex problems is directly linked to the amount of money spent, with the top-spec systems costing many thousands of pounds.

There's a perception that modern vehicle diagnostics is easy if you have the right kit and, to a limited degree this is true. However, those who are fooled into thinking that spending

Oscilloscope-based machines are becoming a basic requirement for serious diagnostic work. Laptop computers loaded with the relevant programming provide perhaps the most convenient and versatile alternative.

A few hundred pounds will buy you a hand-held tester like this Advanced Code Reader from Sykes-Pickavant. Capable of accessing and clearing fault codes, as well as many other useful test functions, this tester requires system-specific software pods.

TECHNICAL TOPIC: *Coolant temperature sensor swap*

The coolant temperature sensor plays a vital role in the engine management system. It's primary job is to inform the fuel injection system (via the ECM) whether the engine is hot or cold and, in this way, it helps to ensure that fuelling remains correct. However, the information it provides is also used by the ignition system, the timing of which is varied when the engine is hot and cold. What's more, modern management systems, on cars with electronically-controlled gearboxes, also make use of engine temperature information when determining appropriate gear shift patterns.

It's unfortunate then that such an influential component in the system suffers from what could best be described as a somewhat random service life. Failure causes significant drivability problems and, to understand these you must appreciate a little about how it works. Essentially it's a component which is able to vary its resistance depending on temperature, hence it's classified as a thermister. To be completely accurate, it's an NTC thermister, with the 'NTC' standing for 'negative temperature coefficient'. This basically means that it works in the opposite way to a normal resistor – the hotter it gets, the more its resistance is lowered. This handy performance means that the thermister is very good at monitoring temperature and reacting to changes by resistance variations.

Under normal conditions the sensor's resistance may be 1,000ohms when the engine is cold, but this drops to perhaps 300ohms when the motor has warmed to normal operating temperature. However, when things go wrong the sensor loses its ability to vary the resistance. It simply gives up the ghost and usually becomes lodged at one resistance value. Often it will get stuck at the high end of the resistance scale, sending a permanent message to the ECM that the engine is cold whether it is or not. This, as you can imagine, sets up a lot of electrical consternation within the ECM, causing the fuel injection system to pump in too much fuel, and the Lambda sensor in the downpipe to have a blue fit at the suddenly terrible condition of the exhaust gases. Confusion and conflict within the system reigns supreme and fault codes are normally registered.

The harsh environment in which the coolant temperature sensor operates – repeated heating and cooling – undoubtedly plays a big part in its deterioration. Once it goes wrong the only solution is to replace it but first it's important to confirm that it is actually the sensor, and not it's wiring, that's at fault.

1 The first job is to detect whether or not it's actually the sensor which is at fault. The other possibility is that there could be a problem further back in the wiring, between the sensor and the ECM. So start by a few simple visual checks, making sure that the connector is a tight fit on to the sensor, and that the terminals inside are dry and free from any sign of corrosion.

2 Next check that there is a supply voltage reaching the sensor. Remember, at this stage, that virtually all sensors in a modern electronic management system work off 5V electrical supplies, so don't expect to find 12V fizzing down the wires. Use a multimeter, set on a low voltage range, and connect one of its leads to the negative terminal on the vehicle's battery. Having switched the ignition on, probe the socket with the other lead clip and touch each of the two terminals in turn. Only one will register a voltage, confirming that the sensor is receiving a supply. Just about the only components to be fed with a 12V supply are the fuel injectors.

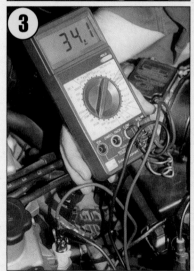

3 So, assuming that power is getting to the sensor, then the problem must lie within the sensor itself. To test this you need to carry out a resistance check, with the multimeter switched to a suitable ohm range. You'll have to refer to the workshop manual to find the appropriate setting. To make the test an effective one you need to take at least two readings, one with the engine cold and the other with it hot, and both should relate to the data quoted in the manual. If you have no data at all then the best you can do is check that the resistance value falls away progressively as the engine warms up.

4 Removing the faulty sensor is a simple job that's best tackled using a ring spanner. You will lose some coolant as the sensor is loosened so either catch it to reuse later or remember to refill with an appropriately mixed water/antifreeze solution once the job is finished.

5 It's a pretty unimpressive component really and, because it's a sealed unit, there's no chance of repairing it. Fortunately a new one is unlikely to break the bank and can usually be bought for around £40 which, considering its influence on the rest of the system, is pretty good value. A word of warning though. Make sure you actually buy the correct replacement. On some vehicles it's possible to get confused with other sensors used for the cooling fan or temperature gauge. Be careful because these are likely to have different resistance tolerances and will prove very confusing for the Electronic Control Module!

6 Because the coolant temperature sensor needs to be a water-tight component, it makes sense to check the threads before fitting the new one. Make sure there is no debris or dirt in the hole which could damage the threads and, whatever you do, don't over-tighten the sensor when re-fitting. The last thing you want is to strip the thread.

Expert assistance

Colchester Institute has a large Automobile Engineering Centre which provides part-time (one day per week) and full-time courses in automobile engineering, body repair and welding.
For more information contact: **Dave Roberts**
Head of Centre for Automobile Engineering, Colchester Institute, Sheepen Road, Colchester, CO3 3LL.

£6,000 on a state-of-the-art diagnostic fault-finder is going to turn them into an expert overnight, will be sadly mistaken. You see, the computers used in modern cars are no different from the one on your desk in the office or at home. The old maxim 'rubbish in, rubbish out' is as true with engine management as it is with all other branches of computing. If a vehicle's ECM is fed with spurious information, then that is exactly what the tester will retrieve. It's important to appreciate that diagnostic equipment can only ever act as a link between the operator and the ECM's memory, so it's the interpretation of the data which is the key factor.

The ability to master this vital interpretation is a rare one, which is why there are still so few genuine diagnostic experts working successfully in the UK. In my experience a worryingly high proportion of dealerships struggle to correct even the most fundamental problems, while a significant proportion of the independents are floundering.

The upshot is that you, the customer, are paying the price for the trade's lack of knowledge and unwillingness to learn. With vehicle diagnostics, a little knowledge really is a very bad thing indeed. It's frightening but plenty of workshops haven't a clue about what's causing the problems they are presented with, and their solution is to replace component after component until the fault goes away.

Most owners are understandably ignorant about the inner workings of these management systems, and so they accept what the workshop tells them. Presented with a list of replaced components including a Lambda sensor, an airflow meter, a throttle position switch, an air temperature sensor and an ECM, who among us is prepared to question the service manager about exactly why so much was needed? The bill, of perhaps £800, could well be £600 over the top because all that actually needed doing was the replacement of one component instead of five. It's little short of a scandal.

So, in next month's instalment we'll be looking in more detail at the most common types of component failure on modern systems, and explaining how to recognise these problems as they occur. In this way we intend to empower you the owners, giving you the confidence at least to question what's being done to your vehicle.

Next Month
Engine management failures

TOOLKIT BUILDER:
Hacksaws and files

Unless you're planning a prison breakout, hacksaws and files are not the types of tool guaranteed to set the pulse racing. However, they are both stalwarts of the automotive toolkit and, as such, deserve a mention in this series.

Files come in all shapes and sizes and so choosing which to buy can be a problem. The good news, though, is that for general automotive applications, the choice can be whittled down to just a handful of basic options. The only real factors to watch for concern blade shape and design plus overall size. The pattern of teeth cut on the blade varies depending on the application but, you should seek out examples featuring what's called a 'second cut' blade. Don't go for anything that's too harsh (chunky teeth) as you'll probably find such a tool awkward and clumsy to use. Really, though, it's largely a matter of trial and error.

As far as blade shape is concerned there are a couple of basic designs you should look out for. The common flat blade, with teeth on both faces, is an obvious choice and you'll certainly need one or two of these for general work. Another valuable tool is the round file which, as its name suggests, has a circular cross section and is ideal for cleaning up drilled holes etc. Perhaps less useful on an everyday basis are the 'square' and 'half-round' (flat on one side, rounded on the other) files which

This is typical of the type of general-purpose hacksaw that's ideal for automotive applications. Make sure your tool is fitted with a 24tpi blade.

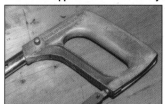

Handle design is an important factor for the serious user. Plastic versions tend to be more comfortable than metal examples like this.

Blade tensioning is set using this wing nut. It's a matter of judgement but getting it wrong increases the risk of wasteful blade snapping.

are both rather more specialised.

As far as the blade length is concerned, you're really looking at something about six inches long to provide the ideal compromise between convenience and effectiveness. The much longer, old-style engineers' files really are too cumbersome for many modern applications. Opt for good quality plastic handles too if you can. These are much easier and more comfortable to use than the old-style bulbous wooden ones, which always had a tendency to split as they aged.

One final option worth considering is buying a set of miniature files, rather like those tiny jewellers'-type screwdrivers we mentioned recently. These can be particularly useful for delicate work on modern engines – deburring or filing connectors etc.

Hacksaws are an even simpler option to buy. Most general purpose tools are

supplied with a 12-inch blade mounted in a metal frame. Handle design is an important factor because it needs to be comfortable. Don't forget that, when in use, you'll be pushing quite a lot of pressure through the grip, so it needs to be good. Modern tools feature moulded plastic handles which are great.

Blade type is probably the most significant issue. All are classified by the number of teeth which have been cut per inch (TPI) and, as a general rule, the most appropriate specification for general automotive metalwork is 24tpi. Hard metals need more teeth per inch, soft ones require fewer. The other option is the Junior Hacksaw which is simply a scaled down version of the main tool – about half the size. This will normally be fitted with a five-inch blade and is very useful when space is tight. Blade quality can vary too and the only real way to judge this is on cost. Buying a packet

of blades for a pound is not advisable as these will probably snap the first time you use them in earnest. Even if you're lucky and they don't break, the teeth will probably give up the ghost at the first sight of metal!

Blades in the traditional full-size hack saw are mounted under tension which is adjusted with a wing nut at the front of the frame. Some modern designs feature a sprung frame which eliminates the need to set the blade tension manually. This is a good idea because getting it wrong – either too tight or too lose – increases the risk of blade snapping. As a rule of thumb you shouldn't be able to twist the blade any more than 45° from one extreme to the other.

One final practical issue is that all hacksaw blades are designed to cut in one direction only, and it's important that you mount replacements correctly in the frame. Usually an arrow indicates the direction of cut, and should be pointed away from the handle. Remember that the saw should be cutting on the push, rather than the pull stroke for the best results.

Old fashioned wooden-handled engineering files are commonly available at boot sales, but will often be too large and cumbersome for automotive uses.

Files with plastic handles and six-inch blades are the best option for general use.

Back to Basics

Part 8:
Know thy enemy! Chris Graham exposes the engine management offenders.

As I hinted in last month's episode, while vehicle electronics are certainly reaching an impressive level of complexity, reliability continues to be a significant issue. Certainly most new cars are magnificent machines, offering their owners bags of reliability and wallet-soothing levels of efficiency, but question marks remain. Things are all very well in the early days, as the company reps. thrash their steeds mercilessly up and down the motorway. But it's when these cars fall into the hands of their second or third owner – poor souls like you and I – that the electronic chickens start coming home to roost!

Tired and ageing engine management systems can be bedevilled by niggling, inconvenient and expensive problems. There are certain components within all systems which are prone to causing trouble. Some fail prematurely, others are over-sensitive to the clumsy fiddling of inexperienced technicians, but all have the potential to make your car all but undrivable. So, in a valiant bid to push back the boundaries of automotive awareness, we've singled out five of the most common offenders here, and explained what they do, why they fail and how to recognise it when they do.

1. CRANKSHAFT POSITION SENSOR

This is one of the most fundamental sensors in any engine management system. Quite simply, without it nothing happens so its failure is pretty disastrous. This component has two basic functions although both are equally important. Firstly, as you might have guessed from the name, it informs the ECM about the crankshaft's position, so that the controller is aware, at any time, which piston is nearing TDC. But in addition to this, it also monitors the speed of the engine. The ECM uses this speed and position data in its calculations of correct fuelling and ignition settings.

The crankshaft position sensor is based around a magnet which is influenced by a spinning, toothed wheel (reluctor) that's attached to the end of the crank. Every time one of the teeth passes close to the tip of the sensor, a small voltage is induced and sent away down the signal wire to the ECM. The toothed wheel features 36 teeth with one larger gap which denotes TDC for number one piston, thus giving the ECM a basic point of reference. Most crank position sensors are simple two-wire components – one carrying the signal and the other making an earth connection. No power is supplied to the sensor.

Failure tends to be caused by general deterioration. Both the magnet and it's electrical windings suffer with age, but the magnetic aspect can have another consequence too. This sensor is often prone to the build up of metallic debris on it's tip. Often this component is located close to the clutch, and the tiny metal fragments created as the linings wear get drawn to the sensor through magnetic attraction. This build-up may seem insignificant but it can become sufficient to distort the reading produced by the sensor, thus leading to engine running problems.

The proximity of the sensor to the teeth on the reluctor wheel is a key factor in successful operation, but there are a number of factors which can disturb this. For a start the teeth can get broken or badly distorted by technicians who use the reluctor wheel as a convenient point of leverage. Also, if the air gap between the sensor's tip and the reluctor wheel is wrong, the signal will be distorted. This is a crucial measurement (check your workshop manual) which normally ranges between 0.75 and 1.5mm, depending on the application. It must be set accurately.

This sensor is a straightforward screw-fit and so tightening it into place will normally ensure the correct gap. However, dirt in the thread or on the contact faces can affect this, so be warned. Also, note that some manufacturers (including BMW) have used adjustable sensors in the past which need to be correctly set up and adjusted. The air gap must be checked using a feeler gauge but, because the sensor is magnetic, it's best to use plastic or brass feelers otherwise you wont easily be able to assess the 'sliding fit'.

Failure tends to be a random affair and so it's impossible to predict. If the problem relates to metallic debris build-up, then gradually worsening intermittent misfires may well be noticed. This sensor, being so important, is normally included in the fault code system, and so any problems should be flagged up with an appropriate numerical code accompanied by the dash-mounted warning light.

If you suspect that the crankshaft position sensor is faulty, then confirming this with a test is quite easy. Use a multimeter (set to AC volts) to test the output voltage. Anything less than one volt, while the engine is being cranked, will normally spell trouble. Defective sensors cannot be repaired and replacements cost about £30.

2. THROTTLE POSITION SENSOR

This is another of the key components in any engine management system. It's purpose is to provide the ECM with vital information about the position of the throttle, which obviously has a direct bearing on engine fuelling.

On early vehicle applications (running to about the mid-1980s), a throttle position switch, rather than a sensor, was used to determine if the throttle was open or closed. However, as engine management technology developed this basic approach became far too imprecise and was replaced by a more accurate sensor that could monitor degrees of throttle opening. In both cases, the component is bolted directly on to the outside of the throttle body, and takes its input from the main throttle spindle.

The throttle position switch/sensor is a relatively frequent cause of trouble, although it rarely fails completely. The switch type, being the simpler of the two, tends to present more obvious faults. It utilises a pair of contacts, one of which is closed when the throttle is shut, and the other which is activated when on full throttle. Because this is a physical switching action problems can develop. Wear, burning and pitting of the contact faces will lead to inefficient switching, causing spurious messages to be sent to the ECM. For example, if the throttle is in the shut position (engine at idle) but the corresponding contacts within the switch are worn and unable to close completely, the message wont get through. As far as the ECM is concerned, the throttle is set somewhere between fully closed and fully open, even though in reality, it's closed. Fuelling and ignition timing will be adjusted accordingly and chaos will result. The idle will become rough and there will be noticeable hesitation during acceleration. In fact, the only time the engine is likely to operate correctly is under hard acceleration, when the throttle is fully open.

The symptoms of a problem with the more complex throttle position sensor are almost identical, but it will be more difficult to detect without advanced diagnostic equipment. The sensor relies on an arm which sweeps along an electrical track in direct response to throttle position. So the same potential exists for dirt and wear to upset the electrical contact. Unfortunately, though, with this type of component, the fault can arise at any point across the throttle setting range, rather than just in the throttle 'open' or 'closed' positions. Faults will present themselves as noticeable hesitation or 'flat spots' (momentarily reduced engine performance) at a specific point or points in the throttle range.

One of the biggest practical problems associated with testing a throttle position switch/sensor is actually identifying the connector wires so you know which to check. You really must refer to an accurate circuit diagram to be sure about this before diving in. Use a multimeter, set to 'ohms', to carry out a simple resistance check by probing the input and output wires. With a switch you should expect to see a low resistance in the 'closed throttle' position, but this should change instantly to an 'open circuit' reading (very high resistance) the moment the throttle is opened. At the other end of the throttle travel, the resistance level should drop again once the 'fully open' position is reached, but this is measured on a seperate terminal. The workshop manual should detail exact resistance values as well as correct terminals.

With a sensor the same sort of thing happens in that the resistance varies across the throttle position range, although it will be a smooth progression

this time. Once again, the manual should include appropriate resistance values, however it's the smoothness of the resistance increase which is the important thing here. In reality it's unlikely that you'll be able to spot any 'glitches' in the progression with a straightforward digital multimeter. All you're likely to see is a series of changing figures. To be sure of the problem the resistance increase must be plotted in graphical form using an oscilloscope. Only in this way will any small anomalies responsible for drivability problems, become obvious.

Failure of this sensor is a random business and there is no hope of cleaning and re-using an already failed component. Replacement switches/sensors cost about £35 each, but it should be noted that in many cases there will be a specific setting-up procedure designed to ensure that the new component works correctly. So fitting is not always as simple as you might imagine.

3. OXYGEN SENSOR

Up until last year new cars were fitted with just one oxygen sensor, normally in the exhaust downpipe close to the engine. But, recent emissions legislation dictates that cars must now be fitted with two, the second being positioned downstream of the catalytic converter.

The function of the oxygen sensor (often still referred to as a Lambda sensor) is to make sure that the air/fuel ratio does not deviate from the 14.7:1 ideal. Remember, this is the ratio at which combustion of the fuel occurs most efficiently, thus minimising exhaust emissions. The sensor monitors this by measuring the oxygen content in the exhaust gas – a factor which is directly linked to the efficiency of the burn. The richer the mixture, the lower the oxygen content in the exhaust gas, and vice versa.

The oxygen sensor is a clever device which reacts to differing oxygen content by producing a varying voltage output. It does not require a power supply to do

this, although it is temperature sensitive and starts to work effectively only once it's been heated to around 300°C. The more oxygen the sensor detects, the greater its voltage output to the ECM, although actual values are never greater than one volt. Typically an oxygen sensor will work over a voltage output range on 0.1-0.8V.

In actual fact, the sensor operates by switching continuously between these two voltage extremes, normally at a rate of about once every second (a frequency of one Hertz). In effect, the sensor is playing a never-ending game of catch-up as it reacts to variations in oxygen content within the exhaust gas. For example, if it senses low oxygen levels, its output will rise to 0.8V, and the ECM will interpret this as a 'go lean' command and will cut fuel supply accordingly. But this reduction in fuel will then weaken the mixture and create higher levels of oxygen in the exhaust gas. The sensor will immediately pick this up and decrease its voltage output towards the 'go lean' 0.1V end of the scale. From this the ECM will gather that the mixture needs to be made richer again, and so the process continues. This seesawing action continues as the engine runs, but the ECM is clever enough to average out the two extremes so that fuelling levels settle somewhere in the middle.

The oxygen sensor is one of the worst performers in reliability terms and when it fails it does so either because it's switching action becomes slowed, or it stops altogether. When it stops it tends to stick at one or other end of the range – most commonly at the lean end (0.1V). Detecting whether or not the switching is taking place using a multimeter can be tricky, as many units will simply average the voltage output, presenting you with a reading of, say, 0.5V. However, even this should be sufficient to tell you that it is actually switching. A permanent reading of either 0.1V or 0.8V should be regarded with a deal more suspicion. But, the best way of confirming a

problem with the oxygen sensor is by using a gas analyser, which will show that emissions are way out of tolerance.

In normal driving terms, the effects of a problem can be fairly minor. Some fastidious drivers may notice an increase in fuel consumption, or you may pick up engine surging when driving at cruising speeds on light throttle settings, if the sensor is switching slowly. But defects shouldn't be ignored because there are potentially serious consequences for the catalytic converter as well. Cats are extremely sensitive to variations in exhaust gas constituents. An over-rich mixture will cause excess fuel blown into the cat to clog up its honeycomb with lacquer. On the other hand, a weak mixture will promote overheating. Either way, the cat will become unserviceable and need to be expensively replaced.

Early oxygen sensors were single-wire units that earthed themselves through their mountings. However, the threads had a tendency to corrode, reducing the effectiveness of the earth, which led to failure. In those cases, removing the sensor, cleaning up the threads and refitting would often rejuvenate things for a while.

Then the designers switched to two-wire versions to overcome the problem, with a reliable and permanent earth connection back at the ECM. The latest four-wire examples are heated as well so that they start working after about 30 seconds.

A typical replacement will cost about £85, and is a simple screw fit into the exhaust.

4. AIRFLOW SENSOR

There have been a variety of airflow sensing devices fitted over the years. Things began in the 1980s with vane or flap types, but these were replaced by the more efficient 'hot wire' versions in the 1990s. Both types perform the same function, which is to measure the quantity of air being sucked into the engine. This information is used by the ECM

The throttle position sensor is a vital component on any modern engine and problems with it are common.

Compared to an old-style airflow meter, modern 'hot wire' versions are much smaller and more reliable because there are no moving parts inside.

The Lambda or oxygen sensor is another important component which is, linked directly to the vehicles ECM and plays a vital role in setting correct fuelling. It's a regular failure point.

Catalytic converters are extremely sensitive to their operating conditions. An engine that is running rich or lean will quickly ruin this expensive component.

TECHNICAL TOPIC: *Airflow meter cleaning*

So, as you should have gathered by now, there is still a fair bit that the keen amateur can usefully do when it comes to DIY diagnostics and fault rectification. Of course, many owners will feel a reluctance to get too heavily involved in such work, which is perfectly natural. Vehicle electrics has always been a bit of an automotive 'grey area' for most home mechanics and nowadays, with the electronic complexity of even relatively ordinary cars reaching NASA proportions, the situation is even worse.

Nevertheless, with care, patience and a methodical approach useful progress can be made. A perfect example of this is the difference that can be made by spending an hour or two cleaning and inspecting the air intake system on your vehicle. On older vehicles, with engines that are starting to consume oil, this can become contaminated with residue that will gradually work its way out towards the sensitive and vitally important airflow meter. It should never be allowed to get this far! Also, you need to be sure that the system is airtight, which means carefully checking the condition of the trunking and clips.

What follows is a step-by-step guide to 'overhauling' the system on a typical airflow meter-equipped family saloon.

(1) Old-style airflow meters, which employ a hinged flap that's deflected by the incoming air, are hefty devices. They can give plenty of problems but respond well to a bit of TLC. It's electronic 'brain' is contained in the small box on the top.

(2) Remove the main air trunking which runs between the air filter housing and the throttle body – normally secured by straightforward Jubilee clips. Inspect it carefully for any signs of damage. Splits that allow extra air to bypass the airflow meter will cause real fuelling problems. Flex the trunking to expose any hidden cracks.

(3) Check for signs of oil residue inside both the trunking and in the entrance to the throttle body. You're more likely to find this in the throttle body but, in bad cases, it can have worked its way down the trunking too. Any contamination you find here is not a particularly healthy sign because it indicates that the engine is burning oil. If oil finds its way into the airflow meter it will cause trouble, so removed it.

(4) In most cases the airflow meter will be part of the air filter housing. Having released the clips securing this, lift it clear and have a look inside to inspect the condition of the vane or flap itself. Keep an eye out for signs of dark coloured deposits and residues, much as you might expect to find when looking into an old-fashioned carburettor.

(5) Use a good quality carburettor cleaner to flush out any impurities. Brake cleaner, petrol or methylated spirits are not suitable, and may even damage some of the rubber seals within the component. Avoid inserting brushes or cloth-wrapped screwdrivers as these may cause damage. It's a very sensitive component. The orientation of the airflow meter as you apply the carburettor cleaner is important because the fluid must be kept away from the electronics, which are in a box on the top. For the best results, position the assembly vertically so that the cleaner is encouraged to drain out as it works.

(6) Once you've removed all visible deposits, use a finger to ensure that there is free movement of the vane. Do this gently, feeling for any sticking points in its travel. If the movement is not perfectly smooth then the component may well be seriously damaged, in which case a replacement will almost certainly be necessary.

(7) With the trunking removed, it makes sense at this stage to give the throttle body a squirt of carburettor cleaner as well.

(8) Next, switch your attention to the electronics side of the component. Removing the cover can be tricky because it will have been silicone-sealed at the factory to keep the innards protected against water ingress. It will need to be carefully prised off with a screwdriver to break the seal without damaging the lid or its seat. After the cleaning operations are finished, you must be sure to reseal the cover back into place using a good quality silicone sealant.

(9) Try to avoid touching any of the circuitry inside with your fingers, and certainly resist the temptation to attack any grime you may find with cloths or, worse still, abrasive paper. It's all very delicate in here! It's also important to use the correct cleaning product at this stage. You must specify an electrical contact cleaner. Automotive alternatives such as brake or carburettor cleaner, paraffin or petrol are certainly not appropriate for this job. All will leave residues which could affect the efficiency of the electrical contact being made.

(10) To be sure of a thorough cleaning action, gently move the contact arm across its travel, at which point you will have done all you can to correct any wayward performance, and you can start putting it all back together.

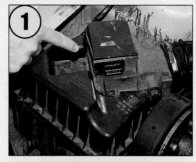

Handy Hints

- Never use abrasives to clean electronic components.
- Always use and LED-based circuit tester for engine management work.
- Be careful to avoid dirty threads when fitting screw-in sensors.
- Remember that a knock sensor's tightening torque is an essential factor.

Expert assistance

Colchester Institute has a large Automobile Engineering Centre which provides part-time (one day per week) and full-time courses in automobile engineering, body repair and welding.
For more information contact: **Dave Roberts**
Head of Centre for Automobile Engineering, Colchester Institute, Sheepen Road, Colchester, CO3 3LL.

to calculate the precise amount of fuel that needs to be added to achieve the correct 14.7:1 mixture ratio. A varying DC voltage output from the sensor correlates with the air flow – low voltage means little air and *vice versa*. A typical signal varies from about one to 4.5V.

On the older, flap types, a smooth progression between the two voltage extremes is the most important requirement. Symptoms of problems can include increased fuel consumption, lack of power, hesitation, flat spots – very similar to throttle position sensor problems – and ultimate failure causes the ECM to inject incorrect amounts of fuel. In common with the throttle position sensor, this component also relies on an electrical track which is swept by an arm, in response to the amount of air being drawn in. The track is susceptible to dirt and contamination and the mechanical hinging action of the flap can suffer with wear, damage and seizure as well. What's more, the trunking between it and the engine must remain completely airtight. Any air that gets into the engine, without having been accounted for through the airflow meter first, will cause real fuelling problems.

You can test a suspect airflow sensor with a voltmeter but, as before, you must be sure about the wiring. Normally there will be at least seven terminals and it's important that you probe the right one so that the output signal can be monitored. Measure the voltage output at idle then steadily open the throttle and check that the output increases progressively. Specific data will be included in the workshop manual.

Hot-wire types are much more reliable and failure is rare, but they are delicate. Inside there is a thin wire, like a light bulb filament, which is stretched across the trunking aperture. This wire is heated to a fixed temperature and the amount of air entering the engine is gauged by the cooling effect it has on the wire as it rushes by. Don't poke about inside with a screwdriver because it's very easy to snap the wire.

Unfortunately, replacements can be expensive. An up to date 'hot wire' unit can cost up to £500, while the older flap design will be about £100. Refitting is a simple bolt-on job, but you should take time to ensure that all trunking and vacuum pipes are tightly secured.

5. KNOCK SENSOR

The humble knock sensor is one of the unsung heroes of the modern engine because it performs a vital and often overlooked function. It's sole purpose in life is to guard against that old-fashioned mechanical bugbear called detonation. More commonly known as 'pinking', this unfortunate and potentially very destructive phenomenon is caused by early detonation of the fuel/air mixture within the combustion chamber. The mixture is ignites just before the spark plug actually fires so, in effect, there are two explosions within the combustion chamber. When the opposing shock waves meet, all hell breaks loose, literally. Prolonged periods of detonation can cause valve damage and, in the worst cases, will blow a hole in the top of the piston.

The need for the knock sensor arose when lead – the original pinking inhibitor – was removed from petrol for health reasons. The old solution to pinking was to manually retard the ignition timing but, although effective, this also reduced engine performance. A knock sensor does exactly the same thing but much more quickly and automatically. In essence the sensor is a very sensitive listening device which bolts on to the side of the engine block so it can pick up the characteristic knocking sound of detonation. It's able to do this thanks to a clever little crystal which is compressed by the vibration and produces a small electrical voltage as it does so. This signal is sent to the ECM so that appropriate action can be taken. This all happens within the blink of an eye and means that 'pinking' is a thing of the past on modern engines. However, the sensor does go wrong, which is when the fun starts.

The crystal used inside the knock sensor is the same as those found in 'electronic' cigarette lighters, and it wears out. On most systems the sensor will be coded and so, as well as the noticeable presence of engine pinking, it's failure should trigger the dashboard light. It's a very difficult sensor to test electronically because the voltage output is so small. Really it requires an oscilloscope to do the job properly, but there is a useful practical check which involves activating the sensor manually and watching for ignition retardation. Use a spanner to tap the side of the engine block, as close to the knock sensor as possible, while observing the engine's ignition timing marks using a timing light. If the sensor is working, it should react to the tap and trigger the ECM to adjust the ignition timing accordingly.

Fitting is an important issue and it's vital to make sure that the sensor threads and its mating faces are spotlessly clean. Any obstructing which may hold the sensor away from the block surface, even if only by a fraction of an inch, will affect its ability to work. Even a layer of oil spray on the block can be sufficient to upset operation, so be scrupulous about cleaning. It's also important for the threads to be clean because this sensor must be tightened to a specific torque (refer to manual) to ensure that the crystal within is pre-tensioned. Replacements cost about £40.

Next Month
Electrical do and dont's

TOOLKIT BUILDER:
Circuit testers

The good old fashioned type of circuit tester, like a small screwdriver with a 12-volt bulb in the handle, is no longer suitable for use on modern engine management systems. Certainly it's still useful for checking basic electrical circuits, such as those supplying the headlamps, for example, but for anything more electronics based, it's a definite no-no. The big risk is that, because of its 12-volt bulb, it could draw excessive currents through sensitive circuits which were never designed to handle them, resulting in potentially expensive damage. As a rule, you should avoid any testers that contain bulbs, opting instead for tools based around LEDs or LCDs.

These more modern units work in basically the same way, using a sharp probe, a length of wire and a crocodile clip but, because LEDs and LCDs only require tiny current draws to activate then, there is no danger of creating any problems.

There are a number of alternatives around but the only real difference between them is the way in which they display the information. The most basic units have just one or two LEDs which are lit to signify that a

Bulb-type circuit testers like this one are fine for use on basic electrical systems, such as lighting circuits. But don't go near anything related to the engine management side of the vehicle or you will almost certainly cause damage.

current is flowing. Slightly more advanced tools are able to distinguish between positive and negative current flows and, generally speaking, the more you pay, the greater the range of voltage that can be measured. Obviously, the bottom end of the voltage range is an important factor for modern circuitry, with many sensors operating at five volts and below.

The LCD display-equipped tools don't always display an

Modern LED-based testers like this one are inexpensive but essential for anyone contemplating even the most basic engine management-based testing.

actual voltage figure, but may instead present a message such as 'Circuit OK'. It's horses for courses

One of the most modern developments has be the introduction of neat testers which do not require an earth lead connection at all. Instead, they rely on the user to provide the electrical earth by touching a spare hand on a convenient piece of metal bodywork or engine component! The older style machines, with the conventional earth lead, can be a little restrictive in some situations. The leads are never terribly long and can complicate matters when working up behind a dashboard, for example, or where space is extremely limited.

Prices start at three of four pounds, and rise to a maximum of around £15 for a good, branded tool. We'd certainly advise paying top dollar for your tester as it's hardly going to break the bank and will certainly provide years of trouble-free and valuable service.

Back to Basics

Part 9:
Chris Graham advises on avoiding some common electrical blunders.

The unfortunate truth is that as engine management systems become ever more sophisticated, so their accessibility to all but the most experienced and well-equipped technician diminishes. With this greater complexity comes increased sensitivity, and it's this that poses the biggest threat for the amateur fiddler. So much so that, nowadays, it can take little more than having your multimeter mistakenly set on the wrong function, as you carry out a seemingly innocent sensor check, to blow and expensive ECM.

So the stakes are high. The consequences of making a mistake can be very costly and, usually, you don't get a second chance. Touch the wrong probe on the incorrect terminal, however fleetingly, and the damage will be done. For this reason alone the 'hands on' testing of engine management systems is something best left to those with a good technical knowledge. The old maxim about a little knowledge being a dangerous thing was perhaps never more apt!

But having said all this, there is still a lot of useful work that a proficient DIYer can undertake, as long as he or she observes a few basic rules. It's vital to bear in mind that modern systems are extremely sensitive to power surges (spikes) finding their way back to the ECM. You must be very wary when testing any circuit that's linked directly to the main control unit. This applies to all the primary sensors on a vehicle and, as a general rule, the safest approach is to disconnect any sensor before starting any sort of test on it.

As I hinted earlier, use of even a straightforward multimeter can

be fraught with problems for the uninitiated. Most people imagine these commonly available convenience tools are as simple to operate as they appear, but this is not quite the case. And, of course, most are supplied with woefully inadequate instructions so the potential for mistakes is usually high.

The first thing to avoid is using the ohm meter function on any sensitive electronic circuit in an attempt to measure resistance. To perform this test the multimeter relies on an internal 9V battery to generate the necessary voltage and,

although this is only a small current, it's certainly quite sufficient to upset many sensitive circuits. Resistance checks are actively encouraged in many technical manuals as one of the first options when carrying out diagnostic investigation. Many technicians feel comfortable working with resistance because they've done it so much in the past but, nowadays, the potential pitfalls are great. To be on the safe side, it's far better to test for problems using a multimeter that's been set to read voltages rather than resistance.

Multimeters are convenient tools to use for modern diagnostic purposes, but you must be sure about what you're trying to do. Correct function setting is vitally important.

The same general warning applies to the use of the Amp Meter function, because this operation utilises a very low built-in resistance which can allow excessive and potentially damaging current to flow. Of course, these dangers only arise while the circuit remains intact and linked to the ECM. It's perfectly safe to test individual sensors within a system, once they've been disconnected, in any way you choose.

Another auto-electrician's favourite old short cut from yesteryear – the widespread use of a jumper lead – can also land the hapless user in the brown stuff. By 'jumper lead' I don't mean those chunky cables used for emergency engine starting on frosty January mornings. No, here I'm talking about a short length of single-cored wire, often with a crocodile clip on each end, that's used to 'bridge' across terminals.

A classic example of the sort of mistake which can be made when using a jumper lead is as follows. It can be tempting, when you suspect that a particular component isn't working because it's not receiving a power supply, to use the lead to bring power from a known source somewhere else on the vehicle, and feed it directly on to the component terminal. The big danger is that you could unwittingly supply component-munching levels of current because the jumper lead will not be of the same resistance as the o/e wiring. So unless you are absolutely sure that the resistances match, then leave well alone.

Another much vaunted approach to vehicle diagnostic testing is the use of a pointed probe to pierce a wire's plastic insulation, so that readings can be taken. Well, in theory this approach makes a lot of sense, and it's convenient too.

Unfortunately, the reality is that it's becoming less and less appropriate for use on modern applications. All the latest automotive circuitry is extremely sensitive to changes in resistance, even tiny variations. Breaching a wire's insulation in this way will allow in moisture which, in turn, causes corrosion on the metal within. The regrettable but inevitable consequence of this rusting is an increase in resistance that will eventually prove sufficient to throw the ECM into a muck

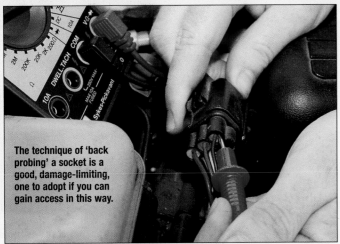

The technique of 'back probing' a socket is a good, damage-limiting, one to adopt if you can gain access in this way.

If you must probe directly into a wire – because the relevant connector is completely sealed – then make sure that the pinprick you create is sealed up afterwards. However small the damage, moisture will get inside and start the rusting process.

Be careful when going into the female terminal of a connector because it's all too easy to splay the terminals inside, thus ruining the connection thereafter. Work gently!

sweat. Fault codes will be triggered and the warning light on the dashboard will burst into life, with all the potential confusion that this may cause.

The problems caused by a single insulation piercing can strike within a couple of years on a state-of-the-art system, although they will probably take longer to develop on older, less sensitive systems. Of course, when multiple wires have been 'attacked' in this way, then the deterioration process is speeded up significantly.

The preferable alternative to the indiscriminate piercing of wires is to use a technique known as 'back probing'. This is far less intrusive and, when done properly, causes no damage at all. It involves taking test readings from the connector rather than from the wire itself. The pointed probe is used carefully to enter the connector, following the route of the wire being tested. In this way the tip can be slid inside until it makes contact with the terminal and a reading can be taken. Adopting this method ensures that no seals are broken and the system remains intact. Unfortunately, a recent trend in system manufacture means that many of the latest connectors are sealed up against the elements, which makes them impossible to access without causing damage.

The textbook approach to modern, non-intrusive diagnostics involves the use of a piece of kit called a break-out box. This clever instrument can be plugged into the circuit being tested, and allows convenient and disruption-free access to all of the wires involved. The one problem with this solution is the cost. Break-out boxes are normally supplied as part of a kit, and so purchase prices can be beyond the average DIYers budget. Also, the box's usefulness is completely dependent upon the number and variety of socket adaptors that are bought with it. As you can imagine, a modern engine utilises a great number of socket

designs, from the simplest two-wire type right up to the hefty multi-pin connectors that plug directly into the ECM. To be able to tap into any circuit you fancy requires a complete set of loom adaptors, and these don't come cheap.

So if you have no alternative but to continue testing circuits using the old-fashioned probing method, then you must take steps immediately afterwards to minimise the risk of corrosion setting in. Thankfully it's now possible to buy special plastic sheathing from dealerships and good motor factors. This is designed to be heat-shrunk into place over the damaged section using a hot air gun. It's a method of protection which is guaranteed to produce an air and watertight seal, and it's certainly the approach favoured by dealership workshops whenever they are forced to cut into a loom while making a repair.

As you might expect, the vehicle manufacturers are only too well aware of the sorts of problems that can afflict the sensitive wiring systems used on their vehicles, and all are working hard to reduce the potential for niggling problems. Not only have most redoubled their efforts to keep all electrical connectors effectively protected from water and dirt, but most have also switched to the use of gold as a coating for the vital pin terminals within. This precious metal is very resistant to tarnishing and therefore works well at preserving the all-important electrical contact.

However, the benefit of this gold coating can be easily lost by clumsy probing within the connector block. Out of necessity, the gold layer is very thin and, because it's a soft metal, it's easily scratched off. So great care should be taken when working in this way as it only takes a tiny slip to breach the protective layer. The other big danger with over-enthusiastic probing into a 'female' socket is that you can force the terminal pins apart. Often this can

happen without you realising anything is wrong, usually because most probe points are bigger than the space available inside the socket! The problem is that, from that moment on, the loose fit will mean that the connection will be weak or possibly non-existent. But, because the problem has been caused inadvertently, it'll usually be a while before you get round to suspecting the socket as being at the root of the problem. This sort of scenario can be the cause of a great deal of wasted time and effort.

It's an easy mistake to make but the good news is that it's usually possible to put things right once you've realised. Much depends on the overall design of the socket but in many cases it is possible to use a very small screwdriver to bend the splayed terminals back together. The other alternative is to buy a connector pin refurbishing kit, which is ideal if the terminals have become corroded or even melted. These kits include a special tool that allows you to pinch the terminal together and withdraw it out through the back of the connector block so that a new one can be inserted.

Another common mistake that people make when dealing with contaminated connectors is that they attempt to clean them in unsuitable ways. Reaching for a wire brush or a piece of abrasive paper is potentially disastrous, as anything gritty or sharp will

certainly clean off the dirt all right, but will also remove the important terminal coatings. The metal beneath will be laid bare to the elements and corrosion will be the sure result. Instead, all connectors should be treated with nothing more aggressive than a good quality electrical contact cleaning spray. Terminals that you find showing signs of rusting should be replaced. In reality there is little chance of pulling them back to original condition once corrosion has a hold. Their electrical performance will be compromised for ever more, so there is no sensible alternative other than fitting new ones.

Dirt and corrosion within a connector socket remains one of the most common causes of engine management system problems. It's ironic really that with all the expertise that exists today in the automotive industry, it still takes just a few drops of water, or a tiny piece of grit, to bring even the best system crashing down into operational chaos. For this reason, it makes a lot of sense to carry out a basic inspection before embarking on any sort of electronic fault diagnostic work.

It's important to make sure that all contacts in the circuit you intend to test are clean and tightly secured. This will save a lot of time and should eradicate the likelihood of potentially confusing voltage readings. Remember always to use your eyes first, as

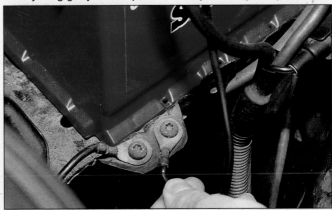

Many people still fail to appreciate the importance of good earth connections. All must be clean and secure if circuits are to function efficiently.

TECHNICAL TOPIC: *Vacuum testing*

Over the years car engines have grown more and more dependent on the use of vacuums in a number of different ways. Nowadays, apart from still being employed in a conventional manner to operate rubber diaphragms, they are also used in more subtle ways, to influence the voltage outputs from certain key components within engine management systems. For this reason, maintaining the system in good running order is perhaps more important now than it's ever been.

Leaks caused by splits in the pipework, or cracks in diaphragms produced as the result of age-related perishing, can all have a marked effect on engine performance. Often the only way to be quite sure when a vacuum circuit has failed is to test it using a hand-held pump. These are available from most good motor factors and perform a unique function. Basically they are precision-engineered pumps used to apply an accurate amount of vacuum, thus simulating that which would be applied under normal operating conditions. An accurately calibrated gauge – normally marked in kilo/pascals or inches or millimetres of mercury – is used to monitor the level of vacuum being produced.

The testers are usually supplied with a kit of pipes and adaptor pieces to cover most eventualities, and the best units have good quality metal construction like the one illustrated here. Although a simple device, the function of the vacuum tester pump can be invaluable for diagnosing a range of potentially serious engine faults, as the examples here show.

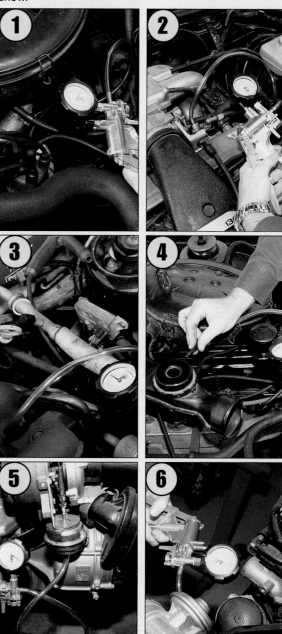

(1) One of the most basic tests that can be carried out using a vacuum pump is to assess the advance unit fitted to an ignition system. It doesn't really matter whether you're working on a engine with an old fashioned points-based ignition system, or one with an early electronic system, the test is equally valid. Remove the vacuum supply pipe from the ignition advance unit and attach the pump's pipe, with appropriate adaptor if necessary, in its place. Set up a timing light on the front pulley and, with the engine running, begin to apply a gradually increasing vacuum with the pump. As this happens you should start to see the ignition being retarded, indicated by movement of the timing mark. Some vehicle manufacturers will provide specific data describing the correlation between the vacuum applied and the degree of ignition retardation. The check is designed to test that the diaphragm inside the advance/retard unit is not punctured or seized, which is a classic occurrence on an ageing vehicle, leading to generally poor performance.

(2) One of the more important components in a fuel injection system is the pressure regulator, which is designed to alter the fuel pressure in response to variations in engine working load. The component can only work if it's able to sense the vacuum within the inlet manifold, and a rubber pipe linking the two allows this to happen. You can check that the regulator is working by replacing its vacuum supply pipe with that from the hand pump, and hooking up a fuel pressure gauge elsewhere in the system – using a convenient Shraeder valve if possible. Then, with the engine running, a gradual increase in the applied vacuum should produce a corresponding alteration in fuel pressure. Once again, it should be possible to source technical data from the vehicle manufacturer to establish the precise relationship between vacuum and fuel pressure so that a definitive check can be made.

(3) One of the key engine management inputs on many modern systems is provided by the MAP sensor, which is another component that relies on the accurate monitoring of a vacuum. In this case, it converts pressure variations into voltage outputs which are then sent directly to the ECM where they are used to help calculate correct ignition timing and fuelling settings. To test a MAP sensor, disconnect its vacuum feed pipe from the inlet manifold and attach the vacuum pump. Variations in applied vacuum should cause the voltage output to change so, having identified the correct terminals using a circuit diagram, you'll need to probe into the socket and use a multimeter to monitor the output. The key thing to look for here is that the voltage does change as the vacuum is altered; the specifics of the change are not so important in this case.

(4) On older carburettor-equipped engines, warming-up on cold mornings was often assisted by a vacuum-driven flap that caused inlet air to be drawn in from around the exhaust manifold, rather from outside the vehicle. In this way warm-up times were reduced. As soon as the desired temperature had been reached, the flap was lowered to open the normal intake channel. The vacuum applied to the flap is controlled by the switching of a heat-sensitive, bi-metallic strip. These flaps are prone to getting stuck because they get clogged up with contaminants, and this often results in slower warm-up times. Testing the operation of the flap is a simple matter of connecting the pump, applying the vacuum and checking that the flap operates. With the forward section of inlet trunking removed, it's easy to see the flap for visual confirmation.

(5) Engines fitted with turbochargers require a mechanically-operated wastegate to ensure that the boost pressure is released when the motor is being driven hard. The wastegate allows excess exhaust gas to bypass the turbo, effectively limiting its maximum performance and preventing the engine being excessively strained by too much boost. The wastegate is controlled by a vacuum which acts on a rubber diaphragm but the latter deteriorates with age, vacuum pressure is lost and the mechanical consequences can be very serious indeed. To double check that all is well, connect the pump to the wastegate, apply a vacuum and watch for the obvious movement as the wastegate is opened. If nothing moves then there's a problem. Some vehicle manufacturers may provide specific vacuum levels at which things should start to happen.

(6) The exhaust gas recirculation (EGR) valve is included on most new vehicles now as an anti-emissions measure. It's job is to allow a certain percentage of the exhaust gas to be circulated back into the inlet manifold, so that it's passed through the combustion process for a second time. It's been found that doing this reduces cylinder temperatures which, in turn, lowers production rates of some of the nastier pollutants, including NOx. The EGR valve is controlled by the ECM, which switches a solenoid to apply the vacuum and operate the valve at the correct time. Problems arise because these valves are subjected to harsh operating conditions, and are prone to contaminant build-up which causes them to stick. Use the hand pump to activate the valve 'manually', thus confirming that the internal diaphragm is intact.

Handy Hints

- Learn to use your multimeter properly – they can do plenty of damage in careless hands.
- Avoid over-enthusiastic probing into female sockets.
- Remember that earth connections are as important as power supply.
- Always check a fault memory twice to eliminate spurious codes.
- Use your eyes to check the obvious. They are the best tool you have!

Expert assistance

Colchester Institute has a large Automobile Engineering Centre which provides part-time (one day per week) and full-time courses in automobile engineering, body repair and welding.
For more information contact: **Dave Roberts**
Head of Centre for Automobile Engineering, Colchester Institute, Sheepen Road, Colchester, CO3 3LL.

While break-out box kits can be expensive, they represent the best and most professional way to access a modern circuit without causing any damage at all.

they are one of the best tools you have. Missing something obvious because you've rushed into a job without being methodical is likely to cost time and money, not to mention temper!

The same applies to earth points, which are another commonly overlooked but vitally important aspect of any electrical circuit. Many professionals ignore these most basic of connections, and it always leads to trouble. Likewise, the same happens at the diagnostic stage, with many investigators neglecting the earth point in favour of 'more interesting' potential causes. As a consequence hours can be wasted on fruitless investigation elsewhere in the system when, all along, the defect was being caused by nothing more complicated that a poor earth. It's also worth bearing in mind that every ECM is equipped with a single earth pin, and that this should be another key check point in times of trouble. Problems with this connection will shut the whole system down every bit as effectively as a fault with the power supply.

The ECM's earth connection is best checked using a voltmeter. You should probe the relevant pin (as indicated on the circuit diagram), leaving the earth wire connected, and ideally expect to see a reading of zero volts recorded. Anything significantly higher than this (more than 0.5V) will indicate that there is a resistance somewhere in the earth connection and, hence, a problem to be dealt with.

It is possible to check an earth connection using an ohm meter but it's vital to remember, particularly when dealing with the ECM, that the wire should be disconnected first. Under normal circumstances you would expect to find a resistance reading of about 0.5ohms when the earth connection is a good one. Once again, anything significantly above this points towards a problem that needs sorting. Good earth connections are more important now than they have ever been, as far as engine management systems are concerned. All ECMs rely heavily on the quality of their earth connection to provide a reference for all other operations.

For example, the EGR valve is powered by a constant 5V supply. The ECM basically acts as an electronic switch, operating this valve simply by providing a route to earth for the 5V supply. So, as the current flows, the component is triggered. To switch it off again the ECM simply cuts the ground connection. But, if the ECM's ground is inefficient or non-existent then it loses the ability to switch important actuators like the EGR valve. An appreciation of this sort of subtlety is vital for anyone attempting to diagnose electronic problems. Also, you must avoid the mindset which causes so many people to look primarily at the power supply as the most likely cause of trouble, often disregarding the earth side of the circuit completely.

Finally, remember that whenever you disconnect a sensor socket on a modern engine you'll almost certainly induce a fault code within the ECM's memory. While this won't necessarily cause a running problem, it will illuminate the dashboard warning light and register a potentially confusing fault code. For this reason it's good practice, whenever investigating a vehicle's memory for the first time, to note down and then clear all stored faults codes found there. Then, following a test run, re-check the memory and see what's there. Any of the originals which have appeared again can then be regarded as genuine problems, while those from the first list which are missing will probably be spurious.

Next Month
Charging Systems

TOOLKIT BUILDER:
Power drills

Whether it's for drilling, screw driving or nut running, there are times when nothing other than a power drill will do. The convenience, speed and sheer ease of use these handy tools offer makes them an attractive proposition for anyone building a toolkit. But the big question, of course, is which one should you choose?

The first, and probably most basic decision to be made, is whether you want a corded or a cordless tool. There are pros and cons in both cases, and prices can vary enormously with both options. Conventional corded tools are certainly the bargain product, with basic models being available for less than £15. However, for this money it's unlikely that you'll find yourself a machine bristling with attractive and desirable features. Preferable specification

that includes a reversible action, variable speed and a 'keyless' chuck usually costs somewhat more, although there are always bargains to be had. The biggest minus point of the conventional electric drill is its lead, which can be a nuisance, potentially dangerous and operationally restrictive. Trailing leads in a workshop always represent an accident waiting to happen, with the added spice of the mains supply within should the protective insulation get accidentally frayed or cut!

On the face of it then, the cordless drill might appear to be the preferable option but it's not all plain sailing as far as these are concerned either. For a start they are generally a good deal more expensive than their corded cousins – convenience never comes cheap! Also, unless you pick a high-spec model, they can lack power compared to a conventional plug-in. This can be a very important factor when drilling hard metals. However, if you can afford the difference, and find a tool that matches your performance needs, then a

cordless drill is a great machine to own. It's a luxury to be able to drill when and where you want, in fact, in the early days you'll probably find yourself creating jobs in the most unusual places just to maximise this operational freedom!

Cordless drills are commonly available in a range of power ratings – 7.2, 9.6, 12, 14.4 and 24V – and the price goes up enormously for the beefier machines. In reality it's likely that you'll need nothing bigger than a 12-volt drill for everyday automotive work. Seek out the same specification as for corded drills, and also check on battery recharge time and whether or not a spare is included in the kit. Unbranded, cheap and cheerful machines can be found in discount stores and look attractive but, remember you'll probably need to set aside just under three weeks each time the battery needs a boost. Rechargeable battery technology is a subject in itself, but all you need to know here is that the more expensive the tool, the better its battery will be. As a guide expect recharge times to be around the one hour mark.

Conventional corded electric drills are powerful but inconveniently reliant on a wall socket. These days reasonable quality machines are available for peanuts. Always opt for a chuck size of 10-12mm.

The convenience of a cordless drill isn't in doubt, assuming you find one that offers the right power output, isn't too heavy for prolonged use and doesn't break the bank.

Back to Basics

Part 10:
Alternators, batteries and regulators. Chris Graham investigates charging systems.

Although modern batteries are labelled 'maintenance free' because they feature sealed caps, they will still suffer if abused.

Winter has an unfortunate habit of exposing weaknesses. Unlagged pipes freeze, blocked drains flood and central heating boilers pack up. From the motorist's point of view, the cold weather ushers in a whole set of nasties including slippery roads, frozen radiators and, of course, the old favourite, flat batteries. This last annoyance – the one that always seems to strike on the morning of that vital business trip – is less common on new vehicles, but still does occur. As well as being an extreme nuisance, an exhausted battery also signals the end of a struggle for survival which has, more than likely, been going on for weeks, if not months. You see, batteries need TLC. They crave regular care and attention just as much as any other important component on your car, yet many are ignored completely.

To appreciate how best to look after a vehicle's battery we must cover a few basics first. For a start, it's important to realise that the primary function of a battery is to start the engine – it plays no part in proceedings once the motor is running. But also it provides a source of power for running the various ancillaries that may be used when the engine is stopped, such as sidelights, radio, interior lights or hazard warning lights. Starting the engine and running ancillary systems represents hard work for the battery and, without help, it would quickly become exhausted. Thankfully, all modern cars are fitted with an alternator, which is basically an electrical generator that's driven by the engine. Once on the move, the alternator takes over power

supply, meeting the requirements of the whole vehicle as it's being used. But the alternator is also designed to divert some of its electrical output back into the battery, to replace any energy that's been lost.

Alternators replaced dynamos as the automotive engine's source of electricity way back in the late 1960s, although both rely on the principles established by Michael Faraday some 140 years before that. His great discovery was that when a magnet was brought close to a coil of wire, a measurable current was generated in that wire. Dynamos utilised this phenomenon by spinning coiled wire around a fixed magnet, but

the results were crude by modern standards. The alternator appeared when it became possible to produce much lighter magnets which could themselves be spun around a stationary winding. The weight saving allowed the magnets to be spun much faster, greatly boosting the electrical efficiency and output of the alternator.

This engineering leap forward came in the nick of time as the old fashioned dynamo technology had just about reached the limit of its development potential. The arrival of engine management systems, together with advances in vehicle lighting, heating and

It's always best to charge a battery off the vehicle, and outside if possible. Using a multimeter across the terminals to check when the stored voltage reached 12.5V will help confirm when charging can stop.

in-car entertainment, sent power consumption needs sky-rocketing to levels that would have been unimaginable 20 years ago. The alternator was able to match these needs and today remains an integral part of every vehicle's electrical system.

Like the dynamo, the alternator relies on the vehicle's engine for its impetus, taking its drive directly from a simple rubber belt.

One of the keys to the alternator's success is its output flexibility. It's able to vary the current levels produced according to demand, and achieves this thanks to a component called the voltage regulator. These are built directly into the alternator's body, and worked by monitoring overall electrical demand and adjusting generation levels accordingly. In times of heavy loading, when electrical demand is high, the voltage regulator acts to increase the strength of the alternator's electromagnets, to boost current output. When demand is low, the reverse happens.

Unfortunately, the system isn't infallible, and it's the battery that continues to provide a relatively weak link in the chain. Fundamentally, we're dealing with 100-year-old technology, certainly as far as lead/acid batteries are concerned. While things have moved on a little in recent years, most conventional box batteries still contain plates coated with lead-based paste that are surrounded by an electrolyte solution of weak sulphuric acid – how archaic is that? But the fact that this technology has lived on over the past 100 years says much for its overall suitability. The approach works well in the harsh under-bonnet environment. Batteries of this type are easily charged, they store a lot of energy and can deliver it reliably on demand.

But there are disadvantages too. Electrolyte levels are the key to good performance. Car batteries are divided into cells and each of these must be correctly filled with electrolyte so that the plates within are submerged. The problem is that as the battery is used the electrolyte is consumed – primarily by evaporation. If levels fall too low then power delivery and recharging functions become badly inhibited.

But even when electrolyte

levels are kept spot on, car batteries do have a finite service life. They eventually become exhausted, at which point the chemical reaction stops and power output is lost. A typical lead/acid battery will normally provide about three years service, although service life will be considerably shorter if maintenance issues are ignored. In a bid to assist owners, the battery manufactures introduced the so called 'maintenance free' battery in the 1980s, featuring improved lead plate coating materials and a sealed lid design which greatly reduced electrolyte loss. Life expectancy was pushed up to between four and five years and the servicing requirement was virtually eliminated.

In the past five years though, there's been a real step forward in battery technology. Mounting concern about the disposal of waste lead from the millions of expired car batteries discarded every year has driven researchers to seek an alternative operating mechanism. It was also accepted that lead was a restrictive component in terms of ultimate power output and service life.

The solution involves a switch away from lead to a calcium/silver mix as the plating material, and this has now been adopted by every major motor manufacturer as the standard O/E fit. As a result, service life has been pushed to well over five years (assuming normal operation) and voltage output has been boosted too. However, on the downside, these new batteries demand a more sophisticated charging system – the standard alternator/regulator approach is simply too crude.

Calcium batteries are very sensitive to the way they are charged, and require a well managed, slow trickle-type of delivery. To provide this the conventional voltage regulator has been ditched in favour of a much more sophisticated and accurate control module. In some cases this is actually a separate unit but, more often, it's incorporated within the vehicle's main ECM. The level of technology built into these charge monitoring systems has resulted in the process earning the tag 'smart charging'. Of course, the increase in complexity means that fault diagnosis is that much more complicated as well, and these systems tend not to be terribly multimeter-friendly anymore. In most cases access is only possible using a well matched diagnostic tester. These expensive machines run through a sequence of important tests – including battery voltage, alternator output, reserve capacity and cold cranking –

Remember to remove the cell caps whenever charging an older-style battery so that the gas produced can escape safely.

Beware of the 'rapid charge' function unless you have a state-of-the-art automatic charger. Slow charging usually works best.

The alternator meets all a car's electrical needs once the engine is running. It recharges the battery as you drive too.

Shielding batteries from extremes in temperature is important. Some manufacturers like Nissan use a simple plastic box, while others employ quilted padding.

HEAVY DUTY	063	DIN EQUIV	54434	
AMP HOUR	44	AH	CCA SAE	370	AMPS
OTHER EQUIV			IEC	245	AMPS
RESERVE CAPACITY	62	MINS	CCA DIN	210	AMPS
12 VOLTS					

There are all sorts of technical battery classifications but most 'high street' suppliers tend to simplify things nowadays, preferring to use quick-reference model application charts, which makes purchase much easier.

simulating realistic operational conditions.

The knock-on effect of this technology, for you and me, is that we need to be extra careful whenever recharging or replacement is required. Don't imagine for one minute that a flattened calcium-type battery can be effectively brought back to life by hooking it up to your trusty 15-year-old battery charger. The two are simply incompatible and the only way to tackle the problem is to go and buy a new-generation 'smart' charger. Also, resist the temptation to save a few quid by replacing an exhausted calcium battery with an older-style lead/acid type. Vehicle charging systems designed to work with calcium batteries will prove ineffective at maintaining a cheap and cheerful lead/acid unit.

Nevertheless, despite the technological advances, battery failure remains very high on the list of vehicle breakdown causes. Incorrect charging rate is a persistent cause of trouble.

Problems with the voltage regulator can lead to both under- and overcharging, but it's the latter that does most damage. Pushing too much energy into a battery will cause it to heat up and promotes evaporation of the electrolyte and, in extreme cases, buckling of the plates. Of course, the hot under bonnet environment doesn't help matters either. Car designers have long been aware of the need to keep vehicle batteries at a stable operating temperature to ensure maximum service life and reliability. But placing the box next to the engine makes things tricky.

Manufacturers have tried various ways of overcoming the problem of heat build-up. Jaguar, for example, opted to fit an electric cooling fan directed at the battery on the XJS! So why not move the battery right out of the engine bay? That seems a sensible idea but few manufacturers appear keen. Mercedes-Benz and BMW spring to mind as a couple who have relocated the box on some models, but most prefer to struggle on with the old arrangement. The latest idea is to lag the battery with a sort of quilted insulator material, designed to keep the unit warm in winter and cooler in summer.

Dealing with a flat battery is becoming increasingly involved as well. Starting the engine with jump leads is fraught with potential problems on modern vehicles, and some manufacturers actively warn against this technique because of the risk of damaging the sensitive on-board electronics. But many owners still choose the apparent convenience of a 'jump start', and imagine that getting the car going and giving it a good run will recharge the battery and bring everything back to normal. Unfortunately, this just isn't the case. The vehicle's own charging system is designed to provide a modest top-up charge, but nothing more. It can't cope with a heavily discharged battery, so even a high speed journey from Land's End to John O'Groats won't bump the battery back into full working order again – it will probably recharge to no more than 75% of the original capacity. Then, continuing to use the battery in that partially charged state will cause the uncharged 25% to 'die' permanently. Thereafter, you're left with a battery only capable of operating at three-quarters of its original power, which is bound to cause problems with cold weather starting in the future.

The only thing to do with a completely discharged battery is to remove it from the car and bench charge it in the traditional manner. In this way it will be completely replenished and all performance will be restored.

However, one word of warning here. It's worth checking with your vehicle's operating manual, or at your dealership, concerning whether or not it's advisable to disconnect the battery. This may sound ridiculous but severing the main power supply can cause increasingly severe problems these days with engine management systems, not to mention security coded car radios. So be sure before you act.

Another myth is that a battery can only withstand one or two total discharges before failing altogether. In fact, batteries work better if they are thoroughly cycled. Ironically, treating them as we do nowadays – continually

TECHNICAL TOPIC: *Battery care*

Car batteries lead a hard life, suffering from all the common and most unpleasant ills that modern society has to offer – neglect, abuse, disrespect, starvation and torture. If ever there was a prime candidate for the automotive social services, the poor, downtrodden car battery is it! Most drivers regard these boring boxes as a truly 'fit and forget' component when, in reality, they are anything but. The manufacturers don't help much either, by encouraging us all in the belief that their products are completely 'maintenance free'.

Batteries really are a 'distress purchase'. We only buy them when we absolutely have to, and most of us try to get away with spending as little as possible. We're unaware when things start to go wrong and, because of that, we take no action. Battery failure is an irritating and frequently premature occurrence. But there's a lot that the enthusiast can do to help ensure maximum service life, and help to keep the inevitable failure a predictable event rather than an unforeseen nuisance.

1 You can still use a multimeter to carry out some basic checks on a car battery while it's on the vehicle. With the ignition switched off and the meter set on the most appropriate voltage range (0-20V), take a reading across the terminals and, assuming all is well you should find 12.5V or more. Then, to assess alternator output, carry out the same check with the engine running at 2,000-3,000rpm. This time the voltage reading should have increased to 14.5V, although this can be higher on some cars nowadays. Renault, for example, has pushed the performance of its voltage regulators so you'll find anything up to 15.5V on some models.

2 Although car batteries seem heavy and strong, their plastic cases can be vulnerable to damage, particularly on the baseplate. So, it's a good idea to make sure that the battery tray is completely cleared of any sharp stones or other hard debris that might have accumulated there, and could cause a casing puncture. Use a brush or vacuum cleaner to remove all loose material before the battery is replaced.

3 Keep a wary eye on the condition of all battery cabling. Splits, cuts and corrosion will all inhibit electrical efficiency, so any leads found to be suffering in this sort of way should be replaced. Also take time to check that the battery's earth connection is both clean and secure. This is a vital and often overlooked factor.

4 The tension and condition of the alternator belt is another very important factor, both for the well being of the battery as well as bearing condition in the alternator and elsewhere in the system. If it's too slack battery charging will suffer while with it set too tight all bearings that it acts on will be over stressed. Keep an eye out for nicks or signs of age-related perishing. Any visible damage means a new belt.

5 All car batteries will be held in place by some sort of restraining device, and it's vital that this is both tight and secure. Units that are lose in their mountings will almost certainly suffer from the destructive effects of operational vibration, which will significantly shorten service life. Don't imagine that the battery's own weight will be sufficient to hold it in place because it won't. Elasticated straps are worse than useless too.

6 Battery terminal design has varied quite a lot over the years, but one fact remains constant. Connections must be clean, tight and adequately lubricated to guarantee effective operation. However, be careful not to over-tighten the fixing and make sure that the collar is fully down on to the terminal post before reaching for your spanner or socket.

7 To ensure a good electrical contact, and so efficient operation, terminals should be coated in a specialist electrical grease or a petroleum-based product such as Vaseline. Avoid the use of other apparently suitable lubricants or general purpose greases because these are unlikely to have the necessary levels of electrical conductivity, and could actually hinder rather than help the battery's operation. If you find terminals that are coated in a white, crystalline substance, this is a classic sign of electrolyte loss. This sort of contamination must be removed because it reduces the contact area and will inhibit power delivery and recharging capability.

8 Electrolyte levels are absolutely crucial to the operation of any battery. This important liquid is consumed as the battery works although the so-called 'maintenance free' versions limit this loss with almost completely sealed lids. Nevertheless, the cells still have to breathe so the potential exists for fluid loss, particularly if the battery gets overheated due to a charging fault. If you're able to top-up, make sure you use distilled water rather than normal tap water. Also, be careful not to fill the cells up to the brim. The level should be just above the top of the plates, to allow for expansion.

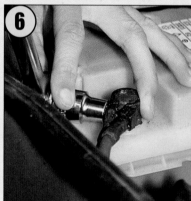

Handy Hints

- Always charge your battery off the car
- Avoid jump starting if possible
- Charge slowly instead of rapidly
- Never top up a battery with tap water
- Check with manufacturer before disconnecting a battery

topping up their charge – is one of the least efficient ways of utilising a battery's full performance!

We've already touched on the need for care and attention when recharging a battery, but this is a very important aspect which must be understood by all DIY enthusiasts. Many chargers are fitted with a 'Rapid' charge function and you need to be wary of using this. In normal operation, a charger begins its job by assessing the state of the battery by measuring its internal resistance. Based on this information it will then set an appropriate charge rate designed to slowly bring the battery back to a fully charged state. All recharging operations create heat as a by-product and this needs to be given time to dissipate so that internal damage is avoided. The beauty of slow, trickle charging is that the many hours it takes allows ample time for the heat to soak away quite naturally, so that levels never become worryingly high.

Switching to the 'rapid charge' function however, attempts to condense ten hours of charging into just a couple. The only way that the charger can achieve this is by upping the charge rate

dramatically which, inevitably, leads to much greater heat build up. This has to be controlled and modern, good quality 'automatic' chargers achieve this by regulating their own operation during the charging process. Cheaper, manual machines usually don't boast this control luxury but, nevertheless, often offer a 'rapid charge' function, and this is where the danger lies. It's down to the user to avoid cooking the battery. In days gone by one of the accepted methods of preventing this was to keep a check on the temperature of the electrolyte. But, of course, this isn't possible anymore with modern sealed units, so the only other alternative is to monitor the battery's voltage output using a multimeter. To avoid plate damage this should not be allowed to exceed 14.5V, but keeping a constant eye on this can test the patience of a Saint!

Don't forget, though, that it's not always the battery that will be at fault. Sometimes the alternator can be just as problematic. These current generators contain a set of contacts which provide the connection between the rotating electromagnets and the electrical winding. These are

called brushes and because they run in contact with moving parts, they do wear out. Although in most cases they should last for 100,000+ miles, premature failure is not impossible. When this happens, alternator performance tends to deteriorate and the most noticeable consequence of this will be a reduced battery charging rate. The first sign for the driver is likely to be a flickering dashboard warning light when engine revs are low.

The alternator's drive belt is another potential source of trouble. The tension of this is a critical issue, and problems will be caused if it's too tight or too loose. A belt that is too slack wont drive the alternator at the correct speed, leading to undercharging of the battery and reduced output for the rest of the electrical system. Apart from testing the belt tension using the procedure outlined in the workshop manual, a loose belt

will also produce that characteristic screeching noise as it slips, especially in cold weather when the alternator is having to work harder than usual.

A tight alternator belt is probably even worse because it will unnecessarily load every bearing in the system. The components affected vary from engine to engine, but often you'll find that the belt will also be used to drive important items such as the water pump and power steering pump. The increased loading will accelerate bearing wear rates (sometimes halving the life of a component) but, outwardly, there will be no sign of the damage being done. Being made of rubber, the belts also suffer with time so it's wise to keep an eye on their condition, and replace those showing any signs of wear and tear.

Next Month
Clutch technology

TOOLKIT BUILDER:

Battery chargers

Battery chargers have undergone something of a technological revolution over the past few years. The changing face of battery design and operation has meant they've had to. All of a sudden these once simple devices have become all high-tech, with flashing LEDs, brightly coloured labelling and purposeful sounding names.

However, cutting through the marketing hype, there remain a number of fundamentals you must consider before buying a new battery charger. For a start

you have to make sure that the model you're interested in actually delivers enough punch to be useful. All battery chargers have a rated current output, classified in amps, and it's important, for car battery work, not to buy anything rated too low. As a general rule you should look for a machine with a 'max charge' figure of between five and 10A for general purpose operations. If the output of a charger is too small, then all that it will do is provide a very slow trickle charge that will be insufficient to deal with a flat battery. It will act like the alternator on your car, providing a top-up function rather than genuine full charging potential. To simplify the choice Halfords now classifies its chargers by engine capacity, which is a good idea that should

leave customers in no doubt about which machine they need.

The other basic choice to be made is whether to buy an 'automatic' or a 'manual' machine. Models that boast automatic control are highly recommended for use on modern batteries which require sensitive, well-controlled charging. These machines eliminate the risk of overcharging thanks to the ability to vary their electrical output in response to battery condition. The more basic, cheaper manual versions don't work in the same way, relying instead on greater vigilance from the user who must remain on hand to switch off the machine before things get too hot.

Knowing when a battery is fully charged, and avoiding the dreaded overcharging that can so drastically shorten service life, is a vital factor. Thankfully, many of the better chargers

now feature handy LED indicators to help with this. Some even include a light which illuminates if the user mistakenly connects the charger clamps to the wrong terminals – what a sad reflection on the great British public that is! After all, if you're not confident about whether to connect the red lead to the positive or negative terminal on the battery, then perhaps you shouldn't even be lifting the bonnet, let alone fiddling with the battery.

Prices do vary a lot but really there should be little need to pay much more than £35-£40 for a good quality machine that will perform safely and reliably. The presence of a rapid charge function is not something I'd worry too much about. It's a feature which needs to be handled with great care and should only ever be used as a last resort. Also, many of the higher spec chargers aimed at the semi-professional and professional markets will offer a jump or boost start facility, allowing an engine with a flat battery to be started instantly. Once again, this is great for emergency use but, while such treatment will certainly get the motor running, it's unlikely to replace much of the lost charge from the battery. Remember, there really is no substitute for effective, slow-rate bench charging.

Old-style chargers like this can wreck modern batteries if used incorrectly. They can still be used but demand constant supervision to avoid problems.

Modern battery chargers come in all shapes and sizes but the greater electronic sophistication they offer is much more appropriate for use on today's car batteries.

LED indicators are great for keeping tabs on the charging process. They make battery charging almost foolproof.

Back to Basics

Part 11:
The clutch performs a vital function. Chris Graham explains how it does it.

Measuring clutch pedal position.

W e all like to think of ourselves as good drivers. Car enthusiasts take a pride in their vehicle and the way they use it. Mechanical sympathy is high on the list of motoring priorities, which is why the sound of graunching gears is guaranteed to send shivers down the spine. Hearing a fellow driver battling with the cogs actually makes me wince, as I imagine the pain and suffering being inflicted on the poor, unsuspecting gearbox. Of course, things aren't as bad as they used to be. In many ways we're spoilt these days, with modern gearbox and clutch combinations offering tremendous levels of change slickness and pedal lightness. How different it all is now from the old days when changing gear required genuine muscle power, and the prospect of a lengthy spell in stop/start traffic appalled everyone apart from professional footballers and Olympic sprinters!

But, even with all the advantages of modern design, it's still perfectly possible to make mistakes with your gear-changing and, if we're honest, we're all guilty of the odd noisy lapse every now and again. Driving smoothly with a manual gearbox requires good clutch control and this, in turn, demands effective timing and skilled pedal operation. Failure in either respect will lead to juddery progress, causing increased wear and tear right through the vehicle's drivetrain – engine, clutch, gearbox and driveshafts.

In practical terms, the clutch is the key to everything. It provides a vital and variable link between the engine and the driven wheels, allowing power to be transmitted in a controlled manner best suited to the speed of the vehicle and its engine. The trouble is that the internal combustion engine is a poor performer at low revs, unlike steam engines or electric motors. We all know that you simply can't get your car moving without a fistful of revs. Trying to pull away at less than 1,200rpm or so will usually cause the engine to stall because there is very little power available at the bottom end of the rev range. For a comfortable getaway most engines need at least 2,000rpm if the clutch is to be operated normally.

This lack of power (torque) at low speeds is one of the primary reasons why petrol and diesel engines need a clutch. But also, the clutch provides a handy way of completely disconnecting the driving force between the engine and the gearbox, allowing gears to be changed and a temporary 'neutral' to be used during everyday motoring manoeuvres such as parking. It's very important to be able to break the link between the engine and gearbox on demand, otherwise changing to a higher or lower gear ratio would be virtually impossible. Without this facility to disconnect, the gear cogs which have to become interlinked so that the gear can be changed, simply wouldn't be able to do so – the speed differential between them would be too great.

So it was very fortunate that some bright spark, way back in the mists of motoring history, invented the clutch. His concept was to create a device which, thanks to the clever use of spring pressure and the phenomenon of friction, would enable the rotary motion needed to spin the gearbox and drive the wheels, to be switched on and off without affecting the running of the engine. While modern clutches are pretty complex, high-tech contraptions, not too much has changed in terms of the basic principles and primary components used. Put simply an automotive clutch can be broken down into three basic parts; the driven plate, the pressure plate and the clutch housing assembly (see diagram).

The success of the whole concept relies on the driven plate being pressed and held tightly against the engine's main flywheel, so that the two can spin as one. When this is happening the clutch is said to be 'engaged', and rotary drive is transmitted from the engine, down the input shaft and straight to the heart of the gearbox. The engine-end of the gearbox's input shaft is splined so that the driven plate is locked to it (although it can slide back and forth) so that all the time it's spinning, drive is transmitted to the gearbox. The driven plate is able to cling tenaciously to the flywheel thanks to a coating of high-friction material similar to that used on brake pads. In the old days this used to be an asbestos-based compound but, nowadays, with health issues in mind, the industry has switched to more environmentally-friendly alternatives such as kevlar.

However, the driven plate grips the flywheel only while it's clamped tightly against it. To break the link between the engine and gearbox the clutch must be 'disengaged', by levering the pressure plate back towards the gearbox, which releases the clamping force on the driven plate causing it to slip. As the release continues the plate eventually stops spinning when all contact with the flywheel is lost. The transition between these two extremes allows the clutch to slip, so that power from the engine can be fed progressively to the gearbox and the car can be driven smoothly.

In its 'natural' state though, the clutch remains engaged, with the driven plate tightly clamped against the flywheel by a strong sprung-steel diaphragm built

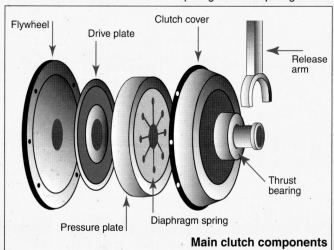

Flywheel

Drive plate

Clutch cover

Release arm

Thrust bearing

Diaphragm spring

Pressure plate

Main clutch components

into the cover assembly. Originally clamping pressure was supplied by coil springs but the 'fingered' diaphragm took over for a number of reasons, including the fact that it was more resistant to centrifugal forces and lowered the pedal pressure required to operate it.

Clutch control is achieved via the foot pedal which is linked to the release arm by either a cable or hydraulic pipework with a slave cylinder at the end. The industry has drifted between cable-based systems and hydraulic ones over the years, with the latter enjoying a bit of a resurgence at the moment. This may well be because as engine power increases so the clamping force has to be upped to match. Hydraulic actuation systems allow greater pressure to be applied without creating excessively heavy clutch pedal feel for the driver. However, irrespective of which is used, the key factor is that the clutch release mechanism is correctly adjusted. There is a reasonably fine tolerance on this and, as we'll see later, inappropriate setting can quickly lead to serious clutch faults and potentially expensive repair bills.

But it's not only the drive plate which enjoys a close relationship with the flywheel, because the clutch housing is bolted to it as well. The whole lot spins as a unit, centred on the gearbox's input shaft, whenever the engine is running. It's a neat solution to a tricky problem and yet it's not perfect and there is certainly plenty of potential for problems.

For a start, the clutch must endure the rigours of a harsh operating environment, sandwiched as it is between the engine and the gearbox. Although protected from external influences by a cast metal cover called the bell housing, the unit remains susceptible to overheating, oil contamination and, perhaps most common of all, the consequences of poor adjustment.

Everyday levels of wear and tear will eventually destroy a clutch's ability to grip the flywheel, as the anti-slip friction material is worn away from the surface of the drive plate. Under normal circumstances though, wear should only occur when the clutch is being slipped, so overall service life has much to do with driving style and type of use. Cars which carry heavy loads, tow trailers/caravans or are tortured by drivers who habitually slip the clutch, or regularly use it instead of the handbrake during hill starts, will suffer with premature clutch failure. But these are all rather extreme cases, certainly as far as most of us are concerned. So if you're not an encyclopaedia seller, a clutch

slipper or someone who helps to clog up the West Country with a caravan every summer, then the sort of clutch-related problems you are likely to encounter can be divided into three types.

The first of these is straightforward clutch slip, which occurs when the clutch becomes unable to cope with the transfer of power from the engine to the gearbox. This will first become apparent when the clutch is placed under the greatest load, usually as the car is being driven up a steep hill, and it will gradually get worse, occurring more frequently with less and less provocation. The cause can be

Clutch casing with diaphragm fingers, drive plate on right.

a variety of factors including a worn clutch, poor adjustment or even oil splash on to the friction plate from leaking lubricant seals. Clutch replacement is normally the only solution.

The second common fault is the opposite of slip, and is called clutch drag. This occurs when, even though the pedal has been pressed right the way to the floor, the clutch fails to disengage completely and so drive to the gearbox does not stop. The consequence of this is that it becomes difficult to change gear and the cause can be poor clutch adjustment, distortion from overheating or semi-seizure of the main thrust bearing on its spline. Once again, major investigation and probably clutch replacement will be needed to put things right.

The third and final common complaint is clutch judder where, instead of providing a smooth power take-up as the clutch is engaged and the engine revs increased, an unpleasant jerkiness creeps into the equation. This happens because the grip between the flywheel and the drive plate has been disturbed for some reason, resulting in uneven levels of friction between the two. Juddering like this always relates to a fault with the clutch itself, rather than poor adjustment or driver error. Usually, some form or clutch plate contamination or distortion will be at the root of the problem, but the only way to be

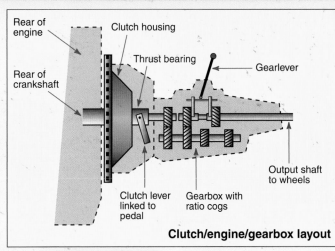

Clutch/engine/gearbox layout

Release mechanism operated by lever from outside the bell housing. Release bearing inside is a wear item.

sure is to get the clutch out and have a poke about.

It's clear then that dealing with clutch faults can be a time-consuming and expensive process, so it's important to do all we can to maximise service life. One of the key factors in prolonging this, apart from driving style, is correct adjustment. The method for achieving this tends to vary from vehicle to vehicle but, with cable-operated clutches there are two basic alternatives. The adjustment can either be manual or automatic, with the latter being preferable until things go wrong. Cars equipped with a manually adjusted clutch require regular checking to make sure that the settings are adjusted to compensate for clutch wear. The name of the game is to ensure that sufficient play exists so that the clutch can be fully released when the pedal is at rest. In the worst cases of over-adjustment

the clutch will remain partially applied even though the driver's foot is off the pedal.

The opposite condition – under adjustment – occurs when there is too much free play in the pedal so the clutch can never be completely disengaged, even when the pedal reaches the full extent of its travel. This condition promotes a difficult and awkward gear change because the clutch is never fully disengaged. There are various ways to check clutch adjustment on cable-operated applications and, once again, the manual must be your guide. Some involve a measurement being taken between the clutch pedal and the floor or the steering wheel, while others specify a setting for the amount of free play at the clutch lever at the gearbox. Adjustments are made as required, using the nut which is run up and down the threaded extension on the end of the cable.

Automatic adjustment is a more convenient alternative which usually makes use of a sliding ratchet arrangement fitted on top of the clutch pedal. It's quite difficult to explain how this actually works and, in all honesty, it's probably beyond the scope of this feature because putting it right when it fails is a devil's own job! Access is very limited and much has to be done by feel alone because, even when lying on your back in the driver's footwell, some parts of the assembly can still be out of sight. The alternative to this is when the auto-adjust mechanism is fitted to the clutch cable, usually conveniently within reach in the engine bay, rather than above the pedal. In these cases it's a different arrangement with a large spring which acts to maintain the correct tension on the cable.

The biggest cause of problems with the pedal-mounted adjuster mechanism is a 'heavy' clutch. This places excessive strain on the toothed quadrant of the ratchet – most of which are made of plastic these days – and inevitably one or two

TECHNICAL TOPIC: *Clutch craft*

You may be lucky and find that what you thought was a clutch problem is in fact a fault with its operating mechanism, but those are in the minority; it is a fact that the vast majority of clutch problems have just one solution – renew the clutch! How easy this is varies a lot from vehicle to vehicle. Some modern cars are designed so that clutch renewal is remarkably easy and does not even involve gearbox removal. On others – Citroen Xantias for example – it's a pretty major task.

Generally though, with modern front wheel drive vehicles it's basically a matter of removing both driveshafts and then sliding the gearbox off the end of the engine. How easy all this is depends on the vehicle's layout and how much other stuff has to be disturbed. With most 'conventional' rear wheel drive vehicles, the job is a bit easier technically as once the car is on axle stands, you can get to the gearbox fairly easily. However the job needs a fair bit of brute strength; conventional gearboxes are heavy and a bit bulky, and you definitely need an assistant to help you with removal and refitting.

In all cases, we strongly recommend studying the appropriate workshop manual to see exactly what the job involves and deciding whether it's something you want to tackle yourself. You may well decide that it's better to let your friendly independent garage do the job on their hoist, than try it yourself. There are also clutch 'fast fit' centres in some areas. Some of these do a good job; others do not. If you do use one of these, try to find out where they source their parts; some use reconditioned clutches to keep cost down, but in our experience these are a false economy. The major part of most clutch jobs is the labour, so it makes sense to pay a bit more for parts if that means significantly longer service life.

There are, however, a number of useful clutch related jobs that anyone can do, as follows.

1 On cable-operated clutches with a manual adjustment facility you'll normally find the adjuster nut on a threaded stud arrangement at the engine-end of the cable. This is used to adjust the length of the inner cable in relation to its outer casing, so that the correct setting can be maintained as the clutch itself wears. It's important that a working clearance is maintained at all times, so that the clutch can be completely disengaged when not in use. Your vehicle's workshop manual will specify how this adjustment should be made and measured.

2 Often measurements relating to the clutch pedal will be quoted. The method used varies. Sometimes it may be the height of the pedal which has to be measured. Other times it will be the amount of free play present between the end of the cable and the clutch actuator arm.

3 Some clutch cables are fitted with the automatic adjuster along the cable, rather than on top of the pedal. These are normally positioned on a convenient section that's easy to get at in the engine bay, and are a good deal simpler to deal with. These fittings were particularly favoured by Rover.

4 Clutch fluid is an important factor on hydraulically-operated clutches. There is a standard service interval for fluid but this is a frequently overlooked aspect, particularly on vehicles which are serviced independently. As a general rule the clutch fluid (and brake fluid) should be replaced every two years, regardless of the mileage covered. The biggest problem is that, given time, the fluid will absorb moisture, which will reduce it's boiling point and can lead to air pockets forming within the system. This, obviously, is a far more serious problem as far as the brakes are concerned, but it can also lead to a spongy-feeling clutch pedal and inefficient operation, which will make gear selection more difficult and increase the overall rate of wear.

5 The colour of the fluid is a good indicator as to its overall condition – clear is best. Watch for signs of sludging too, as in this case. Removing this potentially harmful sludge is another reason for regular fluid changes. In most cases the system will not need to be flushed before the fresh fluid is poured in, but it's important to make sure the system is correctly bled, so that no air pockets remain. Don't skimp on the quality of brake/clutch fluid you use. Your car's manual will have details of the precise specification needed, and you should stick to this rigidly.

6 Before removing the top of the clutch fluid reservoir, always make sure that it's free from dirt and grime. You must guard against the risk of small particles being allowed to drop down into the reservoir as you lift off the top.

7 The route taken by a clutch cable is an important factor as far as smooth operation is concerned. Any curves should be gentle to avoid pinching the cable within. Also watch for any signs of damage and, if additional sections of protective sheathing have been added, as in this case, make sure they are in the right place and haven't been allowed to slide further along the cable leaving a vulnerable spot nearby.

8 If you do ever get to the stage where you've removed and stripped down a clutch, this is the sort of drive plate you're likely to find inside. Note the excessive wear – the friction material coating has been worn away right back to the shiny metal beneath. The four small coil springs are included to help reduce clutch judder as power is taken up.

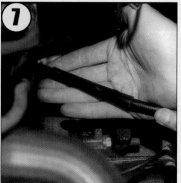

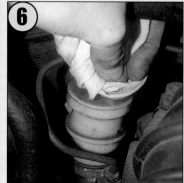

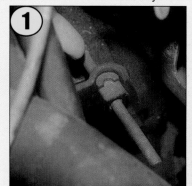

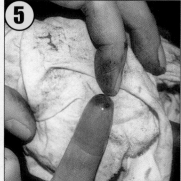

Handy Hints

● When dealing with a heavy clutch remember that you'll have to sort out the original cause first, otherwise the same thing will happen again. This can happen for a number of reasons, including an old, worn or kinked cable, or wear in the clutch itself. Modern nylon cables should not be lubricated and are designed to run dry.

will sheer off. The clutch can become heavy for a number of reasons, but often the cause relates to the cable itself. One possibility is that it has been wrongly routed after some other engine work, so it's now following a tortuous route which includes a number of tight curves that promote wear and pinch the cable within its sheath.

For this reason, if you ever find yourself having to replace a clutch cable, it's important before you start to make sure you are familiar with the correct route and the various anchor points along the way. Take some time to check that things are as they should be and, if you're in any

doubt, refer to the manual or look at a similar model to make certain. A heavy clutch is the sort of problem which can sneak up unnoticed on us all, because it develops so gradually. It's a hard condition to quantify in any meaningful manner, apart from a practical comparison with another clutch. Of course, it's very important to make sure the other clutch is on the exact same model otherwise the exercise will be pointless.

The situation is rather different with a hydraulically-operated system in that the same sort of adjustment checks are not necessary. But obviously, you must keep a weather eye out for

leaks and damage to the pipework. as well as ensuring that the fluid is changed as the manufacturer recommends. You will also find that some vehicles make use of a dual purpose reservoir that supplies fluid for both the clutch and the brakes. In these cases you should note that the outlet for the clutch system will always be considerably higher up the side

of the container than that for the brake. This is a safety-related feature which ensures that if there is a problem with the clutch system, and fluid is lost, enough will remain in the reservoir to ensure that the braking system keeps operating as normal.

Expert assistance

Colchester Institute has a large Automobile Engineering Centre which provides part-time (one day per week) and full-time courses in automobile engineering, body repair and welding.
For more information contact: **Dave Roberts**
Head of Centre for Automobile Engineering, Colchester Institute, Sheepen Road, Colchester, CO3 3LL.

Next Month
Inside gearboxes.

TOOLKIT BUILDER:

Torque wrenches

A torque wrench might not seem like the most essential tool for a new and enthusiastic workshop dabbler, but you'd be surprised just how useful one can be. Essentially it's a clever variation on the spanner theme which enables the user to accurately control the degree to which a nut or bolt is tightened. In the good old days when we had a motor industry of our own, and block exemption still had something to do with drains, tightening force, or torque, used to be expressed in quaint units called foot-pounds (ft/lb). But now we live in a different world and it's classified in the much more EC-friendly, but equally baffling Newton-metres (Nm). However, the point is that these measurements provide a standard to work to.

There are many instances with car maintenance and repair when nuts or bolts have to be tightened to a specific degree – head bolts, crank bearing journals, pulley nuts, wheel bearings, etc., etc. But, in addition to this, the increasing use of alloy components on modern vehicles means that over-tightening is something to be avoided like the plague. The torque wrench is the only tool which can help prevent expensive damage in both cases. Old fashioned versions used to rely on a sprung pointer which was deflected as the turning pressure increased. But these were quite difficult and imprecise to use, so that approach was dropped in favour

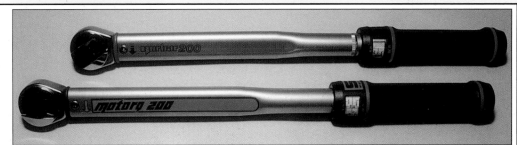

You can get solid metal torque wrenches like these with plastic handles. While these might be more comfortable to use, the plastic will be less robust.

An easy-to-read setting scale can make a big practical difference if you're using the tool on a regular basis. A silk finish will ensure that the numbers remain clearly visible under all lighting conditions.

of a spring-loaded toggle arrangement. The spring is tensioned to increase the pressure on the toggle which, in turn, raises the amount of torque required to 'click' the head and signify that the desired tightness has been achieved. A scale incorporated into the shaft allows specific torques to be set and the tool is used just like a giant ratchet handle. Only, with a torque wrench you can't pull and pull to your heart's content because, at the pre-set torque level, the toggle does a flip and the wrench clicks into neutral to prevent further pressure being applied.

Of course, as you might imagine, the level of sophistication and engineering which goes into these tools means that they don't normally come cheap. It's unlikely that you'll find much worth owning below about £40. Accuracy is the

There is no substitute for quality if you want reliability and accuracy from a torque wrench.

key factor with a torque wrench – you need to know that it's doing what it should, otherwise it's worse than useless. Most tools from established manufacturers will be built to exacting standards and will have been calibrated to confirm their performance. However, reliability does suffer over the years as the main spring starts to get tired, which is why all wrenches should be re-calibrated every year or so – your local tool

specialist will advise on the nearest calibration agent.

For this reason buying a second-hand tool can be a bit of a lottery and much depends on the make and how it's been treated. The best advice is to stick to the well known suppliers to be sure of getting a quality product. Some of the equipment arriving here from the Far East leaves a lot to be desired in terms of performance accuracy and internal components used.

The presence of a rubber or plastic seal between the head and the top of the shaft is a good sign. This will keep dirt and debris from getting down inside the shaft and gumming up the works.

Being able to lock the torque setting you have dialled in easily and securely is an important factor as far as accuracy is concerned. Locking methods vary. This retractable lever on a Britool torque wrench works really well.

Back to Basics

Part 12:
Chris Graham delves inside the typical automotive gearbox.

Gearbox oil usually is usally supplied in a squeezy-type bottle with a flexible plastic filling tube that allows the fluid to be transferred conveniently and easily. The oil is squeezed into the gearbox, rather than poured.

Layshafts, dog clutches, baulking cones and mating teeth may sound like the stuff of pantomime but they are, in fact, all terms, which relate to the motor vehicle gearbox. This essential of motoring life is responsible for ensuring that your car can speed along a motorway just as comfortably as it can dawdle in town traffic. The gearbox also enables you to accomplish awkward hill starts and tricky reverse parking manoeuvres without a second thought.

One of the fundamental limitations of the internal combustion engine, as we mentioned in Part 11 of this series, is that power output is relatively poor at low revs. Typically, a standard engine will produce its greatest power output (maximum torque) at between 3,000 and 4,000rpm. At lower revs the engine's grunt falls away dramatically and its performance becomes far less useful. This problem is compounded because, by and large, most cars are relatively large and heavy when compared to the size and power output of their engines. This is where the gearbox comes into play.

This clever box of tricks contains a number of shaft-mounted metal cogs, which are more correctly known as pinions or gear wheels. These vary in size and can be brought together to increase or decrease the speed of the driven wheels in relation to the speed of the engine. In this way, at any given engine speed, the output to the driven wheels can be varied to best suit the vehicle's overall speed and the road conditions. A single shaft, called the input, primary or first motion shaft, transfers the rotation of the engine's crankshaft, through the

clutch and into the gearbox. From here it's the interaction between the various gear pinions and wheels that controls the speed and direction of the drive output.

Virtually all modern saloon car gearboxes offer five speeds plus reverse. First gear is a low ratio setting, which means that the rotational output from the gearbox is a good deal slower than that of the crankshaft. It's perhaps easiest to understand the fundamentals of gear ratios by relating things to the set-up on a multi-geared mountain bike. When set in the lowest gear the chain runs from a relatively small pedal sprocket back to the rear wheel where it's routed around the largest sprocket there.

The comparative size difference between the two sprockets is what governs the gearing. If the pedal sprocket is small and the wheel sprocket large, then the bike is very easy to pedal, although your feet move fast and overall progress is pretty slow. This gear is great

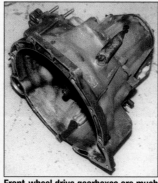

Front-wheel drive gearboxes are much more compact than their rwd cousins because they usually have to be mated to a transversely-mounted engine.

for moving off or tackling the steepest of hills, but no use at all for high-speed cruising.

As the speed builds, the rider must change progressively up through the gears so that the relationship between the pedal and wheel sprockets becomes reversed. At top speed the rear wheel sprocket is much smaller than the pedal sprocket, meaning that the feet can move more slowly even though the back wheel is rotating much faster. With a car's gearbox, this situation is rather more exaggerated, although the principle remains the same.

With first gear selected, the ratio between the two gear wheels being used can be anything up to 4:1 – one gear wheel is four times the size of the other. The consequence of this intentional mis-match is that for every complete rotation of the gearbox's output shaft (which transmits drive from the gearbox to the wheels), the primary shaft has to spin four times. This ensures that the engine runs good and fast, even though the car is only moving slowly. Accordingly, plenty of torque is produced and the car pulls away from a standstill with ease.

Like the bike though, as the car's speed increases it becomes impossible to remain in first gear because the engine quickly begins to rev dangerously high. A change to the next, higher ratio is necessary to save the engine's blushes, and keep it at it's most productive rev level.

Each successive gear offers a slightly higher ratio until fourth gear is selected when most gearboxes are running at just about 1:1, meaning that the engine is turning at the same speed as the gearbox wheels.

Fifth gear tips the balance in favour of the engine, as it then runs slower than the gearbox to promote better fuel consumption while cruising. In the old days this sort of ratio used to be referred to as an 'overdrive', a name which simply indicated that the prop shaft was turning faster than the engine.

As you can imagine, there is plenty of scope to play about with ratios and vehicle designers put a great deal of effort into ensuring that the gears chosen ideally suit the vehicle application. Most saloon cars nowadays offer what's called a 'wide ratio' gearbox, which is best suited to general everyday motoring. Gear changes can be fairly relaxed, the engine isn't over-stressed and the ratio difference between first and fifth is a wide one.

For competition use, however, engineers opt for a 'close ratio' alternative, with gears chosen especially to keep the engine's rev level at the high end of the scale, thus maximising power output. Using a close ratio gearbox is hard work as the gear changes necessarily come thick and fast.

Over the years gearbox technology has developed tremendously so that, nowadays, a manual 'box is very forgiving and easy to use. But things weren't always so pleasant! Back in the halcyon days of motoring, when driving

The rear-wheel drive gearbox can be more elongated, which allows for the use of straightforward gear selector rods.

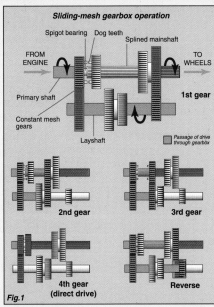

Sliding-mesh gearbox operation

FROM ENGINE — Spigot bearing — Dog teeth — Splined mainshaft — TO WHEELS

Primary shaft

Constant mesh gears

Layshaft

1st gear

Passage of drive through gearbox

2nd gear — 3rd gear

4th gear (direct drive) — Reverse

Fig.1

was generally a calm and civilised affair, drivers were nevertheless forced to grapple with an awkward beast called the sliding-mesh gearbox. Most cars from the early 1900s were fitted with this type of unit, which demanded both skill and style from the user. The problem was one of gear selection and, in particular, ensuring a smooth transition between successive gears. For this reason the unit was commonly known as the 'crash box' but, despite its operational limitations, its efficiency levels were high and the design provided the basis of what we all use today.

The typical four-speed sliding-mesh gearbox used on a rear wheel drive car contained an assortment of toothed gear wheels mounted on three shafts – the primary shaft, the layshaft and the mainshaft (refer to Fig.1).

As we've already noted, the primary shaft transfers drive from the engine to the gearbox, and is fitted with a fixed pinion wheel that is permanently engaged with a similar but larger wheel on the end of the layshaft. These two are collectively known as the constant-mesh gears and ensure that the layshaft spins continuously. The layshaft itself is mounted, supported by bearings, within the gearbox casing, and is fitted with three other fixed gear pinions. Above it, the mainshaft is splined and carries a further three gear wheels. The engine-end of this

This is the oil filler on a 'traditional' rear-wheel drive gearbox. Oil condition and specification are important factors for reliable and efficient gearbox operation.

shaft is supported by a spigot bearing built into the end of the primary shaft. The splines allow the gear wheels to be slid back and forth to engage with those on the layshaft, as various ratios are selected. Selector forks are used to initiate this sliding motion and these is linked, either directly or remotely, to the gear lever inside the car. A four-speed 'box requires three selector forks.

The problem with gear selection on this type of gearbox arises because of the speed differential that exists between the constantly driven layshaft and the mainshaft. You can imagine that trying to slide two spinning toothed gear wheels together, when they are rotating at different speeds, is a tricky business which all too easily results in spine-tingling and tooth chipping chaos. The obvious solution is to synchronise the speeds so that the gear wheels can be slid together and intermeshed without damage. To achieve this, the technique of 'double-declutching' was devised, and was based around the careful and deliberate use of the clutch pedal during the change.

For example, when changing from first to second, it was important to allow time for the mainshaft to slow down before selecting the higher gear. Achieving this involved engaging the clutch and selecting neutral, at which point the clutch was released. Then it had to be engaged once more so that the gearbox layshaft would be braked by the engine as the revs fell away. Only then could the higher gear be selected.

Good timing was vital to the success of this operation, together with the longevity of the gearbox! But, if you thought that was bad, changes down were even more difficult because they required that the engine/gearbox speed be increased before the lower gear could be safely selected.

This involved a blip of the throttle with the gearbox set in neutral, and the clutch engaged, so that the speed of the layshaft was increased to match the anticipated engine speed once the lower gear was engaged. It called for good mechanical judgement and a lot of practice!

With all these gnashing teeth and spinning shafts to deal with, effective and reliable lubrication was a vital factor. The solution was a simple one though. The gearbox was filled with oil to the

level of the layshaft, so that the gear wheels would splash the lubricant all over the place during operation.

But despite the good soaking they got from the oil, the gear wheels and pinions remained very noisy, producing a characteristic whine. The primary cause of this was the fact that their teeth were straight-cut and this, coupled with the difficulty and slowness associated with using the sliding-mesh gearbox, outweighed its high level of mechanical efficiency.

A simpler approach was desperately needed and, in particular, one that boasted a much more user-friendly gear change method. Key among the objectives was to rid the motoring world of the need for cumbersome double-declutching. But, to do this it was necessary to overcome the gear wheel speed imbalance problems. The first attempt at this was the introduction of the constant-mesh gearbox, which arrived just before the Second World War.

Although it was only a stepping-stone towards the modern approach we have today, the constant-mesh gearbox introduced a couple of ground-breaking ideas. First the straight-cut gear wheels were swapped for ones with a helical tooth pattern, which made them stronger and much quieter. But, perhaps more fundamentally, the pairs of gear wheels on the layshaft and mainshaft became permanently intermeshed, and thus in constant motion. Those on the mainshaft were mounted on bushes or roller bearings so they spun freely. But, obviously, to transfer any drive the wheels had to be locked to the shaft, and this was achieved using sliding dog clutches splined to the shaft so they could be moved across to interlock with the appropriate gear wheels when required.

While not a perfect solution, the constant-mesh gearbox was a big improvement and, although the dreaded double-declutching was still required, any damage that resulted from mis-timed changes was restricted to the dog clutch teeth, rather than the more expensive gear wheels. A measure of its success is that the constant-mesh gearbox lives on in many commercial and agricultural vehicles to this day. But, it wasn't good enough for us pampered car drivers, so the designers worked on and came up with the synchromesh gearbox. This was basically a variation on the constant-mesh idea, but with the

Selector forks, helical gear wheels and synchromesh assemblies inside a typical rwd gearbox.

important addition of cone clutches to smooth the union between the dog teeth on the gear wheel and dog clutch. I know this all sounds complicated, but that's because it is! In reality, of course, there is probably no need for those of us not intending to dismantle and rebuild a gearbox next week, to understand how the synchromesh device works. But, if you're anything like me, you feel happier with at least a basic comprehension of what's going on. So here goes!

To engage the gear, whichever it is, the freewheeling gear wheel on the mainshaft must be locked so that it turns with the shaft and drive can be transmitted. Locking it to the shaft means that the splined dog clutch must slide along the shaft (driven by the gear selector fork) and interlock with the dog teeth on the gear sprocket.

The big problem is that it's very unlikely that these two will ever be rotating at exactly the same speed, so a perfect union straight away is improbable. Accordingly, they need to be synchronised before the teeth can be finally engaged. Are you with me so far? Equalising the speed is the job of the cone clutch, which is machined into the hub of the synchromesh

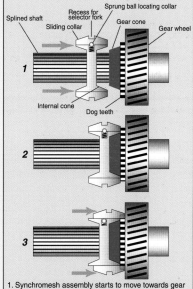

Splined shaft — Recess for selector fork — Sprung ball locating collar — Gear cone — Gear wheel

Sliding collar

Internal cone — Dog teeth

1

2

3

1. Synchromesh assembly starts to move towards gear wheel, activated by selector fork.

2. Gear cone and internal cone engage and resultant friction equalises gear wheel and shaft speed

3. Further pressure from selector fork overcomes spring-loaded ball bearing and causes collar to slide on its splines and interlock with dog teeth on gear wheel.

Fig. 2

assembly (refer to Fig.2). As this is slid towards the gear wheel, the female cone in the hub locates on to a male cone machined on to the side of the gear. Imagine two wafer ice cream cones being slid one inside the other, and you'll get the picture.

As the gap closes, friction is set up between the two cones and it's this, which begins to alter the gear wheel's rotational speed, matching it to the shaft. Once the two have been equalised, the locking process can take place. To achieve this the sliding collar, which rings the synchromesh unit and is driven by the selector fork, must be moved across to interlock with the dog teeth on the gear wheel. This can only happen, of course, if the splines/teeth are in perfect alignment and, to assist with this, those on the gear wheel are machined with narrowing tips.

Think of the interlocking process as like securing a bayonet-fit electric light bulb. If you imagine the bulb having 20 lugs instead of just two, and the socket offering a similar number of slots, then fitting would involve little more than pushing the two together once they were lined up.

However, the issue of alignment remained an important one because, as far as the synchromesh/gear wheel combination was concerned, it still offered the potential for baulking. The possibility that the teeth/splines might foul on each other as they came together still existed, particularly if the gear was being changed quickly.

In the early days of synchromesh it was quite common for an enthusiastic driver to 'beat the box', an action that was met by a crashing of gears as the splines and teeth battled to engage. To overcome this problem the boffins introduced something called a baulk ring system, which ensured a more rapid equalisation of speed between

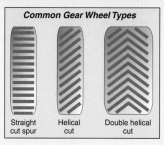

Common Gear Wheel Types

Straight cut spur | Helical cut | Double helical cut

gear wheel and synchromesh unit, thus producing a quicker and cleaner change.

The explosion of front-wheel drive saloons, which hit our roads in the 1970s, threw a bit of a spanner in the works as far as gearboxes were concerned. All of

TECHNICAL TOPIC: *Gearbox maintenance*

Tackling any sort of serious repair on a gearbox is certainly not for the feint-hearted. I wouldn't advise anyone who doesn't have a good deal of experience, plus a well-equipped workshop, to undertake rebuild or internal repair work. This type of job really is best left to the professionals who have the expertise and the often specialised tools needed.

Nevertheless, there are a few things which the keen DIYer can do and keep and eye on to help ensure continued, trouble-free operation. As is so often the case with motor vehicle maintenance, a little well-informed vigilance goes a long way as far as gearboxes are concerned.

(1) Control for the reversing lights normally comes from the gearbox so don't forget to check here if your lights mysteriously fail. A simple on/off switch activates the lights when reverse gear is selected. In most cases these devices are kept very simple to ensure reliability. Usually a slotted shaft inside the gearbox moves as reverse gear is engaged, allowing the switch to be activated. Externally the switch connection can be vulnerable to damage and the ingress of water or dirt. Replacement is a simple unplug/unscrew job. In this particular example, the switch is sited above the gearbox oil level plug, so no lubricant will be lost if the switch has to be replaced. If oil is lost then this must be replenished with the correct grade. Always refer to the workshop manual to be completely sure of transmission oil specification.

(2) When checking gearbox oil levels it is very important to make sure that the vehicle is standing evenly, whether it's on the ground, raised on axle stands or suspended on a hoist. Jacking up the front end and then checking the level will give a false reading. Don't be surprised if automatic transmission fluid or even engine oil is specified as the recommended refill lubricant on your vehicle. Requirements vary from manufacturer to manufacturer. Some gearboxes are not fitted with an oil drain plug at all, and are only designed to be topped up. When refilling add enough fluid so that it just starts to run out of the filler hole. The bottom of the hole provides the correct filling level.

(3) Oil leaks are one of the most common problems to afflict a gearbox, and can spring from a number of places. But the most usual culprits are the driveshaft seals. These are simple rubber or Neoprene seals and, with age, they deteriorate and lose their sealing ability. To replace them the driveshaft will have to be removed, which is easy on some vehicles, but more involved on others. If you have to tackle this job yourself, always make sure that new seals are well lubricated with grease to help the bedding-in process and prevent burning. New ones are supplied dry but should never be fitted in this state.

(4) There are two main types of speedometer drive – electrical or cable. In most cases both usually take their drive from a metal worm gear inside the gearbox, which acts on a plastic pinion, and it's this, which can wear out. Also, the simple cable drive versions have a tendency to snap with age and fitting a new one can be a bit of a struggle. It's usually pretty straightforward to disconnect here at the gearbox end, but is often trickier to release from behind the speedometer because of limited access. The important thing to remember is that the routing must be exactly as specified in the manual. Also, the hole in the bulkhead through which the cable passes needs be resealed with its rubber grommet when the new cable is fitted. Failure to do this will increase the likelihood of destructive chafing and will allow water to find its way into the passenger compartment.

(5) Selector mechanisms are another potential source of problems although putting them right isn't really a DIY type of job. On front-wheel drive cars the mechanism is operated by a remote linkage from the gear lever. It is absolutely critical that the connection between the lever and the gearbox is accurately set. The method for doing this varies from manufacturer to manufacturer, and getting it wrong can result in serious problems – first gear being selected instead of reverse, for example! The setting must be precise because of the way the linkage operates – a small movement within the 'box equates to a large movement at the gear lever. Factors that can cause excessive play in the linkage include worn bushes, resulting in a sloppy feel at the lever. Sometimes this can be detected from underneath the car, when it will be possible to rattle the linkage arm in its bush mountings. It's sometimes possible for worn bushes to be replaced but, more often than not these days, a new linkage assembly will have to be fitted. This in itself is not a particularly difficult job, but it's the re-setting afterwards that poses problems for the inexperienced technician. Although specialised tools aren't normally required, the procedure can be complicated.

Handy Hints

- Make sure car is level before checking gearbox oil level ● Sloppy change action could mean selector bush wear
- Never skimp on specification of transmission fluid ● Old gearbox oil is carcinogenic – protect yourself

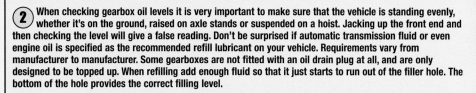

a sudden, designers were faced with the task of re-thinking their conventional rear-wheel drive layouts, so that more compact units could be squeezed on to the new, transversely-mounted engines. Not only did this mean that internal layout had to be radically re-thought, but it also required that the gear selection mechanism be re-vamped.

Until this development, gearboxes had usually run longitudinally on most saloons, with input from the engine entering at the front, and output to the wheels leaving from the back. But the new orientation meant that in most cases input and output had to share the same end of the casing. To facilitate this, the layshaft was dropped in favour of a 'single' rather than 'double-reduction' design (refer to Fig. 3).

The other big consequence of mounting the engine transversely was that it significantly increased the distance between the gearbox and the gear lever. This made it impractical to continue with the established lever linkages for gear selection, as the run was too long. But also the fact that the 'box now had to be mounted transversely meant that the straightforward back and forth change motion had to be switched to a predominantly side-to-side action.

Despite the complexity of the modern gearbox, the good news is that serious problems are relatively few and far between. Catastrophic internal failure is a comparative rarity these days and, although wear and tear of the gear wheels themselves isn't unheard of, it normally takes pretty extreme action to cause a serious problem. Teeth can be snapped off by sudden changes in gearbox loading prompted by bad driving. For example, if you're accelerating hard and take a humpbacked bridge too fast so that the car leaves the ground, the driven wheels will be free to spin even faster. When the car returns to earth, the wheels will be suddenly slowed by reconnection with the road and this will seriously stress and possibly damage the gearbox. Likewise, jumping down a high kerb can have the same effect. This sort of problem is pretty drastic and will often lock up the gearbox completely. In some cases it may be possible to select a different gear, allowing the car to be moved, but usually the broken teeth will really jam up the works.

More commonly failures will relate to oil leaks, worn synchromesh units, failing bearings or badly adjusted selector mechanisms. Tired oil seals are a common cause of lubricant loss on older vehicles, and usually it will be the drive shaft seals on front-wheel drive 'boxes that are most affected. Remember, though, that there is an important seal on the input side of the gearbox which, if it fails, usually results in lubricant finding its way on to the clutch, causing double trouble in the form of gearbox oil loss and clutch slip combined. The tell-tale sign of this, obviously enough, is oil dripping out from the bottom of the clutch housing. However, be careful when diagnosing this one, because it's quite easy to be fooled into thinking the front seal has gone when all you're actually looking at is general oil spray coming from elsewhere on the engine!

Typical symptoms of a failing synchromesh are difficulty in gear selection, often combined with a mechanical grating sound. This might relate to just one or two gears and shouldn't be confused with a clutch actuation problem, which may well present similar symptoms as the car is used. But a clutch problem will affect every gear equally, whereas a tired synchromesh won't. Also, gear selection problems will tend to ease when at a standstill if the synchro is at fault, while remaining just as awkward if the clutch is to blame.

The selector mechanism, in most of its forms, is fairly sensitive to poor adjustment or wear in the system. Bushes, which no longer support the rods as they once did, can lead to gear selection problems, while stripping a system and failing to re-set it correctly will create all sorts of selection confusion. If you come across a vehicle suffering with poor adjustment then it's more than likely that somebody else has been fiddling. Remember that these systems tend not go out of adjustment tolerance just through everyday use.

Unfortunately, the harsh reality of today's hard-pressed motor trade dictates that very few gearbox problems actually get repaired, unless you're dealing with a classic car or something very specialised from the sports or competition markets. The time and expertise required for such work, not to mention the cost of the parts, has priced this sort of job right out of the mainstream workshop. In the majority of cases the simplest, quickest and most cost-effective solution is to fit an exchange unit, either from a vehicle breakers or a reputable reconditioner.

Fig. 3 — Typical front-wheel drive gearbox layout

Typical front-wheel drive gearbox layout

Synchromesh units

Power from engine

Drive to front wheels

Drive to front wheels

Fig. 3

Expert assistance

Colchester Institute has a large Automobile Engineering Centre which provides part-time (one day per week) and full-time courses in automobile engineering, body repair and welding.
For more information contact: **Dave Roberts**
Head of Centre for Automobile Engineering, Colchester Institute, Sheepen Road, Colchester, CO3 3LL.

Next Month
Driveshafts

TOOLKIT BUILDER:

Barrier Cream

Whatever level of work you are tackling in the workshop, from changing spark plugs to rebuilding a gearbox, there is one thing you should never forget and that is to use barrier cream on your hands. While such treatment may seem like lily-livered overkill, it certainly isn't. Barrier cream performs a vital function and we definitely recommend its use for all but the simplest and cleanest of jobs.

The cream performs two basic functions. Most importantly it creates a protective layer between your skin and anything sticky, slimy or dirty that you might touch. This is particularly important when it comes to contact with used engine oil or diesel fuel. Both of these two nasties are

Obviously the bigger the container, the cheaper the contents. Motor factors will sell you 'trade-size' dispensers like this which make good financial sense.

carcinogenic, which means they can act to promote the development of cancer if exposure levels are sufficiently high. While this isn't a particular risk to those of you who work on your cars only occasionally, it should be a serious concern to anyone involved in the trade.

The second big advantage of barrier cream is that is makes cleaning you hands so much easier. A well-applied layer will prevent anything you touch making direct contact with your skin, so it's automatically much easier to remove. Of course, the alternative to barrier cream is the use of those thin latex surgical gloves, but not everyone feels happy working with these on.

There are a number of different types of barrier cream on the market. Some come in normal tubs with pump-action dispensers, while others are

When applying barrier cream always take a few moments to make sure that it is thoroughly worked in to all parts of your hand, especially around the nails.

supplied in aerosol form. A visit to your local motor factor or high street discount centre should reveal all. Prices vary accordingly but whichever you choose it's important to check that it is water resistant. Some are more resistant than others and you should make sure you get a good one because the last thing you want is for the protective layer to gradually wash off your hands as you work in wet or damp conditions.

It's also a very good idea to moisturise your hands after you have cleaned them. Most commercially available cleaners are very efficient at removing all the grease from your skin but, while this is great news in terms of getting your hands clean, it also washes away the skin's natural moisturisers. If you don't replenish these then you will greatly increase the risk of developing unpleasant conditions such as dermatitis. Any moisturising cream is good so I'm afraid you have no other option but to brave the beauty counter in Boots!

Back to Basics

Part 13:
Joints and shafts – Chris Graham spins the yarn.

Always remember that, unless you have the luxury of a hoist, vehicles must be supported on axle stands rather than just a jack.

So far in this series we've looked at how an engine operates to generate power and how, with a little help from the driver, that power is controlled by the clutch and gearbox. The final stage of the operation involves transmission of the power to the wheels, so that the car can be driven.

The traditional approach to this was to power the rear wheels and it's only comparatively recently that front-wheel drive has gained so much in popularity. Actually getting the power from the engine to the rear wheels involved the use of a long metal pole called the propshaft, which ran between the gearbox and the rear axle.

But, as time passed and vehicle design developed, the mass market moved away from rear-wheel drive on essentially practical grounds. Turning the engine through 90°, to what's known as the transverse position, allows passenger compartments to be made bigger. Eliminating the need to have the engine and gearbox aligned down the length of the car meant that engine bays could be made smaller and the size of intrusive transmission tunnels reduced.

Of course, rear-wheel drive remains available as the enthusiastic driver's preference, so sports car and sporting saloon designers still work with this configuration. It's generally thought of as much more controllable for life in the fast lane but, at a more day-to-day and practical level, the impressive traction and significant safety benefits of front-wheel drive make this the family choice. However, as rear-wheel drive was first on the scene, we'll start with a quick look at what it involves.

I'm sure you all appreciate that the propshaft has to be strong to withstand the rigours of everyday motoring. Transmitting the ever changing rotational motion from the engine to the rear axle is no mean feat. So you might imagine that these shafts are made from solid metal: well, they're not!

The problem is one of length. Solid metal bars have a tendency to sag under their own weight and this can be disastrous when the bar in question is being spun at high speed. All sorts of vibration problems are set up as centrifugal force distorts the shaft once it's spinning.

The solution is to turn the bar into a tube. By making it hollow, almost all the strength is retained but the overall weight is significantly reduced, which eliminates any risk of sagging. Also, the lower weight means that the shaft is easier to start and stop – it exhibits less inertia – which helps boost the responsiveness of the whole system.

SPLIT SHAFTS

A further development saw the introduction of the two-piece propshaft, for use on vehicles where the distance between the gearbox and the rear axle made splitting the shaft the most sensible option. The centre joint is supported in a bearing assembly.

The fact that the propshaft has to rotate so quickly, particularly in the higher gears, means that it needs to be well balanced. In the same way that a car's wheel vibrates horribly at all but the slowest of speeds if the balance weight drops off, a propshaft can suffer similarly if the metal it's made from varies in thickness. To guard against this all shafts are checked for good balance at the manufacturing stage. Any found wanting are corrected by the addition of small metal plates which are welded into place at the appropriate points.

The other really important point about propshafts is the way in which they are attached to the gearbox and rear axle. The fact that the rear axle is supported by the suspension springs, and the gearbox is located on flexible mountings, means that both fixing points must allow for movement during use. It would be hopeless to bolt flanges together between the rear axle and the propshaft because these would almost certainly be snapped off the moment the wheels went over the first bump. The vertical movement in the rear suspension would cause such an alignment problem that the bolts could never hold it. The clever solution to this poser is a version of the universal joint called the

Driveshafts vary in thickness, depending on whether they are solid or tubular – the latter (above) is thicker.

Common drivetrain layouts

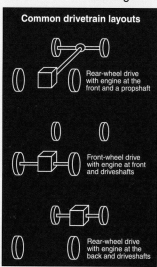

Rear-wheel drive with engine at the front and a propshaft

Front-wheel drive with engine at front and driveshafts

Rear-wheel drive with engine at the back and driveshafts

The maximum angle of operation varies from joint to joint, but is normally 15-25°.

CV gaiters harden and split with age. This is the most common cause of trouble and an MoT failure.

'constant-velocity' or CV joint.

A universal joint is a clever idea, but not a new one. In engineering terms it's a joint which allows drive to be transmitted through a range of angles, thus enabling the components attached to either side of the joint to move independently.

To help clarify the distinction between this and other joints, look at your hard. Imagine you are holding a pistol and your index finger is curled around the trigger. The action of 'pulling' that trigger causes the two finger joints to operate with a simple hinging action as the finger curls, but this is the only direction these joints can move – without extreme pain! The knuckle joint, on the other hand, is a different matter. With your index finger pointing straight out, it's possible to outline a circle with the tip. The ball and socket-type joint in your knuckle allows for a much greater flexibility of movement, although there are still limits.

FLEXIBILITY

A universal joint can be thought of as a type of fixed ball and socket arrangement, where there is good flexibility of movement and yet rotating one half will cause the other half to do the same. Achieving this with bits of metal is relatively easy, as illustrated by the basic Hooke-type joint which has been around for hundreds of years.

This utilises two metal yokes, arranged at 90° to each other, which connect to a small tubular cross called a trunnion block (see diagram). Over the years a number of variations on this idea have been developed, but all have suffered from a fundamental problem. The nature of this linkage means that, when it's operating at anything more than a slight angle, the output speed fluctuates dramatically even when input is kept constant. This is an obvious drawback from a vehicle drive point of view although in other less speed-sensitive applications it's not such a problem. While it is possible to reduce this effect by

This is the triple roller bearing assembly found inside a tripode-type CV joint.

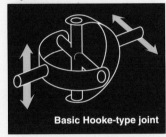

Basic Hooke-type joint

careful angling of the input and output shafts, this extra complication tends to outweigh the advantages from an automotive perspective.

The constant velocity (CV) joint provides the ideal answer. It's greater design complexity ensures that input and output speeds remain the same at all operating angles, producing a smooth and predictable rotational transfer that's perfect for vehicle use. There are a number of different types – Birfield, Rzeppa, Weiss and Tripode – but it's beyond the scope of this feature to explain the workings of each. Suffice to say that the commonly used types rely on steel ball bearings or needle bearings, which tend to be supported in metals cages and packed with thick, greasy lubricant.

Normally, the whole assembly is encased within a rubber bellows-type gaiter, secured by Jubilee clips, which seals it from the elements. Water and dirt will quickly make mechanical mince meat of any CV joint they work their way into.

The advent of independent rear suspension – when each rear wheel could move independently of the other – necessitated the use of a much shorter shaft, complete with CV joints at each end, running between the wheel and the differential unit. These, not unreasonably, were christened driveshafts, and could be either solid or tubular. More commonly nowadays, you'll find driveshafts at the business end of a modern saloon, as they are used to drive the front wheels on virtually all mass-produced cars.

One other aspect that's important to note about driveshafts is that they aren't usually fitted with identical CV joints on each end. The movement of the suspension, as the wheel rides up and down over uneven surfaces or because the car is cornered hard, has the effect of increasing the distance between the gearbox and the wheel. Now, of course, the driveshafts themselves can't stretch to meet this extra requirement, so there has to be some other allowance made for the lateral movement needed.

The neat solution was called the 'plunge joint'. This, when fitted to the gearbox end of the

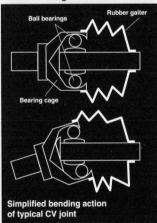

Ball bearings

Rubber gaiter

Bearing cage

Simplified bending action of typical CV joint

Some longer driveshafts are given extra support from a bearing like this.

driveshaft, enables it to slide in and out the few centimetres necessary to accommodate the suspension movement. The sliding action comes courtesy of grooved channels or ball bearings, depending on the design.

Because driveshafts are so much shorter than propshafts, it is rare that they ever need to be balanced, although some specialist units still are. They also rotate much more slowly than the driveshaft (about a quarter of the speed), which makes it less important for them to be absolutely perfect for everyday usage. To give you an idea, when a front-wheel drive family saloon is travelling at 70mph, it's driveshafts will be spinning at about 1,000rpm. So, although driveshafts lead a relatively hard life, structural failures are rare. Actual breakages are uncommon but damage can be sustained by careless jacking or accident impact.

DAMAGE ALERT

The CV joints, however, are a different story. Because of the operating stress they endure, they have a finite service life and this can be dramatically shortened by failure of the rubber gaiter. Loss of lubricant combined with water and dirt ingress will rapidly gum up the works but, quick though the deterioration may be in engineering terms, it's still the type of problem which sneaks up gradually on all but the most attentive of vehicle owners. Apart from picking up the fault by careful inspection, the first most people know about it is from strange grumbling sounds. These vary depending on whether it's the inner or the outer joint which is failing. If there is a knocking sound which becomes particularly apparent when the car is manoeuvring on full lock, it'll be the outer CV joint that's on its last legs.

Alternatively, if you can hear a constant humming noise – rather like you get with a worn wheel bearing – then this tends to point towards a problem with an inner joint. In either case, though, all is not lost because it will often be possible to renew the worn joint without having to buy a complete new driveshaft. Most will be removable with little more than the removal of a spring clip or two although it should be stressed that the method for doing this does vary from manufacturer to manufacturer.

TECHNICAL TOPIC:
CV gaiter swap

Changing a damaged CV joint gaiter really is the type of job which, in most cases, can be tackled by the enthusiastic DIYer. Obviously, the complexity of the operation varies from vehicle to vehicle, and it's certainly potentially more difficult to deal with a newer rather than an older car. To illustrate the basic technique we wheeled in a trusty old MkII Cavalier and attacked the front nearside corner.

1 Jack up the vehicle and make sure it is securely mounted on carefully placed axle stands unless you have the luxury of a vehicle hoist. Undo the wheel hub nut with an air ratchet, if you have one. If not this large nut will have to be 'broken' with the vehicle still on the ground. The hub nut will be very tight and must be reset to the correct torque afterwards – refer to the vehicle's workshop manual. Often the socket required to remove the hub nut will be an odd size – not found in a normal set – so you have to buy it as a one-off. In this case the socket was 30mm.

2 Next disconnect the bottom suspension joint so that the suspension leg can be pulled clear. In this case we had to tackle a tapered ball joint which was 'broken' apart using a combination of pry bar and hide hammer. Fortunately it came apart easily but in cases where it just wont shift, you'll need a special tool called a ball joint breaker.

3 With the bottom joint released, the whole leg can be pulled forward to release the outer end of the driveshaft. Keep an eye out for any brake pipes which may be put under strain as you pull the suspension leg clear. Remember it's easy to stretch these too far. Now you have a choice about whether to work on the gaiter with the shaft still on the car, or to remove it altogether. Obviously, if you're dealing with the CV joint at the gearbox end, then the shaft will have to come off anyway. But if not, and you feel you have enough access to work comfortably, then carry on with the shaft *in situ*.

4 Many people find it more convenient to work with the shaft off the can and on the bench, in which case you'll have to disconnect it from the gearbox too. Normally this is a splined joint that's secured with a simple clip. Careful and even leverage from a pry bar will usually be all that's required to slide it out. Note that removal of this end of the shaft will inevitably result in the loss of some gearbox oil, so have a spill tray standing by. Also remember to recheck the level once the job is finished, and to top up as necessary with the correct grade of lubricant. Finally, if you do remove the driveshaft then it's good practice to fit a new gearbox seal when you replace it. These are sold separately.

5 With the shaft off the vehicle and clamped securely in a vice, pull back or cut off the old gaiter and use circlip pliers to release the spring clip securing the CV joint. In this case this clip had to be opened so that the joint could be slid off the splined end of the shaft. In practice this can be an awkward job, which is one of the reasons why it's often easier to have the shaft on the bench, rather than still on the car.

6 Use a hide hammer to carefully tap the joint as you hold the circlip open. Avoid hitting the joint too hard otherwise you might knock the bearings out and the whole assembly will fall to pieces!

7 New gaiter kits come complete with grease pouch and retaining clips. Nowadays you can buy conventional ones like this or, alternatively, versions which are split to ease fitting. The idea of these is that they can be fitted without the need to remove the CV joint, as they can be wrapped around and then glued to form a watertight seal. The other alternative, if you don't want to remove the CV joint, is to buy a special stretching tool, which allows the boot to be widened sufficiently so that it can be popped over the end.

8 If you're fitting a new CV joint it's vital that you pack as much grease from the pouch as possible in and around the bearings. Any that might be left over can be squeezed into the gaiter before you fit it.

9 Finally, don't forget to slide the gaiter on to the shaft before re-fitting the CV joint. After this it's simply a matter of reversing the dismantling procedure. The joint's retaining clip should open automatically on the taper as you slide the assembly back into place on its splines. Nevertheless, check that it's sitting securely in its groove before continuing. Also, only ever use your hands to manoeuvre the new gaiter. Never be tempted to grab it with pliers because you'll probably split it.

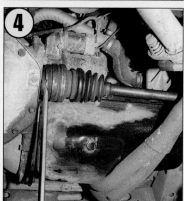

Handy Hints

- Leaking lubricant from a split gaiter is an MoT test failure point.
- Always re-tighten hub nut to correct torque setting.
- CV joint lubricant is horribly sticky stuff, so wear gloves!
- Make sure gaiter retaining clips are fitted the right way.
- Always use a soft hammer when removing CV joints.

Next Month
Steering systems

The One Tool You Can't Be Without

Contents:
- Jacks & Lifting Gear
- Welders
- Starter Chargers
- Booster Cables
- Power Tools
- Electrical Gear
- Plumbing Tools
- Compressors
- Vehicle Service Tools
- Towing & Recovery
- Socket Sets
- Wrenches
- Premier Line
- Hand Tools
- Electrician's Tools
- Engineering Tools
- Lighting
- Grinders
- Safety Products
- Dust Extractors
- Tyre Changers
- Lathes
- Air Tools
- Gauges
- Bandsaws
- Pillar Drills
- Janitorial
- Heaters
- Generators
- Cable Reels
- Inverters
- Shot Blasters
- Sack Trucks
- Hydraulic Pullers
- Cordless Tools
- Spray Guns

☎ 01284 757500
🖷 01284 703534
✉ sales@sealey.co.uk
🌐 www.sealey.co.uk

Catalogue 2005/6

For Your Free Copy Call Us Now On 01284 757525

For your FREE copy of our Catalogue, call us on 01284 757525 or fill in the reply form. Alternatively request a copy via our website at www.sealey.co.uk. We only supply through dealers. Contact us via telephone, fax or email for details of your local stockist.

SEALEY GROUP
KEMPSON WAY,
SUFFOLK BUSINESS PARK,
BURY ST EDMUNDS,
SUFFOLK. IP32 7AR

TEL: 01284 757500
FAX: 01284 703534
WEB: www.sealey.co.uk
E-MAIL: sales@sealey.co.uk

Please send me a FREE copy of your latest printed catalogue and promotions ☐

Name: Mr/Mrs/Miss ....

Address: ....

....

Town: ....

County: ....

Ref: CMBOOK   Postcode: ....

We comply with the requirements of the Data Protection Act and may use these details to send you information about other promotions from the Sealey Group. We may also share this information about you with third parties where we feel their services will be of interest to you. If you do not wish your details to be passed on to these third parties, please tick this box. ☐

Back to Basics

Part 14:
Chris Graham discovers that there's a lot more to vehicle steering than meets the eye.

Until you've driven a car on a skid pan, or been to a rally school with slippery mud like this, it's hard to appreciate just what an influential part of car control the steering is. We're spoilt by normal road conditions when, by and large, our cars go where we point them!

The traditional children's go-kart, made using a few planks of wood, some old pram wheels, a wooden box, string and a mouldy cushion, is the stuff of happy childhood memories. Whether dragged along or let loose down a dusty track, the chances are that most of these rickety little machines relied on a swinging beam front axle for their steering. This simple system was one of the first to be developed, and relied on a central pivot around which the front wheels, that were mounted on either end of a solid beam, could be rotated as a pair.

Now, while this was all fine and dandy on something as primitive as a horse-drawn cart, or for larking around in the playground, it quickly became apparent that more sophistication was needed for proper motor vehicles. One of the biggest problems with the swinging beam idea was that it encouraged a high degree of wheel scuffing, leading to excessive tyre wear. Because the front wheels were turned as a fixed pair, remaining parallel at all times, they were forced to scrub along the ground during virtually every turn. Also, there was a tendency for the wheels to be easily thrown off course by the shocks caused by bumps and potholes, so control could be unpredictable!

FOLLOWING THE LINE

To help understand the scuffing aspect, imagine a car with this type of steering set-up driving on full lock in a perfect circle around a central point. Viewed from directly above, it's clear that the two front wheels are both tracing circles around the centre point.

However, the circle made by the inner wheel is smaller than that traced by the outer. So, to follow the circumference of the smaller circle accurately, the inner wheel actually needs to be set at a greater turning angle – something that was impossible with the swinging beam approach.

Then along came a clever German called Rudolph Ackermann who saw the potential of a double-pivot idea invented by his fellow countryman Lankensperger in 1817. Ackerman patented this set-up, which did away with the swinging axle in favour of individually pivoting wheels, and his name lives on to this day with modern systems being based on the Ackermann layout. However, even this wasn't perfect and another 60 years passed before

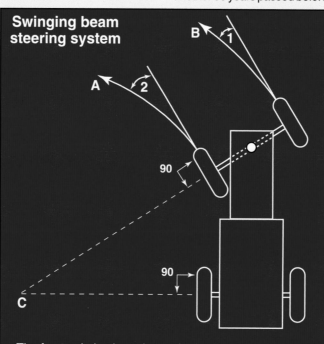

Swinging beam steering system

B
1
A
2
90
90
C

The front axle is pivoted at a single, central point and so both wheels turn as one. Point 'C' represents the centre of the vehicle's turning circle, and the two paths marked 'A' and 'B' indicate the paths the front wheels need to take to negotiate the turn. Angle '2' is bigger than angle '1', illustrating that the inner wheel should turn more sharply than the outer to avoid tyre scuffing. But, because the front wheels are mounted on a swinging axle, this cannot happen.

people started to realise that the turning angles had to differ for the two front wheels.

Significant changes also took place regarding the method by which the wheels were turned. Modern steering requires that the rotary action of the steering wheel is converted into a linear motion which is then used to actually move the wheels. To do this obviously requires some sort of gear mechanism and, over the years, two primary systems came to the fore. The first was the steering box system, which relied on the interaction between a worm gear and a toothed sector or peg. The base of the steering shaft was fitted with a simple spiral thread which was intermeshed with a short run of teeth, or a single peg, attached to a drop arm. In turn, this arm, which was moved forwards and backwards by the rotating spiral worm gear, was linked to the front wheels via a series of rods and joints. The downside of the steering box system is its relative complexity, which means that maintenance and servicing levels can be high.

The more modern alternative to the steering box set-up is the rack and pinion design, which provides a simpler system with the same degree of effectiveness. This time the base of the steering shaft is fitted with a straightforward gear wheel (pinion) which locates against a toothed rack. As the steering wheel is rotated, the pinion turns and this action slides the rack from side to side. Rods are attached to both ends of the rack and these are linked to the front wheels so that they can be steered.

GEARED FOR ACTION

At the heart of both systems is the fact that the driver is steering the wheels through a set of gears, and this is an important point. The front wheels of any car carry a great deal of weight, mostly thanks to the engine, and so the turning action has to be geared down to make things easier for the driver. Anyone who has driven a go-kart for any length of time will appreciate just how 'heavy' and tiring direct steering (with no gear reduction) can be! A typical family saloon is set up so that it takes just under four complete revolutions of the

Wet roads are common throughout the year in this country, and can be quick to highlight problems with a steering set-up. Even top-notch sporting machinery like this Mercedes-Benz can struggle if things are not balanced.

Expert assistance

Colchester Institute has a large Automobile Engineering Centre which provides part-time (one day per week) and full-time courses in automobile engineering, body repair and welding.
For more information contact: **Dave Roberts**
Head of Centre for Automobile Engineering, Colchester Institute, Sheepen Road, Colchester, CO3 3LL.

really is a specialist subject and, as such, is way beyond the scope of this series. But, nevertheless, it's good to have some understanding of the fundamentals, which is why we'll be getting a bit more theoretical next month. So gird your loins and get your thinking heads on!

steering wheel to turn the wheels from lock to lock. But obviously there is a balance to be struck here. Steering feels easier and easier as the gearing is reduced, but a point is reached when the wheel is having to be turned so many times, that it simply becomes impractical.

The arrival of power assistance heralded another revolution for motor vehicle steering, although some of the earliest systems were far from ideal. The basic premiss was a simple one; to use hydraulic pressure to assist with the movement of the steering rack. The key, of course, was to get the level of assistance just right, so that the steering retained that all-important degree of 'feel' which is such an essential of the driving process. It's vital that the driver is able to detect the forces being exerted during turning manoeuvres, and having too much power assistance destroys this ability. Consequently a great deal of emphasis is placed on system control, to ensure that the correct balance is struck between user comfort and safety.

Damage to the track rod end gaiter like this is typical and represents an instant MoT test failure.

All the aspects we've considered so far are relatively straightforward, and so it's quite easy to form the opinion that steering is a simple business. Unfortunately, it's not! Although the actual mechanics involved can be viewed as pretty basic, there is a subtlety to steering which is deceptive. The effectiveness of any system relies on the accuracy of its set-up – the steering geometry. This

The Ackermann steering system

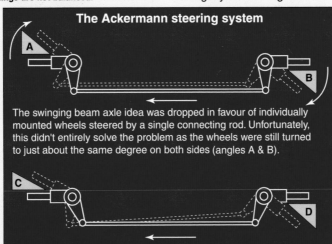

The swinging beam axle idea was dropped in favour of individually mounted wheels steered by a single connecting rod. Unfortunately, this didn't entirely solve the problem as the wheels were still turned to just about the same degree on both sides (angles A & B).

Ackermann's idea, with a little help from Jeantaud, was to angle the two steering arms, which connected to the wheel hubs, in towards the centre line of the vehicle. This ensured that, as the steering was operated, the wheels turned to different degrees, with the inner one always pivoting more (angle D) than the outer (angle C).

A simplified rack and pinion steering system

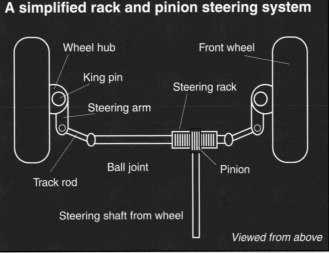

Wheel hub
King pin
Steering arm
Front wheel
Steering rack
Ball joint
Pinion
Track rod
Steering shaft from wheel

Viewed from above

The steering on a Formula One car, such as this Ferrari driven by Jean Alesi, is extremely direct. Unlike you and I in our road saloons, he's not forced to grapple with nearly four turns of the wheel from lock to lock!

STEERING OBJECTIVES

For now though, let's scratch the surface a little deeper with a look at what a good steering system should achieve. For a start it needs to make sure that the front wheels run true, and by this we mean that the tyres are not being forced to go in directions other than that in which they are pointing. A good system should also provide an effective self-centring function, meaning that if released while on lock, the wheels will automatically tend to return to the straight ahead position.

Essentially this is a safety-driven feature but it also provides more of that important 'feel' for the driver while cornering. The impression given about what's happening between the front wheels and the road is fundamental in terms of any action the driver may wish to take. The self-centring system provides a resistance detectable at the steering wheel as you turn, assuming the tyres are gripping as they should. So, the moment this disappears, because you've hit a patch of ice, for example, you will be warned of the danger by a sensation of looseness through the wheel.

The other thing that a good steering system must provide is resistance to shock or violent change. Hitting a bump with one wheel, or getting a sudden tyre puncture, must not be allowed to cause the car to swerve violently to one side. Modern systems are much better at resisting the effects of this sort of problem, thanks to their closer integration with the suspension. But problems can arise if alterations are made. Boy racers who fancy lowering the suspension on their car, or fitting non-standard, wider wheels, can seriously upset the balance of the vehicle if the work is not carried out professionally.

It should always be remembered that the manufacturer's original design combines suspension and steering elements which work as individual parts to produce an overall set-up that's safe and effective. Altering just one aspect has the potential to introduce knock-on effects that will upset all the rest. What's more, while such problems might not be apparent during everyday motoring, it's under emergency conditions when any shortfalls may become cruelly exposed.

TECHNICAL TOPIC: *Track rod end swap*

One of the most common problems encountered by the average steering system is the failure of one or other of the track rod ends, which link the steering rods to the wheel hubs. Rather like the CV joints we discussed last month, these universal joints are protected by flexible rubber gaiters which keep out dirt and moisture. Inside there is a simple ball and socket-type affair, which allows for both up and down and side to side movement, and this is packed with grease. Ageing or impact damage can split the gaiter, at which point the grease will start being washed away. Joint seizure is then inevitable and steering performance will be seriously affected. Consequently, even the smallest split in a gaiter is an MoT test failure point. Replacement of the joint is the only solution but, fortunately, it's not a terribly complicated or expensive business. To illustrate what's involved we ran through the procedure on a Ford Orion.

1 The first thing to establish, of course, is that it is indeed the track rod end which is at fault. Steering and suspension systems are becoming more and more intertwined these days, so it can be tricky actually diagnosing the problem. The best way to check for a worn track rod end, assuming that the gaiter isn't badly split making the fault obvious to spot, is to get a friend to turn the steering wheel while you listen to and feel the joint as it moves. Clonking and grinding will be the tell-tale signs of trouble.

2 Once you have the car securely suspended on well-placed axle stands, or a vehicle hoist, you can begin freeing the joint. The first job is to undo the bottom nut. This will either be a Nylock type or, as in this case, one fitted with a split pin. Remove the pin and discard it as this must be replaced with a new one when you reassemble.

3 This nut will normally be fairly tight, particularly on vehicles where it's not been touched for years. It may also have a specific torque setting, so be sure to check with the workshop manual when you get to the re-tightening stage.

4 Even though you have removed the bottom nut, it's unlikely that you will be able to lift the universal joint clear of the steering arm because it's located on a tapered spindle which, once in place, becomes a very tight fit. The accepted way to separate the two is to use a tool called a ball joint breaker. This is a simple cast metal bracket which fits over the joint, with a threaded bolt that is wound in to exert a force and 'break' the joint apart. It's good workshop practice to protect the thread on the stud being pressed by replacing the nut as shown. In this case, however, this precautionary measure isn't essential as the worn out track rod end is destined for the bin anyway.

5 The ball joint breaker, once in place, is tightened up so that it pushes the stud upwards to separate the two components. However, if the joint does not split after reasonable pressure has been applied, use a carefully aimed soft-headed hammer on the side of the joint, to help shock it apart. It's not a good idea to over-tighten the ball joint breaker.

6 The alternative method, if you don't have a ball joint breaker, is to improvise with a suitable lever and a soft-headed hammer. This method requires rather more caution and you need to pick your leverage point with care. The bar must be used as close to the track rod end as possible, to avoid the risk of distorting the rod itself. Another danger is that you can inadvertently scratch off sections of underbody sealant with the end of the levering bar. This will expose bare metal and promote corrosion. Any such damage should be repaired without delay.

7 With the track rod end disconnected from the steering arm on the wheel hub, it can be unscrewed from the end of the track rod. However, before you do this it's vital to be sure of its position on the track rod, so that the replacement can be screwed on to exactly the same point. Failure to do this will leave the steering out of alignment. The simplest way to ensure you get this right is to make sure that the locking nut on the track rod is held in place as you remove the end. You may also like to count the exposed threads on the far side of the lock nut (before you remove the end!), just to make doubly sure. Then, wind on the new end up to the lock nut and the job's done!

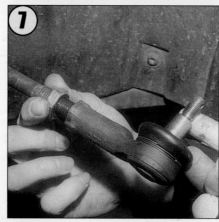

Handy Hints

- After any steering work always make sure wheel alignment is professionally checked.
- Only ever use a soft-headed hammer on steering/suspension parts.
- Uneven tyre wear can be a sign of poor steering set-up.
- Don't forget that the ball joints on the inner ends of the track rods can wear out too.

Next Month
Steering geometry

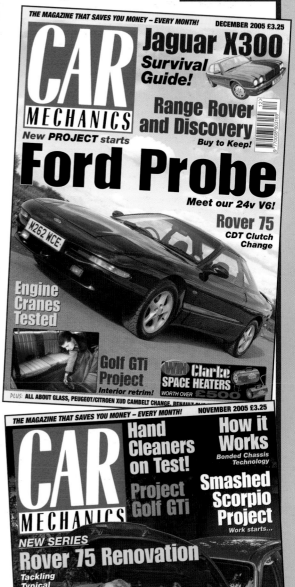

Back to Basics

Part 15:
Chris Graham explains the purpose of springs, dampers and other twangy things!

Body roll is unavoidable during hard cornering and, in some respects, is desirable. However, it must be controlled otherwise suspension geometry starts to be adversely affected and overall handling suffers.

This month we're taking a deep breath and beginning a two-part investigation into vehicle suspension. I say 'taking a deep breath' because it's a deep subject! Even 30 years ago the science of springing was a tricky nut to crack but nowadays, as with virtually every other aspect of modern automotive design, it's become mind-blowingly complicated. Of course, we can only hope to scratch the surface of such a subject in a feature like this so, to begin with, I'm going to take you right back to the fundamentals.

So why have vehicle suspension in the first place? After all, without it vehicle manufacturers could save themselves a fortune in design and production costs. Well the reason, of course, is that cars would be all but undrivable without it. Not only does suspension insulate the occupants from the bumps and crashes caused by poor road surfaces, but it also helps protect the car itself as well.

As we all know, modern vehicles bristle with sophisticated electronics, none of which is particularly partial to being violently shaken for hours at a time. The efforts of the suspension system to smooth out uneven travel, and to minimise the transfer of vibration and impact from the wheels to the vehicle body, has a very positive effect on prolonging overall vehicle life.

SPRING SELECTION

But simply fitting springs isn't really enough to ensure a comfortable and safe ride. While all modern systems are based on the springiness of metal, either in coil, leaf spring or torsion bar form, there is more to it than this. By their very nature, springs bounce and take a while to settle back to their original position after distortion. So simply allowing a vehicle to be suspended on conventional springs would produce an extremely bouncy, uncomfortable and uncontrollable ride. To overcome this, a hydraulic damper is used in conjunction with the spring, to control its movement.

Upward wheel travel, as the vehicle negotiates a bump in the road, compresses the spring and the damper as one unit to absorb the shock. Then the pent-up energy stored in the compressed spring is released progressively as the damper acts to control the descent of the wheel back to it its normal position again.

Most dampers are filled with hydraulic fluid which is compressed by a piston and forced through valves as the unit is compressed and released. Some of the more expensive versions are adjustable, so that they can be 'stiffened' or 'softened' to suit different styles of driving.

As you can imagine, plenty of thought and research has gone into the tweaking of damper performance, as it has such an important effect on passenger comfort and vehicle handling characteristics. The boffins have even considered suspension 'bounce frequency', believing it to be very important to the passengers inside. Research has suggested that bouncing which occurs at a rate of two or more times a second is perceived as harsh and uncomfortable.

Then there's the matter of handling to be considered. Suspension design is perhaps the most important and influential factor in this respect. Control of wheel movement is a key factor here and, with most modern cars now employing fully independent suspension (each wheel is allowed to move independently of the others), the number of variables in the system is high. While this isn't

necessarily a problem when driving in a straight line along a motorway, when the vehicle is cornered more enthusiastically it most certainly can be.

Throwing a car into a tight bend has a number of knock-on effects which can have serious consequences if the suspension system isn't up to the job.

THE ANGLES GAME

Body roll is the first noticeable upshot of entering a bend. The car's body begins to tilt away from the direction of the turn, and the suspension on the outer wheels begins to compress.

This, in turn, affects wheel camber as the suspension geometry begins to alter. Camber is an important concept to understand here because it has some very significant effects on vehicle handling. In simple terms, camber is a measure of the degree to which a wheel is angled. In an ideal world the wheel would sit squarely and at 90° to the road surface, so that the full width of the tyre's tread

Old fashioned leaf springs like this, fitted on back of a Ford Transit, are no longer used on passenger cars. Most modern saloons are now independently sprung at front and back.

A whole industry has grown up around vehicle suspension. Stiffening and lowering kits are popular sellers but enthusiasts should always stick to top quality manufacturers such as Spax. Remember that the vehicle manufacturers spend millions developing the standard systems used on their cars and, by and large, most are pretty good nowadays.

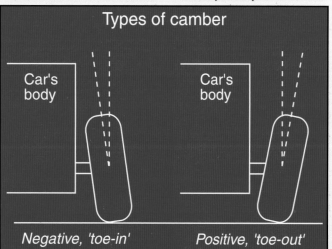

Types of camber

Car's body — Car's body

Negative, 'toe-in' — *Positive, 'toe-out'*

The MacPherson strut-type suspension caused something of a revolution in vehicle design. It provides cheap, reliable and effective springing for most front-wheel drive saloons today.

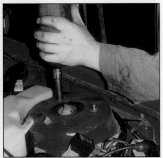

Front suspension struts feature hefty top mountings normally accessed from the engine bay. Dampers which feature variable settings are adjusted from here too.

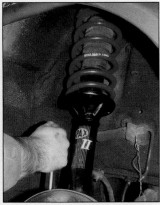

Do-it-yourself suspension work can seem quite straightforward in theory but, in practical terms, there are many mistakes to be made. Suspension geometry is extremely subtle and it's an aspect that many fiddle with at their peril.

makes good contact to maximise grip. Unfortunately, the fact that wheels have to move up and down as the suspension works, means that a tilting effect (away from the vertical) can be introduced and this is known as the camber angle. This value can be either positive or a negative, as we'll see.

You've probably all heard of the terms 'toe-in' and 'toe-out'. Well, these are the popular ways used to indicate the positive or negative nature of the camber angle. Toe-in suggests a negative camber, with the top of the wheel tilted in towards the centre of the car, while toe-out represents the opposite, positive condition, with the wheel tilting outwards. Lots of people fiddle with camber angle in a bid to improve handling, but it can be a

Expert assistance

Colchester Institute has a large Automobile Engineering Centre which provides part-time (one day per week) and full-time courses in automobile engineering, body repair and welding.
For more information contact: **Dave Roberts**
Head of Centre for Automobile Engineering, Colchester Institute, Sheepen Road, Colchester, CO3 3LL.

dangerous business if you don't know what you're doing. It can have significant effects on steering performance, promoting potentially alarming amounts of understeer or oversteer if the settings are badly out.

But, to understand where we're at today, it's necessary to go right back and appreciate how things started. Independent suspension is still a comparatively new concept for run-of-the-mill saloon cars. It didn't really enter the scene until the late 1970s at a mass production level, with the majority of vehicles struggling on with non-independent systems up to this point. And I do mean struggling because, compared to what we have today, the old fixed axle systems were archaic.

Back in the 1960s independent suspension was the preserve of the expensive sports machinery. Nowadays, though, we all take it for granted, revelling in the fact that even a basic Ford Focus can comfortably out handle most exotics from the classic era.

GRIN AND BEAR IT!

Back in the days of yore, wheels were mounted on rigid axles, causing them to react in pairs to anything the road surface might throw up. There were a number of serious disadvantages to this old fashioned set-up but, with no credible alternative available, the average motorist was forced to grin and bear it. For a start these systems could be a nightmare to control on uneven surfaces. With the vehicle supported on leaf springs, body roll was a real problem.

The fact that the front and rear wheels were locked together on solid axles meant that shock was transferred from side to side, causing all sorts of steering imbalance. The driven rear axles, known as 'live axles' were also very heavy, giving them a high 'unsprung weight'. The term unsprung weight refers to everything mounted below the springs, and it's an important factor. The heavier the unsprung weight, the more likely the axle is to bounce and hit it's bump stops at the limit of its travel, giving a very choppy and uncomfortable ride.

An improvement was possible with the use of a DeDion axle at the rear. Although still not an independent set-up, this system offered better handling and ride characteristics, even though

comfort levels were nowhere near independent suspension levels. The fact that the rear wheels were not fixed solidly to an axle, but instead linked by flexible ball joints, allowed neutral camber to be maintained irrespective of body roll. Also, unsprung weight was greatly reduced because the brakes were mounted inboard close to the differential, and neither was attached rigidly to the wheels. A clever telescopic tube, called a DeDion Tube, was mounted transversely across the vehicle, to locate the two wheels but, at the same time, allow for slight variations in track as the suspension moved.

But all of these basic systems posed real problems for the designers as well as the drivers, simply because of the amount of space they took up. The presence of a rigid axle at the front of a car meant that most usually the engine had to be placed behind it, taking up valuable space that could have otherwise been used in the passenger compartment. The knock-on effect of this was that the compartment had to be pushed back within the body, usually extending over the rear axle which was far from ideal. For the greatest passenger comfort, it's generally thought best for all seating to be located within the space between the front and rear wheels. This didn't become a truly achievable standard until the use of independent front suspension became widespread across the automotive market.

STRUTTING AHEAD

Things really took a step forward with the almost universal adoption of a suspension set-up known as the MacPherson strut. This beautifully simple design takes its name from its creator,

Earl MacPherson, who worked for Ford in the 1940s. It first arrived here in the UK during the 1950s, but took some time to establish itself as the designers' (and accountants!) favourite on small family hatchbacks and saloons. The big advantages of the MacPherson strut design, apart from offering independent front suspension, were that it was relatively cheap, very compact and simple to install and maintain. These points made it ideally suited for use on front-wheel drive applications. What's more, from a handling point of view it was, and still is, an impressive performer.

With this type of set-up, each wheel is able to react to road surface changes independently of the other, so there is no transfer of steering imbalance from side to side. Also the unsprung weight is very low, which helps ensure better contact between the tyre and road, by reducing unnecessary bouncing. The compact design liberated plenty of room for the engine, and meant that passengers could be brought forward to fit happily between the front and rear wheels, enhancing ride comfort. Another benefit to the ride characteristics came from the longer spring travel that was possible with the strut arrangement, meaning that softer springing could be used if required.

Like so many of the best ideas, the MacPherson strut marvelled many with its simplicity. A conventional coil spring surrounds a damper and this assembly is secured top and bottom. At the base it locates directly on to the wheel's stub axle assembly, via a lower swivel joint, while at the top it's anchored in a bush to the car's bodywork. Further security is provided at the base by an A-shaped framework called a transverse link. The pointed end is bolted, on a pivot point, to the bottom of the stub axle, while the two anchor points at the inner end of the link are fixed to the body via rubber bushes.

Continues next month.

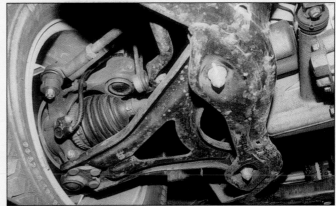

The bottom link arm (A-shaped) is clearly visible here. It features a secure double fixing to the body, designed to resist acceleration and braking torque.

TECHNICAL TOPIC: *Anti-roll bar bush swap*

Worn anti-roll bar bushes are a common failing on older vehicles. Some suffer much more than others, but the first that a lot of owners know about this is when the car fails its annual MoT test. Problems may also be highlighted by strange clonking noises as the vehicle is manoeuvred on tight steering locks while parking, for example.

The stresses and strains placed on the anti-roll bar during normal use mean that its bushes will often be the first in the front suspension system to show signs of wear. What's more, in cases like this 1995 Mondeo, the anti-roll bar is used not only to provide a rigid transverse link between the two front suspension set-ups, but also to provide a lateral tie for both front wheels. As we've already mentioned, suspension geometry is a vital performance and safety-related factor: it must be right if the vehicle is to remain controllable. The fact that the two front wheels are suspended independently on modern cars, meaning they can respond individually to the contours of the road, is great news from a handling point of view, assuming that the movement is well controlled. The wheels must remain within the pre-set suspension tolerances otherwise tyre wear, steering characteristics and brake performance can be shot to pieces.

Preventing the wheels from moving about too much within the wheel arch is a vital factor, and this is controlled in a number of different ways, depending on the suspension system design. In the case of our Mondeo here, it's the anti-roll bar which provides the all important anchor point to stop the front wheels moving backwards and forwards too much, particularly as the car accelerates and brakes. It connects to the transverse link arm, which provides the bottom suspension mounting, running between the body and the wheel hub assembly.

Wear in all of the bushed joints is common in this area, although the outer anti-roll bar bushes do seem to take a particular pounding. Fortunately, swapping them is a relatively straightforward operation.

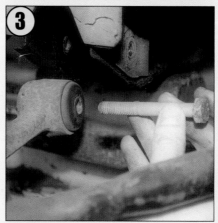

1 Clonking and squeaking from the front suspension usually points towards bush wear. There are a number of bushes which can be affected and in this case all relate to the transverse link arm. However, before you do anything else, you must secure the car safely on axle stands, or a vehicle hoist, so that the suspension is hanging down, unloaded. Remove the front wheel.

2 The outer end of the anti-roll bar is secured just over half way along the transverse link arm, in a large rubberised bush. Its end is threaded and a tightened nut holds it in place. Often this will be extremely tight, particularly if it's not been undone for years. Its exposed position ensures it suffers at the hands of the elements. Take care when undoing it because it's not unheard of to sheer the end off the ant-roll bar when trying to loosen seized retaining bolts. This is a disastrous mistake to make as you'll then be forced to replace the whole bar! If in any doubt, use plenty of penetrating oil and allow it time to work.

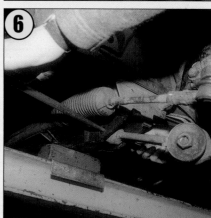

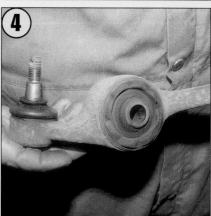

3 To provide clearance to allow the end of the anti-roll bar to be removed from its bush, it's necessary to free the inner end of the transverse arm link. Once again, lubricate this as necessary and remove the pin. This can be tricky to get out because of the tension in the anti-roll bar, so it may require some jiggling!

4 In some cases the anti-roll bar's rubber bush will be in two parts, so that it can be easily removed from the transverse arm link. Unfortunately, this is not so with this one, which is a more conventional, tight friction fit. Consequently it will need to be removed using a hydraulic press and, to do this the complete arm must be removed from the vehicle, which entails also releasing its outer fixing (bottom joint), where it connects to the wheel hub. You'll need to take the transverse arm to a friendly workshop with pressing facilities.

5 The outer anti-roll bar bush is protected by a pair of dished plastic covers – one for each side – and it's a good idea to lubricate these with an anti-sieze grease such as Copperslip during reassembly. The lubrication of these can also be monitored during normal servicing work, to help reduce general squeaking.

6 Reassembly is simply a matter of reversing the stripping sequence. Locating the inner transverse arm mounting bolt can be tricky during because of the tension in the anti-roll bar. It can help to use a suitably sized bar to align the holes while applying pressure to the wheel hub assembly.

Next Month
Rear Suspension and Dampers

Handy Hints

● Never retighten suspension bushes if the suspension is not in its normal, loaded position. If you tighten everything up with the suspension hanging low, then when the vehicle is returned to the ground and the springing takes up the weight, the bushes will all be immediately stressed which will dramatically shorten their service lives.

● Always double-check torque settings when working on suspension.

● Never renew components on just one side of the vehicle. Swap parts in pairs to avoid potentially dangerous handling imbalances.

● If you have to remove split pins during stripping operations, always replace them with new when it comes to reassembly.

Back to Basics

Last month's untimely end to the episode left the story rather hanging in the air, like some part-dismantled MacPherson strut! What's more, that abrupt finish means that I'm forced to start this episode at a similarly arbitrary point. But don't worry, dear reader, because when this whole series is published as another successful *Car Mechanics* book, one episode will join seamlessly to the next, and nobody will be any the wiser!

So where were we? Ah yes, transverse links. The whole idea of these is to help counter the natural tendency of the wheels to move forwards and backwards as the car brakes and accelerates. This is yet another important potential variable which must be kept in check. Unfortunately, it's not all good news for the MacPherson strut approach, and the system does have its weaknesses. One of the most serious is changes in wheel camber as the suspension operates, which can have an adverse affect on handling.

Perhaps the more complete solution, as far as independent front suspension is concerned, is the double wishbone design. Much favoured over the years by racing car manufacturers and sports car producers such as Lotus, this set-up is generally regarded as the best available, in pure performance terms. It's been around for years and remains the system of choice for Formula One designers to this day. The typical system consists of a pair of wishbones, rather like the A-shaped transverse link mentioned in the previous episode, which are located at their pointed ends to the top and bottom of the stub axle assembly with swivel joints. The inner ends are hinged on to the vehicle's

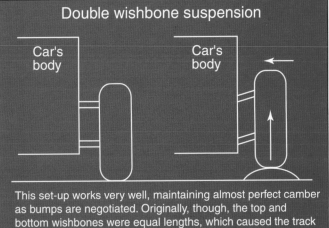

Double wishbone suspension

Car's body · Car's body

This set-up works very well, maintaining almost perfect camber as bumps are negotiated. Originally, though, the top and bottom wishbones were equal lengths, which caused the track to reduce, resulting in high levels of tyre scuffing.

Car's body · Car's body

Then somebody had the bright idea of using a longer lower wishbone to cure the scuffing problem. Unfortunately, the side effect of this design switch was to introduce a degree of negative camber. Perhaps the lesser of two evils.

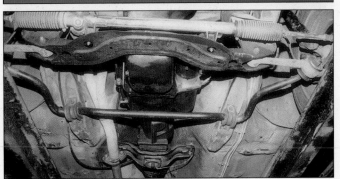

This is fairly typical of a front anti-roll bar, shaped to provide maximum side-to-side support between suspension assemblies.

body. A damper within a coil spring is angled between the upper and lower wishbones to provide the springing effect.

The early versions of this system featured upper and lower wishbones of the same length but this created problems. Suspension travel caused the track (the distance across the vehicle, between the wheels) to be reduced, leading to excessive tyre wear. So, even though the wheels were held in perfect camber alignment, changes had to be made to make the system more practical for everyday road use. The solution was to lengthen the bottom wishbone and, although this did reduce the tyre scrubbing effect, it wasn't the perfect answer because it also created a slight camber problem. However, this was evidently the lesser of two evils and the design tweak became generally accepted as the norm.

ROCK AND ROLL

The one important suspension component that we haven't really considered so far is the anti-roll bar. Essentially this is a rigid bar which runs across the vehicle to join the suspension set-ups on either side. Most modern cars are fitted with an anti-roll bar at the front and often there's one at the back too. Its primary function is to help control the dramatic body and suspension movement which occurs during hard cornering. If left unchecked, this sort of movement can have all kinds of complicated effects on the suspension geometry, leading to reduced body control and steering performance.

We're back to wheel camber again here. Bodies which roll a lot while cornering dramatically, compress the suspension on the outer side of the vehicle. This, in turn, has an almost inevitable effect on wheel camber, altering the size of the tyre's footprint on the road and potentially reducing overall grip. So controlling the degree of body roll is an important function, although there is a compromise to be struck. Eliminating it altogether, while perhaps a theoretical ideal, would not be a good thing in practice. Body roll provides an important indicator for the driver about how near the car is to loosing grip. You get used to the way your car behaves through corners, and develop a 'feel' for how far you can push it. A major part of that 'feel' is communicated by the attitude of the body, and without that things would be a good deal less predictable.

SWING TIME

Although the front suspension plays a crucial role in establishing the handling performance of a vehicle, and works extremely hard because it's dealing with the weight of the engine, it is important not to overlook things at the back. Rear suspension is a big subject in its own right, and has gone though a number of important transformations over the years. In the old days cars were fitted with big, heavy rear axles that were supported by leaf springs. This set-up was very tough and durable but became less and less practical as vehicle technology developed. The desire for improved vehicle handling and comfort drove the designers away from the reliable old leaf spring and towards independent rear suspension arrangements which better matched the modern systems being used at the front.

One of the first attempts at this utilised what were called 'swinging half axles', but it created rather unpredictable results. Axle tubes were employed to link the rear wheels

Expert assistance

Colchester Institute has a large Automobile Engineering Centre which provides part-time (one day per week) and full-time courses in automobile engineering, body repair and welding.
For more information contact: **Dave Roberts**
Head of Centre for Automobile Engineering, Colchester Institute, Sheepen Road, Colchester, CO3 3LL.

to the centrally-mounted final drive housing, and fitted with universal joints on the inner ends to allow for body movement. But the problem was that if such systems were pushed at all enthusiastically, the resultant body movement played merry hell with wheel camber, leading to all sorts of undesirable handling foibles. For this reason swinging axles were dropped.

BROTHERS IN ARMS

The next big step forward came with the arrival of trailing and semi-trailing arms. Both used wishbone-type arms that were hinged to the vehicle's body at one end, and bolted to the wheel hub assembly at the other. The trailing arm configuration came first, with the arms being mounted at right angles to the direction of travel (see diagram). This firm style of fixing only allows the wheel to move up and down, as bumps are negotiated, which is a plus point. Unfortunately, though, body roll through a

corner has the effect of inducing camber, causing both wheels to lean towards the outside of the bend, promoting understeer.

To cure this the boffins developed the semi-trailing arm set-up, where the arms were fixed to the body at an angle of about 60° to the direction of travel. This effectively ironed out the body roll-induced camber problem and created a much more neutrally-handling suspension set-up altogether. This system was used on many mid-range and large modern saloons, and it's only comparatively recently that it's started to be replaced by multi-link rear suspension, which is a more complicated variation on the double wishbone theme.

DOING THE TWIST

Of course, the advent of front-wheel drive on most modern small/medium saloons meant that rear suspension could be simplified – to cut production costs and save space. Many now utilise a straightforward strut approach, similar to that used for independent front suspension, while others favour a torsion bar set-up. The latter is a great space-saver because the coil springs and dampers needed can be so much smaller than with the MacPherson strut equivalent. Torsion bar suspension relies on a metal bar which is twisted as the wheel moves up and down and it's the resistance to this twisting which provides the springing action. It's been used to great effect on small cars such as the VW Golf and Peugeot 306.

But irrespective of the suspension set-up fitted, virtually all vehicles rely on dampers to keep the springing action in check. For this reason, damper failure is a potentially serious problem. Although the fault is most often diagnosed by the simple vehicle bounce test (dampers are worn if they allow the vehicle to bounce up and down more than two or three times after the corner has been depressed), many motorists fail to check. The loss of the damping effect is normally caused by internal fluid leaks and this reduction in performance can throw up real handling problems, particularly during heavy braking. The front dampers usually work much harder than those at the rear, because of the engine's weight, so these tend to fail first. This, in turn, allows the front end

Rear suspensions is generally much simpler than the set-ups used at the front of the vehicle. In this case the coil spring and the damper are mounted seperately.

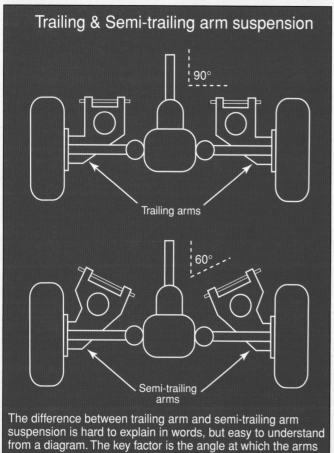
The more modern approach is to adopt the MacPherson strut-like design at the back, with the damper contained within the coil spring.

to dive forwards more than it should during braking, causing an effective lightening at the rear. Not only does this reduce braking effect, but it also greatly increases the risk of skidding.

UNDER PRESSURE

Although today's suspension systems are more durable than ever before, they still suffer from the traditional types of problem – damper failure, bush and joint wear. Unfortunately, the added sophistication of the modern systems adds to the complexity and cost of repair work. Also, because failures occur more infrequently, the price of spares has increased. The most common tell-tale signs of suspension wear at a practical level are a generally spongy feel and/or mysterious clonking. The trouble is that wear usually occurs gradually, which can make it difficult to spot. It has a habit of creeping up on you so that, often, your first inkling of trouble will be when a keen-eyed MoT tester flags-up the problem.

You may also become aware of a condition rather like 'torque steer', when the vehicle appears to pull to one side under acceleration or braking, even though the steering is held straight. This is being caused by worn bushes which are allowing the wheels affected to alter their position slightly as a force is applied.

Trailing & Semi-trailing arm suspension

90°

Trailing arms

60°

Semi-trailing arms

The difference between trailing arm and semi-trailing arm suspension is hard to explain in words, but easy to understand from a diagram. The key factor is the angle at which the arms pivot, in relation to the centreline of the vehicle. The semi-trailing arm approach reduces the pivot angle from 90° to about 60°, and this minimises the degree of wheel camber change caused by body roll, thus improves handling.

Next Month
FRONT BRAKES

TECHNICAL TOPIC: *Rear Damper Swap*

Although front dampers tend to lead the hardest life on most cars, the rears do their fair share of work too, especially on vehicles which are heavily loaded on a regular basis, or used for towing trailers or a caravan. Consequently, it's important not to neglect them and regular inspections should always form part of your routine maintenance programme.

Damper failure can be a gradual process and, often, it's not terribly obvious to the casual observer that a problem even exists. Internal faults are the most common cause of trouble, and it's normally valves or rubber seals which give up the ghost first. Tell-tale signs of leaking hydraulic fluid or a general softness as indicated by a failure of the straightforward bounce test, are the pointers to look for.

Also, it's very important to remember that, although it may just be one damper which is showing signs of distress, it's crucial that you replace the one on the other side as well. Like most other suspension and braking components, dampers must be replaced in pairs, otherwise you risk setting up an imbalance which could have a disastrous effect on vehicle handling and braking performance. There are genuine safety issues to be considered here, so never be tempted to skimp on the repair bill by renewing just one of a pair.

1 Rear suspension design varies from vehicle to vehicle but, there are two or three basic systems which you're likely to encounter. The set-up on this MkII Vauxhall Cavalier is one of the simplest around, and is extremely easy to deal with. The damper is bolted to the vehicle body at the top, and to the end of the suspension arm at the bottom. The coil spring is sandwiched between the centre of the suspension arm and the body, next to the damper. It's actually not fixed there at all, but is held in place by the 'clamping' action of the damper. It would be possible to swap the damper without removing the wheels at all, using a set of ramps. The only requirement is that the car is lifted sufficiently to provide convenient access to the damper's bottom bolt.

2 This simple suspension design means that there is no need for extra equipment such as spring compressors, which are necessary when dealing with a strut-type assembly. In this case it's sufficient to support the vehicle on the bottom suspension joint, as though the car was still on its wheel. Always use axle stands for this type of job. They are much safer and more dependable than a trolley jack, although you will need one of these to get the car up in the first place, so that the wheel can be removed.

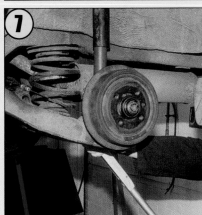

3 Release the damper's bottom mounting. Note that the car is raised on a vehicle hoist for photographic purposes. The suspension is not supported and so the damper could not be freed safely until it is. The damper locates in rubber mountings, top and bottom, which are designed to help minimise the amount of road noise and vibration that's transmitted through the car's body. With time these can wear and perish, so they need to be checked and replaced if necessary. Any play you find is likely to be causing clonking or squeaking, and may be leading to wheel alignment problems too.

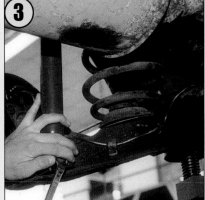

4 The damper's top fixing is usually reached via the boot compartment. This is a very important structural point on the car, and takes a great deal of strain as the suspension operates. The metals around the mounting point is a favourite area for corrosion to strike, so check it carefully. On older vehicles, condensation within the boot plus mud build-up from inside the wheel arch, can both promote the onset of rusting. The dreaded tin worm is an MoT test failure point if it starts to nibble in this region.

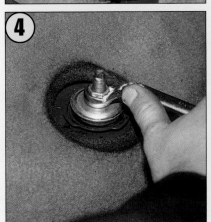

5 With both top and bottom mountings released, and the vehicle safely supported on the bottom suspension link, the damper can be released from the bottom, and extracted.

6 Once the new damper has been manoeuvred into place, it's important to make sure that the top mounting is set correctly. Methods for ensuring this vary, depending on the vehicle manufacturer. In this case a straightforward measurement of the exposed thread is all that's required. You need to get it right because this governs the amount of tension being put on the rubber mounting.

7 The bottom bolt will normally have a specific tightening torque setting and, once again, it's important to get this right. Check the workshop manual to be completely sure.

Handy Hints

● Always manually extend and compress new dampers through their full operating range a few times before fitting. This will bleed out any air which may be inside. It's rare that a damper will ever be fully extended during its working life on a car, so take time to do this when you have the chance.

● Never fit dampers singly – you must ALWAYS replace them in pairs.

● Make totally sure you buy the correct dampers for your vehicle. A practical way to check this is to compare the fully extended length. The thing to avoid is fitting replacements that extend too far, as this could result in the coil springs popping out during excessive suspension travel (over a hump-backed bridge, for example!)

Back to Basics

Part 17: How and why cars stop. Chris Graham reports.

Braking, like steering, suspension and power generation, is one of the four fundamentals of vehicle operation. We've already covered how we get cars moving, how they are manoeuvred and how to keep them comfortable and under control during use. So now it's time to look at how best to stop them.

Vehicle braking systems have developed greatly over the years but the principles behind the problem have never changed. It's all about energy conversion. A moving car possess a store of what's called kinetic energy, and the faster it moves, the more it has. This energy store is what causes the car to continue moving if, when at speed, you dip the clutch and allow the engine to idle.

Eventually, of course, if you continue coasting like this the car will slow to a halt as the kinetic energy ebbs away and is lost to the surroundings. But everyday driving doesn't allow us the time or space for coasting to a stop, and more drastic measures are required to slow the vehicle, particularly under emergency conditions. The application of the vehicle brake ensures a much more rapid consumption of the kinetic energy, by using controlled friction to convert it into heat energy. What's more, in theory, the quicker the kinetic energy is consumed, the quicker the vehicle will stop. In practice, though, there are limitations to this, as we'll see in a minute.

THE GOOD 'OL DAYS

You probably all remember from those old cowboy films, how the man fighting for control of the horse-drawn wagon used to stamp frantically on a big wooden brake lever. All this did was act through a single pivot to force a wooden or metal block against the face of one of the wheels. Slowing down was always a struggle with this sort of primitive set-up, even though it provided state-of-the-art stopping power in those days! Performance wasn't helped by the fact that just the one of the wheels was being braked and that if, by chance, a decent amount of friction was brought to bear, that wheel would simply lock up. And if there's one thing you should know above all others about vehicle braking, it's that locked wheels are about as much use as a chocolate teapot!

Minimising the distance it takes a car to stop is all about maximising the grip, or adhesion, between the tyre and the road surface. As soon as this adhesion is broken, and the wheel locks and begins to skid, the braking effect falls away dramatically and control of the vehicle becomes much harder. Factors such as tyre tread and pressure, road surface and weather conditions all have important affects on this. But the most efficient braking takes place just before the point when the wheels lock up and all adhesion is lost, hence the success of ABS.

A really big step forward in vehicle braking came with the introduction of the drum brake. For the first time it was decided to apply the brakes to something other than the wheel itself. A cast iron drum was bolted on to the axle assembly so that it rotated with the wheel. A fixed back plate was used to mount a pair of crescent-shaped brake shoes which fitted inside the drum and could be pushed outwards to rub against the drum's machined inner face. A coating of relatively soft friction material on the shoes – either riveted or bolted into place – was designed to be consumed as the brakes were used. This 'grippy' formulation, based originally around asbestos, was specially chosen to maximise the adhesion between the shoes and the drum.

The pair of shoes were anchored at the bottom by a pivot point, which provided two important functions. For a start it stopped the shoes from rotating with the drum as the brakes were applied. But it also provided a sort of hinging action which allowed for brake application. The two shoes were pushed apart (in response to pressure on the brake pedal) from the top, so that their friction material-coated faces were brought into contact with the spinning drum (see diagram). Early examples used cam expanders to separate the shoes and apply the brake, but this mechanical method was eventually replaced by hydraulic fluid-operated cylinders.

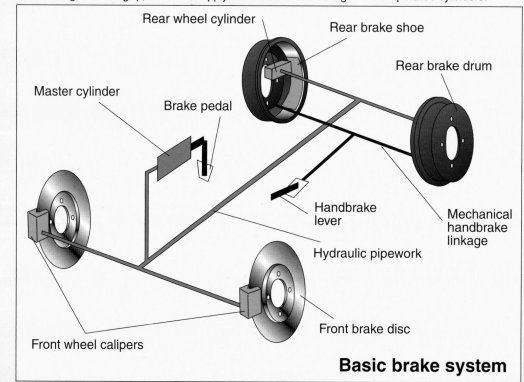

Rear wheel cylinder

Rear brake shoe

Rear brake drum

Master cylinder

Brake pedal

Handbrake lever

Mechanical handbrake linkage

Hydraulic pipework

Front brake disc

Front wheel calipers

Basic brake system

Simplified drum brake

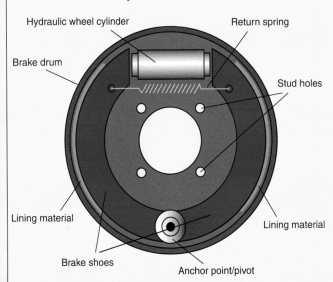

- Hydraulic wheel cylinder
- Brake drum
- Return spring
- Stud holes
- Lining material
- Lining material
- Brake shoes
- Anchor point/pivot

Early brake drums operated mechanically, with a rotating cam that was linked to the brake pedal and used to spread the shoes apart at the top and bring the friction material into contact with the rotating drum. The hydraulic cylinder replaced the cam as a more efficient source of pressure. The return spring connects the two shoes and ensures that they pull back off the drum when the pedal is released. Drum and shoe clearance is kept as small as possible with the use of an adjuster mechanism.

Expert assistance

Colchester Institute has a large Automobile Engineering Centre which provides part-time (one day per week) and full-time courses in automobile engineering, body repair and welding.
For more information contact: **Dave Roberts**
Head of Centre for Automobile Engineering, Colchester Institute, Sheepen Road, Colchester, CO3 3LL.

Kinetic energy converts to heat as a car is slowed by the brakes.

MIND THE GAP!

One other important component of the drum brake system was an adjuster to allow for shoe wear. As the friction material was gradually worn off the face of the shoes, so the gap between shoe and drum would increase. The adjuster was used to re-position the shoes, as part of routine maintenance, and maintain the minimum distance between shoe and drum. This would ensure continued good contact for the minimum amount of pedal movement.

While the drum system worked very effectively under ideal conditions, it did have some serious drawbacks. The amount of heat generated within the drum could cause real problems, leading to a scary condition known as 'brake fade'. Prolonged and heavy use of the brakes could build heat levels to such a degree that the friction material lost its performance, and the brakes literally faded away, sometimes to nothing. The driver's natural reaction to this alarming effect would be to stand on the pedal even harder which, unfortunately, would simply generate more heat and make the situation even worse! It was the enclosed nature of the drum's tambourine-like shape which caused the heat retention problems. Another friction-sapping drawback was that the drums could collect water when driving in wet conditions, also resulting in reduced performance.

But the heat build-up was regarded as the most serious fault and various things were tried to reduce the problem.

Designers came up with drums that were vented, or fitted with cooling fins on the back, but neither really made any significant difference. The best solution came with the arrival of the brake disc. This, fully exposed design featured a single metal disc that was bolted on to the wheel hub and slowed by a pair of friction pads acting from either side in a pinching movement.

Application of the brake pads was controlled by a pair of hydraulic cylinders mounted in a metal caliper that was rigidly fixed to the vehicle. While not actually as efficient as the drum approach – it's much harder to stop something by squeezing it – the more efficient heat dissipation properties made all the difference. Nevertheless, greater system pressure was needed

when applying the pads to achieve the necessary braking effect, and this resulted in the introduction of a pressure-boosting device called a brake servo.

From then on the majority of cars were fitted with discs at the front and drums at the rear, although sporting machinery tended to benefit from discs all round. Drums were retained at the rear on most mass produced cars because they better suited the application of the a handbrake, which still tended to be operated mechanically. We'll be covering this in more detail next month.

Many advances have also been made in the manufacture and formulation of friction materials. Asbestos used to be one of the key ingredients, but the toxic nature of this material meant that it was eventually phased out and replaced by less hazardous alternatives. Friction material durability has been greatly extended and now some pads can last almost as long as the brake discs themselves.

UNDER PRESSURE

Brake application is entirely hydraulic these days. The old mechanical rod and linkage systems were simply too inefficient to provide the consistent and high forces required for today's vehicles. Although modern systems still operate on the same principles as ever, the requirements for greater performance and safety

precautions mean that installations have become a good deal more complex.

Nevertheless, all set-ups still rely on a master cylinder, activated by the foot pedal, which works rather like a giant syringe to push the hydraulic fluid down pipes to the individual wheel cylinders. These are fitted with plungers which extend as the pressure inside builds, and in doing so, press the brake shoes or pads into contact with the drum or disc. Hydraulic pressure in a modern system can be very high, with anything up to 2,000psi being exerted during heavy braking, hence the need for good quality metal pipework.

The big weakness, of course, with hydraulic systems is that they are extremely vulnerable to fluid loss. Leaks or breakages can render the system useless as the ability to build hydraulic pressure is lost. Fortunately, modern vehicles now feature split systems which employ dual hydraulic circuitry so that braking effect on at least two wheels will always be available to the driver if system failure occurs.

Sometimes the system is split diagonally and, although there is only one master cylinder, it's divided into two sections internally. One provides pressure for the front nearside and the rear offside wheels, while the other does the same for the remaining two. In this way a breakage in any one of the pipes will only actually effect the force being applied to two wheels. Obviously, ultimate braking performance will be reduced but it should still be possible to safely control the vehicle.

Drum brake   Disc brake

Drum brakes work as a pair of friction material-coated shoes are pushed outwards on to the machined inside face of a heavy iron drum. They are very effective but suffer from heat build-up due to the enclosed nature of the design. The disc brake was developed to cure the overheating problems associated with drums. An exposed disc was pinched between brake pads to slow the wheel. The force required was greater than with the drum design.

Next Month
Rear Brakes

TECHNICAL TOPIC: Front Brake Inspection

The front brakes play a vital role in stopping your car effectively. In fact, they do about 60% of the work because of the tendency for the vehicle's weight to be thrown forwards as the car slows down. For this reason, the front brakes endure a tougher life than those at the rear, and they wear out more quickly.

Fortunately there's a lot that the enthusiast owner can achieve with brake systems, even on quite modern cars. The most basic of maintenance inspections, as detailed here, will reveal a great deal about the general health of a system. Careful inspection will highlight wear levels and potential trouble spots in terms of corrosion or fluid leakage. We can all easily establish the working life that's left in brake pads and discs, and spotting the signs of leaking wheel cylinders or chafed/split pipes is pretty straightforward too.

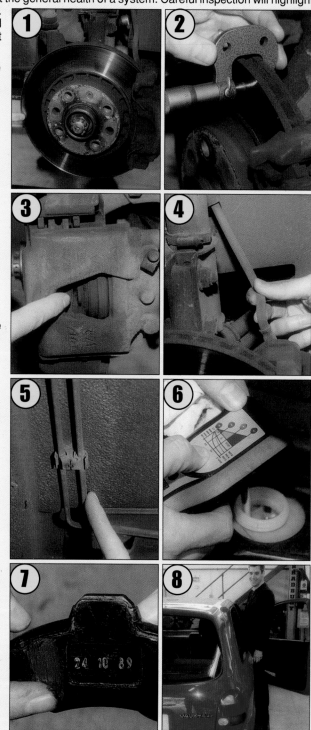

(1) With the car securely supported on a vehicle hoist, or pair of axle stands, remove the front wheels to inspect the disc brake assembly. The primary things to look for are excessive wear of discs/pads, signs of fluid leakage from pipes or on the calipers and wheel cylinder seizure. Some cars are fitted with brake wear warning lights, but plenty are not. Nowadays pads wear more slowly and have a much longer service life, although the harder, more resistant friction materials used mean that the discs wear out faster! The shiny section of the disc is where the brake pads are making contact. On older discs you are likely to feel an appreciable ridge around the edge, indicating how much the disc has been worn down from its original thickness. Keep an eye out for signs of scoring on the disc (like circular scratches or grooves). Also check for 'blueing' or surface cracking, both of which indicate that the disc has been overheated.

(2) The best way to be sure about brake disc wear is to do the job properly and use a micrometer to check the thickness accurately. The minimum acceptable thickness will be quoted in the workshop manual. Any obvious signs of surface deterioration should be treated with caution and disc replacement may be necessary (in pairs, of course!).

(3) Inspecting the brake pad thickness is usually quite straightforward on most vehicles, and can often be done visually. If the degree of wear looks pretty well even on both pads, then it's fairly safe to assume that there are no seizure problems causing one to wear much more quickly than the other. The minimum thickness will be detailed in the workshop manual but, as a rough guide, you shouldn't let them wear down below about 2mm. Although at this thickness the pads will still have stopping power, they become less tolerant to heat build-up and the friction material can start to lift off the pad backing plate.

(4) Although modern brake systems use metal pipework most of the time, the final run to the wheel cylinders is made with flexible rubber hose to allow for suspension movement. These can get damaged by flying stones, or be worn by chafing against brackets or suspension parts. They will also crack with age, so check them carefully. In some cases older pipes will start to perish from the inside, which is a potentially serious problem. The weakness is not usually obvious from a visual inspection unless the fluid inside is pressurised by pressing the brake pedal. MoT inspectors always test pipes in this way, and any internal weakness will cause the pipe to balloon out at the that point.

(5) Check all metal pipes for signs of corrosion on older vehicles – this isn't such a problem on newer cars which have plated pipes. Any rusting is another MoT test failure point. It will often start around the retaining clips, where water is held. Also watch for any signs of pipe fracture and leakage. Another cause of trouble can be if the pipes are not securely located in their retaining clips. You can sometimes find this if sections have been replaced and the technician has not taken enough time with the job. Unclipped pipes are vulnerable to damage through impact damage, stress fracture and friction.

(6) Brake fluid should be checked regularly to ensure that it remains serviceable. As a rule of thumb fluid that appears clear and clean will be okay, and that which has darkened isn't. But, it's best not to take chances so we'd always advise the use of a purpose-made fluid tester. Be careful to avoid dripping the fluid when unscrewing the reservoir lid. Any contact with painted surfaces is potentially disastrous. Also, be aware of any that might have dripped on to your overalls – it's so easy to inadvertently lean this against paintwork on the front wing! Keep it off your skin too. The fluid will last for about two years, but brake fluid absorbs moisture and consequently the boiling point is lowered significantly, which increases the risk of it bubbling-up if the brakes get too hot. This leads to air pockets in the system, which leads to a spongy-feeling pedal and a loss of braking performance. Changing the fluid means draining the whole system, not just topping up! The system will also need to be bled to remove all air pockets. This is relatively easy on older cars, but more involved on newer models fitted with ABS braking.

(7) If you need to fit replacement brake pads then it's a good idea to rub a smear of high temperature grease across the contact points on the back of the pad. This will help guard against irritating brake squeal. Don't be tempted to use an ordinary grease for this because it will simply melt and run off, possibly on to the front of the pad and the disc.

(8) Don't forget the basics either, like actually checking that your brake lights are both working. Doing this on your own means reversing up to a painted wall or other reflective surface. A bulb failure can go unnoticed for weeks and can be the cause of an embarrassing encounter with the 'boys in blue' as well. If just one light is out then it's likely to be a simple bulb failure. If both have gone then it could be a fuse or switch problem.

Handy Hints

- Avoid breathing in brake dust, even when dealing with modern, asbestos-free pads. Damp down the area using a brake cleaner spray and wear a mask.
- Wear gloves or use a good coating of barrier cream when working on brakes.
- If you discover discs which have been overheated then don't automatically assume it's from heavy use. The caliper may well have seized, holding the pad permanently on to the disc.
- Be sure you specify the correct brake fluid for your vehicle. Different grades have different boiling points, so you must get it right.
- Spilt brake fluid should be washed off paintwork immediately using plenty of cold water.

Back to Basics

Part 18:
Chris Graham gets to grips with brake shoes, hydraulics and servo assistance

If you were unlucky enough to be the only person trapped on a runaway railway wagon, and all you had to save yourself from smashing against the solid buffers at the bottom of the hill was a long pole with a friction pad fixed to the end, what would you do? I know this scenario is a little far-fetched but, bear with me because it does illustrate an important principle very well. Essentially, you'd have two options, assuming you rejected the idea of beating yourself to death with the pole, or jumping off the wagon in heroic John Wayne fashion. No, the two most practical choices would be to try and slow the wagon by holding the friction pad-tipped rod against the rail, either from the front or the rear. But which direction would you choose?

DIGGING IN

The correct choice would be to try to brake the wagon from the front. The potential for generating friction is much greater this way, as the pad tends to 'dig in' to the surface of the advancing rail, and grip more ferociously with the minimum of application pressure. The rear-facing approach wouldn't be nearly as effective because of the tendency for the pad to be dragged along the rail, rather than gripping it. The only way to generate any significant stopping power from this direction would be to greatly increase the application pressure which, of course, wouldn't be possible by hand. So what's all this got to do with car brakes? Well, it hopefully provides a reasonably graphic illustration of the distinction between 'leading' and

'trailing' brake shoes in a conventional drum brake set-up.

Drum brakes rely on the friction generated as the semi-circular shoes are pushed into contact with the inside face of the spinning drum. Because the conventional set-up has the shoes pivoted at the bottom, and uses a hydraulically-operated wheel cylinder to push them apart at the top, the two shoes perform with significantly different effectiveness. The leading shoe (see Fig 1, A) does the most work – up to four times as much as the trailing shoe. It's the one that has its top edge pushed into contact with the drum, against the direction of rotation. The combination of these two forces – the rotation of the drum and the movement of the shoe – causes the leading shoe to be 'dragged' tightly on to the drum face, resulting in what's known as a self-servo action.

WEAR'S THE PROBLEM

This is all well and good in theory but, in practice, the picture's not quite so rosy. The disproportionate workload means that leading and trailing shoes wear out at vastly different rates, so servicing requirements can be high. Serious brake fade can be another problem, caused by overheating of the overworked leading shoe. Also, the system

can be very sensitive to pedal pressure, meaning that unpredictable and potentially dangerous wheel lock-up becomes a possibility. To help overcome these disadvantages, the boffins began to experiment with the placing of the friction material. 'Rotating' the linings, to 'lower' that on the leading shoe while, at the same time, lifting the coating on the trailing shoe so that it was much nearer the wheel cylinder (see Fig 1, B), made significant improvements. Then they came up with a 'two leading shoe' configuration, which used a pair of single piston wheel cylinders, at the top and bottom of the drum assembly, to act on the shoes in opposing directions (See Fig.1, C).

The big advantages of this approach were that because both shoes effectively became leading shoes, wear rates were equalised. Overall braking performance was improved considerably, because both shoes were working to good effect and, what's more, the likelihood of brake fade was significantly reduced. On the downside, though, the fact that both shoes were 'leading' when the car was being driven normally meant that they both became 'trailing' when it was reversed, and stopping power was drastically reduced. The final incarnation of the drum brake approach was the 'Duo-servo'

system, which was a variation on the twin leading shoe theme. Ultimately, though, it's probably true to say that the drum brake's days are numbered. Even quite ordinary mass production saloons are being fitted with discs all round these days, as the ever increasing demand for greater operational efficiency and reduced servicing costs drives the trusty old drum brake progressively out of favour.

PRESSURE POINTS

All modern car braking systems rely on the pressure-generating properties of hydraulic fluid. This is the lifeblood of a braking system, and it provides a much more efficient and effective operating solution (no pun intended!) than the old-fashioned mechanical linkages.

One of the biggest problems with the metal rod and wire approach was that it could be hard to equalise the pressure being applied to individual brakes. This is a vital factor for safe and effective braking, but set-ups which relied on an assortment levers, bolted pivot points and mechanical compensation devices were always prone to failure. Exposed locations under the car meant that corrosion and seizure were common problems, making reliable brake operation far more unpredictable than it should be.

The arrival of hydraulic operating systems, with pressurised fluid doing the work of the mechanical levers, represented a tremendous leap forward. Rigid and secure metal pipework carried the fluid to the four corners of the car, where it passed into short lengths of flexible rubber hose to bridge the gap between the vehicle body and the brake assembly. This flexible link allowed for suspension movement and provided another significant advantage of the system.

There also exists the potential to have complete control over the pressure exerted at each brake. The fact that hydraulic fluid transfers pressure equally throughout the system means that simply varying the size of the pistons within the wheel cylinders will alter the force exerted. In this way braking pressures can be tuned between front and rear, and for different types of use.

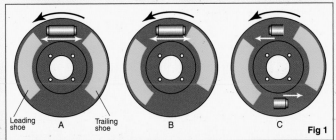

Leading shoe   A   Trailing shoe   B   C   **Fig 1**

As I mentioned in the previous episode, fluid pressure is generated by the master cylinder, which acts like a giant syringe and is connected to the brake pedal. This is all well and good, of course, until the system springs a leak due to a fractured pipe or a perished/split rubber somewhere in the system. The fluid pressure involved means that weaknesses are soon exploited and, if hydraulic pressure is lost, then brake performance falls away drastically and drivers are forced to rely on the mechanically-operated handbrake.

To help guard against this sort of problem split-line systems are more or less the norm nowadays. These are controlled by a tandem master cylinder, employing two pistons which generate operating pressure for opposing front and rear wheels (see diagram).

HELPING HAND

Despite the efficiency of the basic hydraulic system, the increasingly widespread use of disc brakes on cars called for an increase in application force across the board. The advantage of the 'self-servo' action associated with drum brakes, which kept pedal pressure requirements at a minimum, was lost with the arrival of discs.

Consequently, designers had to come up with a convenient way of enhancing the pressure generated at the pedal. The answer was a clever device called a servo, which harnessed the power of a vacuum, generated by the engine, to boost the pressure being produced by the foot pedal.

Servos are complex devices which provide a vital function. In principle, most rely on air pressure differential to operate a large boost piston which acts directly on the hydraulic fluid. The success of the device hinges on the careful control of

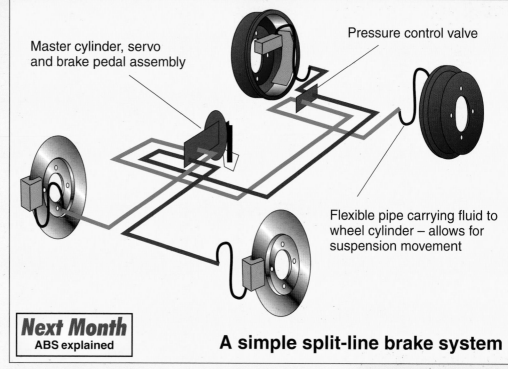

Master cylinder, servo and brake pedal assembly

Pressure control valve

Flexible pipe carrying fluid to wheel cylinder – allows for suspension movement

Next Month
ABS explained

A simple split-line brake system

air flow in and out of the unit, on both sides of the boost piston. Of course, these units have to be 'fail-safe' so that if they stop working some braking performance remains.

Also, they need to be progressive, so that the level of assistance they provide varies according to the pressure applied by the driver on the foot pedal. Light 'check braking' needs to be just that, so the system has to be sensitive enough to translate gentle pedal pressure into gentle brake application.

A graphic illustration of just how effective the servo is on a modern car can be experienced if you try applying the brakes without the engine running. This can sometimes happen during parking manoeuvres and it's amazing (and sometimes shocking!) just how unresponsive and 'heavy' the brakes feel without servo assistance.

LIQUID ASSETS

Finally, it's worth spending a few moments on brake fluid. This is a very important yet often overlooked and frequently misunderstood aspect of the modern motor car. Most fluids are based around a mixture of glycerine and alcohol – usually abbreviated to 'glycol', but there are many other additives mixed in as well. The differences between the formulations mean that it's vital to specify the correct one for your vehicle. Getting it wrong can prove a costly mistake. Brake systems are designed to work with one type and one type only. Pouring in even a few drops of the wrong fluid can have a disastrous effect on the rubber components within the system, causing them to deteriorate and promoting leakage. So make doubly sure that you buy the right stuff before taking it anywhere near the car. Consult the workshop manual, or have a word with the service manager at the dealership, to be certain that you get the right specification.

'Hygroscopic' may not be a word that many of us use often in regular conversation, but it has great relevance as far as most brake fluids are concerned. It describes the tendency that these fluids can have to absorb water from the atmosphere. The amount they 'take in' is determined, quite naturally, by the degree of exposure to normal air, so airtight storage is an important

Handbrakes can pose a lot of awkward problems, particularly as they represent a potential MoT test failure point. One of the most common causes of trouble is frayed wires like this, which have to be replaced.

concern. But given enough time, fluid within the braking system will absorb sufficient moisture to affect its performance, which is why drain intervals are important.

The problem is that water build-up within the fluid lowers its overall boiling point, which is bad news. The possibility then arises that 'heat soak' from extremely hot brake components will boil off the water to produce steam and create air pockets in the system. Because air is compressible (unlike the fluid itself); the result of this is a spongy feel to the pedal and a potentially dangerous reduction in braking performance. The only solution, once this has happened, is to drain the old fluid and refill with fresh, 'bleeding' correctly to make sure that all air is removed. To overcome the moisture problem manufacturers have developed silicon based brake fluids which are not hygroscopic. Unfortunately, they remain expensive but many specialist car owners use them.

The method for securing brake drums varies. This sort is the easiest to deal with because, even though the drum has been removed, the whole wheel bearing assembly remains intact.

Expert assistance

Colchester Institute has a large Automobile Engineering Centre which provides part-time (one day per week) and full-time courses in automobile engineering, body repair and welding.
For more information contact: **Dave Roberts**
Head of Centre for Automobile Engineering, Colchester Institute, Sheepen Road, Colchester, CO3 3LL.

TECHNICAL TOPIC: *Rear Drum Brake Inspection*

Anyone intending to carry out work on their vehicle's brakes should be sure they are clear about the system fitted and how it works. For obvious reasons it's important that DIY enthusiasts are well aware of the risks involved, and that they consult the professionals if in any doubt whatsoever. Remember that with car brakes you may only get one chance to make a mistake. Never assume that you know everything, and always work from a quality workshop manual so that you can be sure about correct procedures, important tightening torques and lubricant/fluid specifications.

1 With the vehicle securely supported on axle stands or a hoist, and having taken off the road wheel, the first job is to take off the brake drum. The method for doing this varies. In this case the drum comes away with the roller bearing, and is held in place with a loose-fitting central nut secured by a split pin. In other cases the drum may be retained by a single grub screw.

2 Drums can be tight to remove and sometimes it can be necessary to shock them loose with a careful blow from a soft-headed hammer. This is a much better approach than trying the lever the drum off with a screwdriver from the side. It can also be a struggle in cases where the drum is badly worn, and the shoes have adjusted themselves out so far that they actually obstruct the drum as you attempt to lift it away. Sometimes it will be possible to 'de-adjust' the shoes, by accessing a mechanism in through a hole in the backplate.

3 When removing this type of drum, which comes away with the wheel bearing assembly, be very careful that the bearings don't fall out and on to a dirty floor. While this may not seem like a disaster at the time, any grit picked up will soon wear out the bearing once it's back in use.

4 With the drum removed, check for brake fluid leakage. This is most likely to come from the wheel cylinder. Any signs of dampness should be regarded as suspicious. Pull back the sealing rubbers and check underneath. The days of reconditioning aged cylinders are gone now, it's simply not worth the hassle. New replacements are the most cost-effective option. Leaking fluid will inevitably get on to the surfaces of the brake shoes, which dramatically reduces their braking efficiency. Contaminated shoes MUST be replaced. They cannot be cleaned up once the friction material has become impregnated with fluid.

5 Don't forget that if the wheel cylinder has been leaking then you will need to clean the inside of the drum as well. Use a spirit-soaked wipe and make sure you do a thorough job otherwise you'll contaminate the new shoes needlessly.

6 The shoes are held to the backplate by retaining pins which must be released if they are to be changed. These ones need to be pushed in and twisted through 90° with pliers before they can be withdrawn, with their springs – take care not to allow these to ping out. On some applications a special pin removal tool will be required.

7 At this stage it's a good idea to make a rough drawing of the layout you find under the drum, in particular noting the way the various springs and connector rods are located. It's quite common for the springs to be specially shaped to fit around various pivot points etc. For this reason they must go back in exactly the same way afterwards. Also, be sure to note down exactly which drillings the springs came from. It's amazing how quickly you can forget such crucial details. You'll probably have to disconnect various linkages, including that for the handbrake, before you can manoeuvre the pair of shoes clear. Consult your workshop manual for the exact procedure on your car.

8 Always be aware of the risks posed by dust inhalation when working on brakes. For this reason it makes good sense to damp down with a brake cleaner spray. Also, if you choose not to wear gloves, use a quality barrier cream on bare skin for added protection. An old paint brush gets into all the nooks and crannies once the shoes have been removed. It's important to clear away any leaked fluid to avoid future contamination.

9 Clean off any areas of the backplate which contact the shoes using a piece of Emery paper, then treat with a good quality brake grease to help avoid squeaking in the future. Never use an ordinary grease because this will melt and run off, risking contamination of the lining material.

10 With the new shoes in place and everything connected correctly, it's likely that you'll have to de-adjust the brake shoes to enable the drum to be refitted over the top. Once again, the method for doing this varies from vehicle to vehicle, so consult the manual.

Handy Hints

- Clean off the contact points on the back of the shoes using a piece of Emery paper to remove any dirt or other contamination. Then treat these areas with a suitable grease to avoid squeaking in the future.
- Make sure that you fit suitable replacement shoes and that they match exactly with the originals you took off. Check for the position of all the drillings before you begin re-fitting.
- If the brake pedal displays noticeably less travel when the hand brake is applied then it's likely that the automatic adjuster mechanism is not working correctly
- After fitting new brake shoes always set-up and adjust the main brakes BEFORE the handbrake. Check manual for exact procedure.
- A simple way to check for hand brake operation is to jack up the rear of the car with the brake applied and try turning the wheels by hand.

Back to Basics

Part 19:
Chris Graham investigates the electronic wizardry of modern ABS.

There can be few automotive innovations which have made more of a difference to everyday motoring safety than anti-lock brakes, commonly abbreviated to ABS.

Keeping control of a car during emergency braking is a problem as old as motoring itself. The comparatively recent wide-spread adoption of ABS has brought safe and effective braking within the grasp of all drivers, whatever their personal skill levels. In the old days, of course, things were very different. Drivers in the 1950s, '60s and '70s were forced to rely on their wits and pure driving ability in emergency situations. Successfully avoiding accidents meant applying just the right amount of pedal pressure so that the car slowed enough without skidding.

DON'T LOCK IT!

As far as most drivers are concerned, the best and quickest way to stop a car is to stamp on the brake pedal with as much force as possible, and to hold it there until everything eventually slithers to a halt.

Before the advent of ABS brake systems this, in fact, was just about the worst thing you could do because it would usually guarantee vehicle skidding. While such stunts still look spectacular in re-runs of *The Sweeney* and *The Professionals*, the reality is rather different. Skidding is bad news unless you are a skilled stunt driver. Stopping a vehicle quickly and safely means maintaining the highest possible level of grip between the tyre and the road surface. This occurs at the point just before the wheel locks and begins to skid.

But applying conventional brakes too savagely will breach this limit in an instant, breaking the adhesion between tyre and road, causing the wheel to lock and skid along the surface.

Loss of grip is potentially disastrous for two important reasons. First it dramatically reduces the rate of vehicle deceleration, lengthening the overall stopping distance and so increasing the likelihood of an impact with whatever object you're trying to avoid.

Secondly, and perhaps even more importantly, a skidding vehicle is essentially out of control because the ability to steer is lost.

Locked wheels tend to slide in straight lines, regardless of where they are pointing. Think back to when you used to drive a conventionally braked car in the snow and ice. Even at low speeds on an icy corner, too much brake pedal pressure would send it sliding off at a tangent towards the verge. The principle is the same on wet and even dry roads, although progressively more speed is needed to create the same effect in each case.

THE RHYTHM METHOD

Precise control over brake application force is the key to avoiding wheel locking. But judging this is a tricky business because there are so many variables to be considered – speed of the vehicle, weather conditions, road surface type, tyre tread depth etc. Drivers need to be very sensitive to the vehicle's performance and behaviour. They must also be able to hold their nerve, resisting the temptation to stand on the pedal in an emergency situation, which is much easier said than done! Slamming on the anchors tends to be the instinctive reaction of all but the best drivers when faced with a sudden drama ahead. But those who remain cool at the wheel know different.

So-called 'cadence braking' was a technique developed specifically to avoid wheel locking. It involved the rhythmical and rapid application and release of the brakes. The idea was to apply enough force to slow the wheels to the point of locking up, then to momentarily release them so they didn't actually lose adhesion before reapplying them again and repeating the sequence. As you might imagine this was a hard skill to master and most ordinary drivers never really got to grips with it.

...but the electronic control unit is separate.

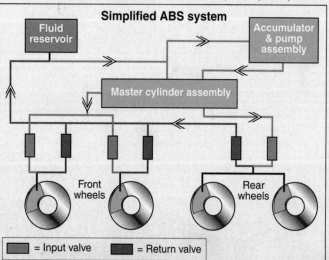

Simplified ABS system

Fluid reservoir

Accumulator & pump assembly

Master cylinder assembly

Front wheels

Rear wheels

■ = Input valve   ■ = Return valve

ABS layouts vary from car to car. In this case the fluid reservoir and brake master cylinder assembly are combined with the ABS modulator valve unit...

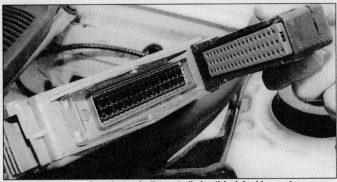

The complex nature of an electronically-controlled anti-lock braking system means that a multi-pin management unit is necessary to process inputs and outputs.

However, as it turned out this didn't really matter because the arrival of ABS braking systems in the 1980s effectively brought perfect cadence braking within the grasp of us all. Advances in automotive electronics made it possible to develop a brake control system which could switch braking effort on and off quickly enough, effectively automating the technique. But it wasn't always this straightforward. One of the early attempts, developed by Lucas-Girling, was a complicated mechanical system using modulator units driven by belts running around the drive shafts! Ford dabbled with this set-up, fitting it on some of the more sporty Escort and Fiesta models (XR3 and XR2), but it really was a little too complex for its own good.

SENSING THE SPIN

To be successful, ABS braking must be reliable and it wasn't until electronics-based systems emerged that genuinely dependable performance levels were achieved. A modern system is based around an electronic control unit (ECU), an ABS module (incorporating the master cylinder, ABS valve block, brake fluid reservoir, electric motor and high pressure fluid pump), road wheel sensors and a dashboard warning light.

The eyes and ears of the system are its wheel sensors. These are simple magnetic devices mounted very close to a toothed gear wheel, called the reluctor. Because it's fitted to either the driveshaft or the wheel hub assembly, the reluctor spins with the road wheel and provides an accurate indicator of rotational speed. The sensors monitor this speed by registering the passing of each tooth on the reluctor, and the tiny voltage they generate is whizzed back to the main ECU for analysis. The voltage output, in the form of a sine wave, varies as the wheel speed changes, and the ECU uses this information to assess whether or not things are as they should be.

The electronic control unit compares the signal inputs being received from all wheel sensors and, in this way, is able to identify anomalies such as one or more wheels which are slowing down significantly quicker than the rest.

This monitoring and comparison job happens continuously at very high speeds – modern ECUs have the capacity to process anything up to 8,000 sensor signals every second! In this way the system is capable of reacting to problems almost instantaneously, which is why today's ABS brakes work so impressively.

RAPID RESPONSE

Of course, knowing about wheel speed changes just a fraction of a second after they've happened is all very well, but acting on that information is another matter.

Obviously, to prevent the wheel from locking, the braking force must be reduced even though the driver has not eased up on the pedal. To do this, the system employs a series of modulator valves in the hydraulic fluid circuit, which are opened and closed electronically to vary the braking pressure being applied.

Typically, each wheel will have its own hydraulic input and return valves, which are operated directly by the ECU and independently of the driver. As the control unit detects that a wheel is slowing too fast, and that lock-up is imminent, the input valve is closed and the return valve opened so that hydraulic pressure is reduced.

The continued monitoring of the wheel highlights when its speed starts to pick up, at which point the valve switching is reversed to build pressure once again. This process will continue for as long as necessary, and the on/off cycle can be repeated more than ten times a second. On most systems you can feel this through the brake pedal as a rapid juddering sensation and, in the early days, many drivers reported this as a fault with the brakes!

Genuine ABS-related faults are not uncommon and, as systems become ever more complex, it's likely that the number of problems will increase, particularly as cars get older. Already many modern set-ups have to be 'interrogated' using sophisticated diagnostic equipment, in much the same way that faults with engine management systems are tackled. Unfortunately, this tends to limit the possible efforts of the keen DIYer.

SEEING THE LIGHT

The ABS control unit stores any fault code information and notifies the driver that a problem exists by illuminating the dashboard warning light. However, it's important to note that ABS faults don't result in complete brake failure. Modern systems are what's known as 'failsafe', which means that whatever may happen on the electronics side, the car is left with conventionally operating, hydraulically-powered brakes, so it can always be stopped. It has to be said, though, that serious faults are relatively rare on modern systems. In most cases any problems which do arise tend to relate to the wheel sensors or faulty connections.

Finally, one interesting spin-off following the advent of ABS was the development of traction control systems (TCS). Originally these were the exclusive preserve of high-performance sports cars but, nowadays, the technology has filtered down to a good many more run-of-the-mill saloons. In fact, the idea of traction control – designed to prevent the wheels from spinning during hard acceleration – is not a new one. Early examples first appeared in the 1950s but it wasn't until comparatively recently that the idea was refined to work effectively under modern electronic control. The ABS wheel sensors double-up as TCS sensors, feeding the main control module with data about unexpected wheel acceleration. In this way the ABS system can be used in 'reverse' to control potentially dangerous wheel spin.

Expert assistance

Colchester Institute has a large Automobile Engineering Centre which provides part-time (one day per week) and full-time courses in automobile engineering, body repair and welding.
For more information contact: **Adam Ward**
Head of Centre for Automobile Engineering, Colchester Institute, Sheepen Road, Colchester, CO3 3LL.

Next Month
Electrical ancillaries

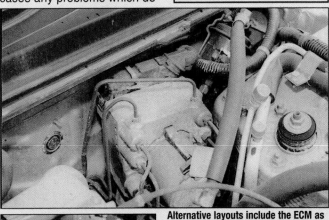

Alternative layouts include the ECM as part of a modular ABS assembly. Here it's bolted on to the back, immediately in front of the bulkhead.

This demonstration set-up shows clearly how close the wheel sensor is to the reluctor wheel.

Modern ABS units are compact and efficient units which provide very few problems.

TECHNICAL TOPIC: *ABS Sensor Cleaning*

The most common problem to afflict a modern ABS system is sensor failure. This can occur for a number of reasons but, usually, it's due to straightforward contamination. Being a magnetic device, the sensor tends to attract any metallic debris that's going, as well as gathering its fair share of road dirt and other detritus due to the relatively exposed position (some are protected by mud shields).

Sensors can also suffer with stone damage, either from simple impact, or from small pieces of grit becoming trapped between the face and the reluctor wheel. While this can sometimes be damaging, most of the time any obstructions will clear themselves because the two run in such close proximity. Dirt encrusted sensors lose their sensitivity and so become less able to accurately monitor the wheel's rotational speed. This sort of problem will trigger the dash light.

The other problem with wheel sensors is that they have a service life and eventually fail. This is normally a simple, age-related problem caused by a breakdown of the internal wiring. Individual sensors can be tested electronically, by assessing their output. However, doing this is a specialised job requiring good knowledge and access to an oscilloscope.

At a practical level just about the best you can hope for is to remove a suspect sensor, clean it up and/or replace it. This is little more than a simple spanner job and should be well within the range of an enthusiast. The sensors don't have a designated service life and failure tends to be a random business.

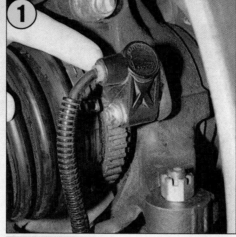
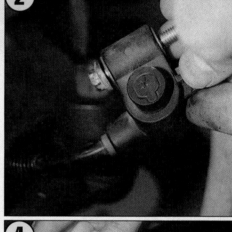

① Wheel sensor retaining methods vary from manufacturer to manufacturer. The key factor is the distance between the reluctor ring and the end of the sensor. Usually the sensor is locked into place by a simple bolt arrangement, and the clearance can't be varied.

② The sensors are self-cleaning to an extent. Because they are located so close to the reluctor ring, larger pieces of debris are brushed clear. However, jammed stones can be a different matter. To check for damage the sensor will have to be removed and, although this is simple in theory, often they become rusted solid in their mountings. Replacements normally cost £20-30 and can be fitted individually as required.

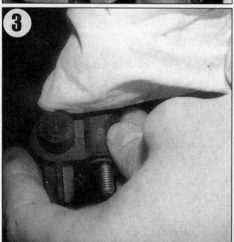
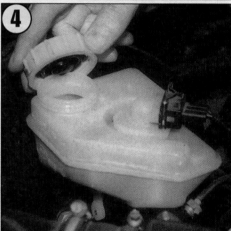

③ Cleaning a sensor needs care, especially if you are using anything other than soapy water. Remember that the plastic-coated connector wires will be vulnerable to attack from spilt solvent cleaner solution. Melted insulation will quickly lead to electrical problems in this environment.

④ An ABS system is more involved to bleed than a more basic set-up. You must refer to the workshop manual to be sure that you adopt the correct method. Remember that the fluid contained within the system's pump will have to be removed along with the rest, otherwise it will simply contaminate the fresh fluid. On some systems the pump has to be run during the bleeding process. This is a potentially tricky business and is best left to the professionals, unless you are extremely familiar with the system. In other instances this can only be tackled using specialised equipment to pressure-bleed the system.

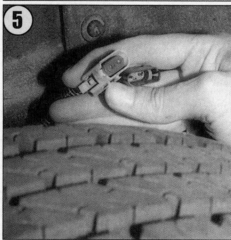
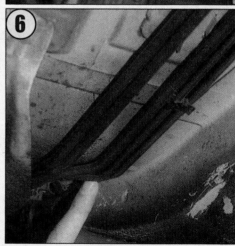

⑤ Wheel sensor terminals can be another cause of problems. A lot of manufacturers bring the connector sockets inside the engine bay to reduce the likelihood of contamination and water ingress. But on older applications the connector may be close to the sensor, laying it open to the worst of the road splash etc. Because these sensors produce such a small voltage output, it takes only a minor problem with the connector socket to throw the whole system into operational chaos. Great care must be taken when separating these connectors for inspection purposes. Be gentle to avoid snapping the casing and avoid losing the rubber seal from inside. Careless handling will simply introduce another fault.

⑥ It's always worth casting an eye over any exposed pipes under the vehicle for obvious signs of damage. In this case the larger diameter pipes are for the fuel system, while the smaller ones carry the brake fluid.

Handy Hints
- Wheel sensor retaining bolts may require a specific tightening torque, so don't forget to check the manual.
- Clean sensors with warm soapy water to avoid damaging associated wiring.
- Wheel sensors can be replaced individually as their failure is a random business.
- If you entrust your ABS problems to a 'specialist' make sure they have adequate diagnostic equipment and experience to match. There are plenty of 'experts' out there who charge a fortune for doing more harm than good!

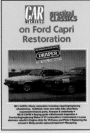   

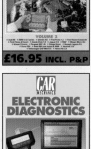

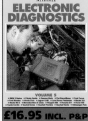

Back to Basics

Part 20: *Fundamental electrics, fuses and relays. Chris Graham reports.*

A simple multimeter can still be used to good effect for checking all sorts of electrical data around a car. The biggest problem nowadays, though, can be identifying and gaining access to the relevant wires.

I'd been hoping to begin this episode with a pithy explanation of exactly what electricity is. Unfortunately, the more I've read about the subject, the more bewildering everything has become. Even the name 'electricity' is shrouded in confusion and contradiction. A simple definition seems nigh on impossible, let alone an explanation. It's a subject which evidently baffles the biggest brains around, so what chance is there for you and me?

Just about the only thing I've discovered, with any reasonable degree of certainty, is that electrical energy is a flow of charged particles which can be usefully channelled down a wire.

These particles operate at a sub-atomic level to create a sort of chain reaction in whichever direction they are travelling. 'Electricity' is just one of a number of energy types which include X-rays, radio signals, light, microwaves and telephone signals. They are all variations on a theme, but each has a characteristically different frequency. See, it's getting far too complicated already!

So I think it's best if we move on before brain-fade gets a grip. However, before we do, just let me plant one amazing and vaguely relevant image in your mind. I've been reading Bill Bryson's excellent new book 'A Short History of Nearly Everything', in which he includes a mind-boggling explanation about the structure of atoms. We all know that atoms consist of a central, extremely dense nucleus (made up of protons and neutrons), and that this is surrounded by a fizzing cloud of electrons. But perhaps what isn't so widely known is the relative size and weight of these parts. To help appreciate this imagine an atom enlarged up to the size

of a cathedral – Salisbury, Durham, Canterbury – it doesn't matter which. Then place a single fly inside the building and think of this as the atom's nucleus. This, in itself, is a pretty impressive comparison but it gets even better when you learn that, for a true representation, the fly would have to be many thousands of times heavier than the cathedral!

POWER STORAGE

Cars use electrical energy in a number of different ways. Most obviously the power is harnessed to provide a spark which ignites the fuel/air mixture and forces the engine to run. But also, at a rather less spectacular level, electrical power is wired around the vehicle and used to operate a whole host of assorted components known generally as 'auxiliaries'. Some of these are

designed to operate while the engine is running (wipers, heater, headlamps etc.), in which case they take their power from the alternator. Others, like the interior lights, clock, sidelights and radio, are often used when the engine is switched off, when they are powered by the vehicle's battery.

One other very important component that uses the battery's store of power is the starter motor. In fundamental terms, operating the starter is the battery's primary function as, without this, the car would be useless. Once the engine is running though, the alternator takes over as the vehicle's primary power source, with some of the electrical charge it generates being diverted back to replenish the battery.

A car's battery produces what's known as a direct current (DC) of about 12 volts, although this figure does vary slightly

depending on battery condition. A DC current is characterised by a continuous flow of energy down a wire in one direction. This is in contrast to an alternating current (AC) supply, where the flow rapidly and repeatedly switches direction. All domestic appliances found in the home are powered by AC and, ideally, this would be used on cars as well. However, the problem is that AC cannot be stored in a battery so DC is the only option.

I'm sure you've all heard of the various terms used in association with electricity – volts, amps, ohms etc. Each has a specific relevance although this is not the time for detailed explanations. For a basic understanding of electricity it's helpful to liken an electric wire to a hose pipe. The pressure of the water flowing through the pipe equates to the voltage – it's a measure of 'power'. The amount of water flowing through the pipe is equivalent to the amps. Then, If you kink the hose pipe, the water flow is dramatically slowed as it negotiates the obstacle, and this equates to an electrical resistance, which is measured in ohms.

RESISTANCE LEVELS

The resistance in a simple electrical circuit normally takes the form of the component that's being powered – a bulb, motor etc. Using the example of the bulb, electricity is being forced through a thin filament which provides a high resistance. This restriction generates heat which causes the filament to glow brightly and thus light the bulb. Forcing too much power through the bulb will generate an excessive amount of heat, melting the filament and causing the bulb to blow. In this way resistance can be used to provide a convenient way of controlling current flow.

An electrical circuit will only operate as such if there is an unbroken link running to and from the power source. When this is a battery the power will flow from the positive terminal around the circuit and back to the negative where it is 'earthed'. In the simplest circuits, which might contain two bulbs and a motor, for example, these components are said to be wired up in 'series'. This approach is used sometimes on vehicle

The good old days! Things were simple before electronics took over as the dominant force under the bonnet. Everything was easy to check and mistakes were rarely costly.

Battery and main fusebox found inside the vehicle for added protection on some modern applications, as this Mercedes-Benz A Class demonstrates neatly.

Old-style fuses featured thin lengths of wire mounted inside small cylindrical containers. Originally these were often made from glass, but then plastic took over.

systems but more commonly you will find components wired up in 'parallel'. This is where wires branch off from the supply side of the circuit, connect up individual components, and then are all linked to a common return lead which runs back to the negative battery terminal and earth.

The big advantage of parallel wiring is that each component in the circuit receives full battery voltage. Wiring components in series inevitably means that the power is shared between components with those at the end receiving less than those at the start.

In general terms any flow of electricity will always tend to seek out a connection to earth. Lightening is perhaps the ultimate example of this phenomenon! As far as cars are concerned, the negative terminal of the battery is connected to the metal chassis/bodywork of the vehicle, and this is sufficient as an earth.

BASIC FAULTS

If, in a simple circuit, one of the wires breaks so that electrical flow is interrupted, the system is said to have gone 'open circuit', and the flow will cease. Obviously from a fault-finding point of view, repairing this sort of problem is dependant upon accurately locating the break. This can be done using a simple multimeter, working back progressively towards the battery until current flow is detected – as if you were detecting a water leak in a pipe. Unfortunately this is easier said than done on

modern motor cars because wiring systems have become so complex. Not only are there literally hundreds of circuits to deal with, but all the wires used tend to be bound together into bundles forming what's known as the vehicle loom.

The wires are colour-coded and a modern circuit diagram provides information about this, but it's the physical access to the relevant wires which can pose the biggest practical problem. Sections of loom are run in the most awkward places – up under the dashboard, low down on the bulkhead, beneath awkward-to-reach trim panels – which makes life very difficult.

Luckily, modern wiring diagrams are extremely comprehensive and the manufacturers build in plenty of connections which can be used to shortcut the testing procedures. The key factor when dealing with an open circuit is to establish the cause of the 'blockage'. The fault may of course lie with one of the components, it may relate to a problem with the wiring itself or one of the connectors within the system.

The other type of fault relates to a condition known as a 'short circuit'. All electrical wires are insulated with a plastic coating which is designed to ensure that the power supply flows down the wire and nowhere else. But if this insulation is broken, because the protective coating has been breached, the current is presented with another potential route to earth. Chafing is a common cause of this sort of problem, as the wire is rubbed repeatedly against a metal bracket or sharp panel edge, for example. When metal-to-metal contact is eventually achieved a second and often easier route to earth will open up. it's likely that the current will be diverted out of the wire and away to earth via the new route and this, in essence, creates what's known as a short circuit.

DOUBLE TROUBLE

Not only does a short circuit interrupt the power supply to any components further along in the original circuit, but it also allows the power supply to rush away to earth in a completely uncontrolled manner. This causes a tremendous power surge as any resistance in the original circuit has been lost. The consequences of this can be serious for the wiring leading up to the point where the short occurs. The sudden increase in power flow is likely to cause overheating, which may then melt the insulation and even cause it to catch alight.

Expert assistance

Colchester Institute has a large Automobile Engineering Centre which provides part-time (one day per week) and full-time courses in automobile engineering, body repair and welding.
For more information contact: **Adam Ward**
Head of Centre for Automobile Engineering, Colchester Institute, Sheepen Road, Colchester, CO3 3LL.

To help guard against this scary outcome, all electrical circuits are fitted with fuses. These are designed to limit the amount of power flowing through any given wire, thus eliminating the risk of overheating. Essentially a fuse consists of a thin length of wire that is designed to burn and break in response to a predetermined current flow. Fuses are rated in amps and work by breaking the circuit before damage is done. A 30A fuse, for example, will allow that much current, but no more, to flow through its circuit. If a 'short' occurs, causing a power surge, the fuse will blow the instant the 30A mark is reached.

As with domestic electrical systems, vehicles are fitted with a number of differently rated fuses, according to the circuit requirements. Interior light circuits, which only require relatively low power, will be fitted with a 5A fuse, while those feeding heating elements such as the rear window heater, need a much higher supply and will therefore be fitted with fuses rated at perhaps 35A.

Fuse design has changed quite a bit over the years. In the old days the fuse filaments were contained inside small glass cylinders which were slotted into metal clips. Nowadays we have moved to a spade connector

Vehicle alarms became a popular electrical add-on in the 1980s. Quality of fit was the vital factor, both in terms of the system's operational efficiency and it's overall durability.

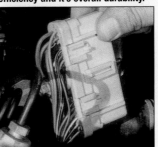

Tapping into a modern electrical system requires knowledge and confidence. Bundles of wires are bound together to form the main loom and usually only become accessible where they enter multi-pin connectors like this one.

type of design, which provides a better and more reliable contact, is smaller and costs less to make.

CONTROLLED SWITCHING

Circuits designed to carry high power supplies need wire of a sufficiently large diameter to withstand the electrical loading and avoid the risk of overheating. Also, high current levels require big switches to control them, to minimise the likelihood of electrical arcing as the switch is operated. Neither of these options are particularly desirable on the motor car, as they are both bulky and add significantly to the cost and design considerations.

The solution, when high current is required, is to run two separate current flow systems. One which carries a low voltage and runs between a small dashboard-mounted switch and a much more heavy-duty switching device called a relay. The relay is linked in to the high voltage circuit and controls its switching. So, pressing the dashboard control sends a small voltage to the relay which then switches the high current circuit to operate high consumption components such as the headlamps.

Relays are essentially simple components which rely on a couple of contact breakers and a magnet. The magnet is energised by the low voltage signal from the separate switch, which causes the contacts to close, allowing the higher voltage connection to be made, and current to flow. Having said this, though, modern relays are becoming increasing complex from an electronic control point of view. More and more they are being designed to include advanced features to enhance their function. Those used for interior lighting now feature delay mechanisms for the courtesy lights, while those wired into the wiper circuit include the wiper arm 'parking' facility. Relays themselves have become a good deal more reliable than they used to be, although failures do still occur. As you might imagine, these modern units contain some pretty intricate componentry so when they fail there is little scope for repair and the scrap bin beckons.

Next Month
All about headlights

TECHNICAL TOPIC: *Electrical Health Check*

Vehicle electrics is one of those areas which many enthusiasts traditionally shy away from, often with good reason. Nobody likes electric shocks at the best of times but, nowadays, there's the additional risk of causing serious damage to the vehicle as well. Modern engine management systems are becoming increasingly sensitive to power surges, so the inadvertent bridging of the wrong two terminals can send ECM-wrecking power spikes fizzing around the whole vehicle.

However, it's not all doom and gloom. While there are a good many things we'd never advise the enthusiast to tackle, there's also quite a lot the keen amateur can check and assess to good effect. But the one golden rule should always be that if you're ever in any doubt, leave well alone. It's a terrible cliché I know, but the old adage about a little knowledge being a dangerous thing could have been written with vehicle electrics in mind. So, if you have any concerns at all, then please stop what you're doing and call in a professional. While it's unlikely that a healthy adult will receive a fatal shock from a vehicle, those with medical conditions may not be so lucky. BE WARNED!

(1) This is a typical blade connector-type fuse, which is compact, cheap to make, reliable and easy to fit. The ratings are clearly marked. Blown fuses are still a relatively common problem, particularly on poorly maintained vehicles. The fusebox should always be one of your first ports of call when sudden failures occur. The lids of most carry an explanatory diagram describing exactly what each fuse is for. If not, check in the owner's handbook or workshop manual.

(2) Earth points are another common cause of electrical problems on vehicles. They always have been and probably always will be. Their location varies from vehicle to vehicle so you'll need to check the literature for your car. Good earth connections are becoming more and more important these days. Retaining bolts must be secure and tight, and the connector lugs clean and dry. Ironically, designers frequently seem to locate these important connections low down on the vehicle, where they are prone to water splash and dirt! They are simple but very worthwhile to check.

(3) Relays are used to control the switching of the higher powered circuits on your vehicle. They usually have simple spade-like connectors which push into the connector board, as seen here. Many are still located under the bonnet and protected by flimsy plastic covers which crack if carelessly handled. Water can be a big problem once it gets inside, leading to corrosion of the terminals. Check them carefully for the obvious signs.

(4) The connection between wires is always a potential weak spot on any vehicle. Over the years manufacturers have tried many different designs in a bid to improve the security of these joints but, in most cases, water can still find its way inside. Once in, of course, it initiates corrosion of the metal terminals which quickly affects their operation. The physical presence of the corrosion forces the terminals apart, which reduces the efficiency of the current flow. It also increases the resistance of the joint, which can be just as debilitating. This can either stop the flow of current completely, causing it to go 'open circuit', or it can reduce the power flow sufficiently to have a serious effect on the components being run. Some of the voltages used in modern circuits are so low that even the slightest variation on signal strength can have an drastic effect.

(5) The variations of design are almost endless. You're likely to find many different types on a single vehicle, even modern ones. Some are a simple push fit, while others are locked together with tiny sprung lugs. Traditionally one of the worst is the 'Scotch-lock' joint, which was much favoured as a simple and quick solution when wiring in additional equipment such as aftermarket alarms or driving lamps etc. These are fraught with potential problems because they usually rely for their connection on pins piercing the wires being joined. The big danger is that, in breaching the wire's insulation like this, the way is opened up for corrosion to attack the wire itself. The best solution when creating any form of electrical joint between two wires is to use a soldering iron and then to heat-shrink a section of insulation around it. But soldering is slow, expensive and time consuming and so it's often not done. Modern alarm manufacturers specify it when their products are fitted.

(6) There are certain areas of modern cars which you need to be very careful with. If there is an airbag system that is controlled electronically you should steer well clear. The cabling which supplies these is normally coloured bright yellow or orange, as a warning. The two big dangers are that you inadvertently disable the system so that the bag won't be triggered when it's actually needed. Secondly, you might set it off as you fiddle. The same rules can apply to some seatbelt tensioning systems which are also electronically controlled.

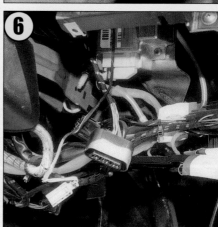

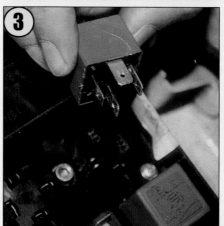

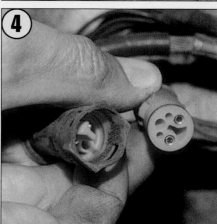

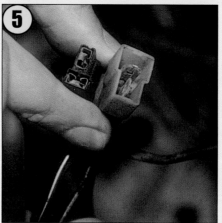

Handy Hints

- Don't 'break' electrical connectors apart for the sake of it. Only open them up if you suspect that water may have got inside.
- Avoid cutting wires whenever possible. If you have to then try to solder the resultant joint to ensure a good quality, corrosion-free result.
- Before tackling any electrical job on a vehicle, however apparently simple, make sure you have an accurate circuit diagram to hand, and that you have studied it before you start. Modern systems are incredibly sensitive to power surges so mistakes can be extremely costly.

Back to Basics

Part 21:
Car headlights just keep getting better, as Chris Graham reports.

Getting old is a cruel business. It gets us all in the end and affects every aspect of life, including our ability to drive. Those of us now in middle age are forced to contend with dulling reflexes, increasingly achy joints and worsening eyesight. It's all very depressing, but don't reach for the razor blades just yet! Car designers are doing a great deal to ease our woes with ever safer cars, increasingly comfortable seats and progressively brighter and more efficient headlights.

This last factor is much more important than you might imagine because the type, or more precisely, the colour of the light produced by car headlamps becomes an increasingly serious issue as we get older. The problem is that, with age, our eyes get less efficient at seeing in the yellow sector of the spectrum. In most cases this isn't a particular problem apart, that is, from driving at night. It's ironic that for decades car headlights were based around tungsten filament bulbs which produce, yes you've guessed it, a yellowish light. So, traditionally, those of advancing years have

When halogen bulbs were first introduced everyone wanted to upgrade to the new wonder light. The manufacturers produced 'universal' bulbs (on the left) that could be fitted into existing headlamps. Bulbs nowadays have locating lugs (right) to ensure correct fitting.

been forced to bumble around at night with the road ahead bathed in a colour of light to which their eyes are becoming increasingly desensitised. It would be funny if it wasn't true!

ALL SEALED UP

The basic components of the headlamp haven't changed that much over the years. All rely on a bulb to provide the light and either a lens or a reflector to focus that light on to the road ahead. The positioning of the bulb within the lamp is an important factor as the distance between the light source and the reflector can have a significant effect on the way the light bounces off the reflector.

In the early days of 'modern' headlamps, cars were fitted with sealed beam units which, as their name suggests, were completely sealed. The whole headlamp unit acted, in effect, as a giant bulb. A tungsten filament was mounted at a fixed point in front of the shiny, aluminised reflector. This was made of coated glass in the old days and was steeply dished to form what's known as a parabolic reflector. A glass lens was bonded on to the front to create an airtight seal. The unit was filled with an inert gas, such as argon, which was held under a slight positive pressure and ensured a good service life for the filament with minimal oxidation. The whole thing worked very well. The fact that the filament could 'burn' in a relatively large space, rather than in a tiny glass envelope as with a conventional bulb, meant that the inevitable tungsten deposits were spread over a wide area. This minimised the discolouring effect which, in time, can dull overall output.

SUDDEN DARKNESS

It wasn't all good news though, because sealed beam units were costly to make and, therefore, expensive to renew when they broke. They also tended to fail very suddenly when problems arose, most commonly when a stone chip in the lens broke the seal.

These limitations prompted the industry to move away from this all-in-one approach back to a separate bulb design. While the basic principles remained the same, the parabolic reflector was made with a hole in the back through which a conventional bulb was poked. This meant that when the bulb eventually failed, replacement was simple, quick and cheap. Lens cracking wasn't such an immediate disaster either, although reflector discolouration still put an ultimate limit on service life.

By the time we all rolled into the psychedelic '70s, and ordinary saloon cars started to get significantly faster, it became obvious that lighting technology had to improve if safety levels at night were to be maintained. The big breakthrough came with the introduction of the tungsten-

halogen bulb, sometimes also referred to as the quartz-halogen. This quickly became the 'must have' motoring accessory and many of the manufacturers began marketing bulbs with universal fittings which allowed owners to fit them to a wide variety of vehicles.

TINY BUT BRIGHT

The bulbs themselves were much smaller and more compact than the conventional tungsten filament variety. The clear envelope was made using quartz rather than ordinary glass, and the space inside was filled with a halogen gas which minimised the oxidation rate of the tungsten filament. The light output was far superior to that generated by the conventional tungsten bulb, being much brighter and a good deal whiter. Power consumption was capped at 55W for everyday use but, of course, more powerful bulbs

One of the most common problems with headlights, even today, relates to incorrect alignment. MoT test centres use beam setters like this to check that everything is within tolerance. If it's not, the car will be failed.

Beam setters are also used to check the alignment of high beam, by measuring the position of the 'hot spots' within the beam pattern. A light meter within the tester measures this.

were available, especially for those involved in rallying. Inevitably, though, enthusiastic owners got hold of these high performance versions and sneakily fitted them to their road cars. Unfortunately, not only did this tend to wind up the boys in blue, but it also frequently put an unbearable strain on the standard vehicle's electrics.

Electrical wiring, as with every other aspect of the mass produced car, is designed to meet a budget. Things are build to a predetermined standard and that's that. As far as the wiring is concerned, this means that there is a built-in overload limit, which is normally about 25% above the stated maximum electrical loading. So fitting headlight bulbs which more than double the recommended power consumption is asking for trouble, and the wiring and connectors will almost always suffer serious damage.

REFLECTED GLORY

Big improvements have also been made to reflector design in recent years. There was a fashion in the 1970s and '80s for rectangular headlamps. However, it's been suggested that round is the ideal and most efficient shape for a light reflector to be. This idea seems to be backed up now by the fact that most modern designs now feature round reflectors once again, even though some are still cleverly built into an essentially rectangular light unit.

Apart from the shape though,

the actual make-up and the function of the reflectors has changed significantly too. Many of the most modern units are now made from plastic, which saves weight and cost, as well as lengthening service life. Also, there's a great trend now for making the reflector as a multi-facetted unit, with lots of differently angled surfaces. The idea of this is that it's the reflector itself, rather than the front lens, which then focusses the light from the bulb on to the road ahead. In this way manufacturers have been able to drop the heavy and light-sapping glass lenses from the front of headlamps, and replace them with swish-looking clear plastic covers. These do little more than protect the light units within and look good.

BRIGHT EYES

The culmination of the headlight designer's art to date has to be the Xenon discharge unit. These achieve much higher levels of light output than a conventional halogen bulb and, more importantly, the colour of the light produced is very much closer to daylight. The units, which produce an electric arc, require much more power than conventional set-ups and so need their own individual transformers to meet this demand. In practice, the difference between Xenon and conventional lighting is fantastic. The quality of light is much better suited to the human eye and so night time illumination (right to the edge of the beam) is greatly improved.

On the minus side, though, the units are very expensive to

The days of complex front lenses like this on a Mondeo are probably gone forever. On modern cars it's the reflector which does all the focussing work.

This headlight unit on a Primera features a 'projector' style dipped beam light, working through a thick lens, and a more conventional round high beam lamp with parabolic reflector.

As this unit on a VW Golf Mk4 illustrates, modern headlamp units can be stylish and interesting as well as effective.

replace (although usual service life is longer), and they require very careful control. Because of the increased brightness, correct alignment is essential to avoid seriously dazzling other

drivers. To achieve this automatic levelling systems are fitted which react to the car's movements and the way it's loaded. This obviously adds to the complexity of the whole system, as well as the potential cost of repairs should things go wrong. Nevertheless, Xenon lighting does appear to be the way forward. Because of the initial cost it was introduced first on top Mercedes-Benz and BMW models, but now the technology is filtering down to more 'ordinary' cars, so we've all got a chance to experience the undoubted benefits. Right now, manufacturers in Germany are developing 'smart' lighting which will swivel the headlights from side to side as the car is steered around bends and at junctions. There looks to be exciting times ahead, particularly for all of us struggling, middle-aged drivers!

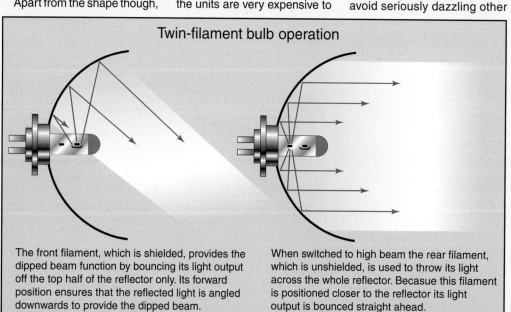

Twin-filament bulb operation

The front filament, which is shielded, provides the dipped beam function by bouncing its light output off the top half of the reflector only. Its forward position ensures that the reflected light is angled downwards to provide the dipped beam.

When switched to high beam the rear filament, which is unshielded, is used to throw its light across the whole reflector. Becasue this filament is positioned closer to the reflector its light output is bounced straight ahead.

Next Month
Automatic Transmission

TECHNICAL TOPIC: *Headlight know-how*

Although headlights have come on in leaps and bounds over the past few years, and have got a good deal more 'high-tech' in some cases, as far as most motorists are concerned the fundamentals haven't altered all that much. The sort of problems which still occur are more or less the same as they always have been, and can be lumped under three general headings; bulb failure, bad alignment, poor earth connections. Obviously, a great deal depends on the age of your vehicle and its general condition. Cars which are past their prime and which have suffered in the hands of less than caring previous owners, can present a whole range of additional niggles. Cracked headlamp lenses that have been ignored are a favourite source of trouble, leading to condensation covered glass and discoloured or corroded reflectors. Previous accident damage is another cause of problems, with poor alignment and weak or insecure fixings providing top traumas.

(1) If you've got a problem headlight, it always makes sense to start with the basics by checking the condition and fit of the electrical connector. If the plastic connector or its wiring looks at all blackened, distorted or melted, then suspect the worst. There are two likely causes. Either a previous owner will have uprated the bulbs by fitting higher wattage units which will have been drawing too much power. The increased current flow will have overheated the wires/sockets. Alternatively, the cause might be more innocent, stemming from little more than a poorly fitted, loose or dirty connector. Any one of these three problems will increase the electrical resistance within the connector, leading to a potentially destructive build up of heat. It's therefore important to make sure that all connections are clean and tight-fitting. Also, watch out for aftermarket alarms which are often wired so that the headlamps will flash when the system is triggered. While usually fine if fitted professionally, a shoddy job with cheap pin connectors can be nothing but trouble.

(2) Although designs vary, the main bulb connector will usually have some form of protection. In this case it's a flexible and tight-fitting rubber cap which keeps the socketry dry and clean. It's obviously very important to make sure that this protection is effective. Sometimes rubber gaiters like this one can be awkward and fiddly to fit properly, so people don't take the time or trouble to do the job correctly. Be sure you do!

(3) Always be particularly careful to avoid touching a quartz-halogen bulb with bare skin. However clean you think your hands may be, natural oil from your skin is bound to be smeared on to the surface of the quartz, which is bad news. The tendency is for this to create hot spots on the surface as the bulb operates, which leads to weakening of the structure and a shortening of service life. So make sure you only ever hold the bulb by its metal base. If you do accidentally touch the quartz then use a cotton cloth and a solvent-based cleaner to treat the affected area thoroughly.

(4) On traditional single headlamp applications the bulb used has two filaments, one to provide the dipped beam function and a second for the high beam. The position of these filaments, in relation to the reflector, is a vital factor (see diagram), which is why correctly seating a bulb in its mounting is so important. The dipped beam filament uses a small metal shield to prevent its output hitting the bottom half of the reflector and being bounced heavenwards. Sometimes, when bulbs get old, this shield breaks away from its tiny mounting, so this is another point to check if your beam pattern suddenly goes a little wayward.

(5) To ensure your headlamps remain as bright as possible the point where they are earthed must be clean and tightly secured to achieve maximum electrical efficiency. In this case the connection is conveniently close to the headlamp and very accessible. But on more recent applications these points can be more difficult to find, and are often shared with other systems on the vehicle. What's more, modern vehicle systems tend to be a good deal more sensitive to variations in earth connection efficiency, because systems such as the engine management are working on much lower voltages (typically 5 volts). Slight fluctuations can be sufficient to cause havoc.

(6) The method for adjusting the headlamps varies from car to car. Sometimes it's easy, other times it's more involved. Normally it's just the up and down adjustment that will need to be altered as this is the one that people fiddle with most. However, there is a side-to-side adjustment available too if necessary.

(7) Many cars nowadays feature an electronic control for adjusting the headlights from the comfort of the driver's seat. Usually there are three or four different settings available, with '0' representing the normal position and each of the others producing a progressive lowering of the lights. This is a straightforward up-and-down movement which is intended to compensate for the loading of the vehicle. A couple of sacks of potatoes in the boot, and your mother-in-law on the back seat, will dip the back of the car sufficiently to start dazzling oncoming motorists if an adjustment isn't made. When checking beam alignment this sort of adjustment control should be set at it's highest level.

(8) It's quite possible to carry out a basic headlight beam alignment assessment at home with only basic equipment. Park your car (unloaded) on level ground about three or four metres from a smooth vertical surface such as a wall or garage door. Measure the vertical distance from the centre of each headlight lens to the ground. Set a metal rule to this figure and then, with the lights switched to dipped beam, hold the rule against the wall or door and note where the top edge of the beam pattern falls. Ideally the two should just about coincide. If there is a big difference then it's likely that the alignment will be sufficiently out to fail the MoT test.

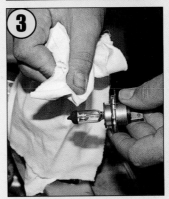

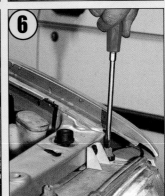

Handy Hints

- Wear surgical-style rubber gloves when handling headlamp bulbs to avoid contact with greasy skin.
- If you have an older lamp suffering with condensation on the reflector and lens, try running it without the rubber seal on the back for a day or two, giving the moisture time to evaporate.
- Use clear nail varnish to plug up chips in old-style glass lenses as soon as you notice them.

Back to Basics

Part 22:
Chris Graham begins his look at auto transmissions by investigating the torque converter.

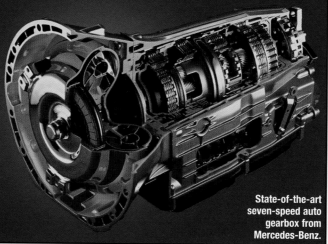

State-of-the-art seven-speed auto gearbox from Mercedes-Benz.

In the old days automatic transmission was for wimps! Nobody with any sort of enthusiasm for driving ever dreamt of owning a car with an auto 'box. They were for lazy drivers to whom the thrill of a snappy double de-clutch down-change meant absolutely nothing. Among the biggest criticisms were that these unfortunate units were usually hopelessly unresponsive, slow-changing and power-sapping. The car would shudder sickeningly when drive was selected, and then proceed to clunk its way up through the three forward gears with varying degrees of smoothness. Lack of oomph was usually a really big problem and if your 'box was bolted to anything less than a gas-guzzling V8, then you were more or less sunk. How times have changed.

Nowadays an automatic gearbox is an increasingly desirable option. They are fitted to all sorts of cars, everything from high-tech, fire-breathing monsters like the BMW M3, right down to the humble Nissan Micra. The traditionally high cost of auto transmission, in terms of economy and performance, really is a thing of the past. Today's electronically-controlled wonder boxes offer a host of interesting and valuable features. In some cases they can be used just like a manual gearbox, and will also think for themselves, adjusting their performance to the driving style of whoever's using the car.

ELECTRONIC CONTROL

Of course, all this technology comes at a price and that price, as usual, is often reliability. The sensitivity of the electronic control systems, coupled with the harsh environment most gearboxes are forced to endure, means that faults and breakdowns become increasingly likely as vehicles get older. What's more, the expense of putting things right if they do go wrong can be astronomic.

The basic function of any automatic gearbox is to save the driver the bother and effort of having to make frequent manual gear changes while driving. It takes away the need to match the gear ratio to the vehicle's speed, and makes life much easier under slow, stop/start driving conditions. But achieving this degree of convenience calls for a stroke of mechanical brilliance and this is exactly what we have in an auto 'box. Any of you who remember reading Part 12 of this series, on manual transmission, need quickly to forget anything you learned from that episode! Automatic transmission is a totally different beast from its manual counterpart. Certainly, in essence, we're looking at a box of cogs, but the way that they are controlled is the truly amazing thing.

NO TIES

The first astonishing point to note is that there is no solid link between the engine and an automatic gearbox! Unlike the manual version, which is rigidly bolted to the end of the crankshaft, via a clutch housing and heavy flywheel, an auto 'box isn't really linked at all. So how on earth is the drive transmitted from the engine? Well, improbable as it may sound, it's done by throwing a bit of oil around!

An incongruous device called a torque converter is what does the business here. It's a type of fluid coupling which is able to harness the power of moving fluid, and transform it into a rotary action that's used to drive the gearbox. I know this all sounds pretty unlikely, but it's true! First developed by a Dr Fottinger in the early 1900s, for use on boat engines, the fluid coupling provided a smooth and effective means of transferring power between the engine and gearbox, without having to physically bolt the two together. By the mid-1920s the technology had been adapted for use on the motor car, and the key point was that it enabled the engine and gearbox to rotate independently.

MASTER OF SPIN

The torque converter is an essentially simple component which performs a complex task. It actually looks not unlike a conventional clutch housing and is bolted on to a lightened flywheel (sometimes referred to as a flexi-wheel) fitted with a conventional ring gear which engages with the startor motor. It consists of three parts: the housing/pump, the turbine and the stator.

The heavy, cast metal housing is the part which bolts to the flywheel, and so it spins all the time the engine is running. Inside it's fitted with angled vanes which are shaped so that fluid is thrown outwards as it rotates, creating a sort of centrifugal pumping action. The oil is introduced at the centre and, as the housing and vanes spin, the tendency is for the fluid to travel outwards and away from the centre, picking up speed as it goes. Think of how a spin dryer works to dry clothes and you'll get the idea. However, this is only half the story.

The other half of the torque converter consists of a large turbine wheel, once again made with carefully angled vanes. This runs independently of the pump assembly, but is connected to the output shaft which links directly to the gearbox itself. Once the oil, which has been accelerated by the spinning pump, reaches its maximum speed and flies out from between the pump vanes, the wall of the housing guides it across the short distance to the curved vanes of the turbine opposite.

ROUND THE BEND

The only option left for the oil at this stage is to follow the course of these curved vanes around a tight bend and off towards the centre of the turbine. This dramatic change of direction which the oil is forced to take is what sets the turbine spinning and this rotary action, believe it or not, is what eventually ends up powering the gearbox, turning the wheels and driving the car. There, I told you it was

Left to right: turbine, stator and pump rotors.

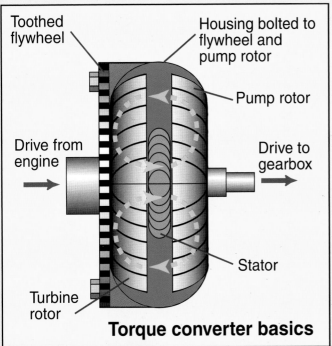

Toothed flywheel

Housing bolted to flywheel and pump rotor

Pump rotor

Drive from engine

Drive to gearbox

Stator

Turbine rotor

Torque converter basics

Expert assistance

Colchester Institute has a large Automobile Engineering Centre which provides part-time (one day per week) and full-time courses in automobile engineering, body repair and welding.
For more information contact: **Adam Ward**
Head of Centre for Automobile Engineering, Colchester Institute, Sheepen Road, Colchester, CO3 3LL.

hard to believe. The idea that a small turbine, no more than a foot or so in diameter and driven by fluid, has the power to push a heavy Vauxhall Omega up hills is a wonder indeed!

Then, of course, the 'spent' oil exiting from the centre of the turbine has to be dealt with. Left to it's own devices it would spray back across and interfere with the running of the pump rotor, particularly as the two are being spun in opposite directions. Obviously, allowing them to meet would cause the pump to be slowed, reducing overall efficiency and exerting a braking effect on the engine. It's the third constituent of the torque converter which stops this from happening. The stator is a much smaller, finned rotor. Once again it has carefully shaped vanes and sits on a shaft in the centre of the unit. It's sole role in life is to deflect the oil exiting from the centre of the turbine and direct it efficiently back towards the pump.

The other important point is that the stator is only allowed to spin in one direction, thanks to a one-way clutch. It cannot rotate in the direction the oil is hitting it, and this resistance is used to redirect the oil so that it arrives back at the centre of the pump rotor, ready to start its journey once again.

TORQUE CONTROL

Unfortunately, the reality is not quite as simple as the explanation so far might suggest – oh that it were! The spin speed differences between the pump and turbine rotors adds a whole raft of complication. You see, it's all a matter of torque, and how this varies during use. Because the pump rotor is driven directly by the engine, it responds quickly to increases in throttle setting. But the nature of the fluid clutch set-up means that these speed variations inevitably take a little longer to be transferred to the turbine. There is 'lag' in the system and it's this principle (replacing the conventional on/off clutch action) which allows the smooth take-up of power, enabling the car to pull away from a standstill without stalling.

When the engine is idling, the pump rotor is being turned relatively slowly and so the energy (torque) being delivered by the fluid to the turbine is insufficient to turn it with any great intent. This is why an idling car with automatic transmission is able to remain still (or creep only slightly) when 'drive' is selected. Touch the throttle, though, and the instant increase in pump speed gives the flying fluid more energy to drive the turbine, and the car will begin to move.

We've already mentioned that the carefully shaped vanes on the turbine rotor are designed to channel the fluid in towards the centre, in preparation for its transfer back to the pump rotor. In fact, the vanes are so tightly curved that they actually reverse the direction of the fluid's travel and, in so doing, enable the turbine to extract the highest possible amount of energy from

the moving fluid. This effectively boosts the torque being generated to a level, improbable though it may seem, higher than that being supplied by the engine in the first place. A well designed torque converter will be capable of at least doubling the torque generated by the engine under the right operating conditions. The limitation on this though is that it only happens at slow speeds, when the pump rotor is running significanlty faster than the turbine. As soon as the latter catches up, the torque increase effect is lost.

ONE FINAL TWIST

But I've saved the trickiest bit until last, mainly because I was trying to put off having to explain it! It concerns the way the stator behaves once vehicle speed gets up around 40-50mph. When things are pottering along the trajectory of the fluid leaving the turbine ensures that it hits the stator's vanes in the ideal way. The force of the fluid pushes the stator against the solid resistance of its one-way clutch and so the only option left to the fluid is to follow the vanes and be shot off back towards the pump. However, this isn't always the case.

Once the turbine attains sufficient speed it starts to throw the fluid out in a different direction, and this is where it begins to get really hard to visualise. Think of a large water wheel which, instead of having the usual flat, horizontal blades, is fitted with curved ones which are all angled in towards the centre. Water from a high pressure hose aimed at the circumference of the wheel in an effort to turn it, would be guided down each curved vane and exit in a stream heading towards the wheel's spindle. Viewed from the side, it would be clear that the water leaving the vanes is actually travelling in the opposite direction to the rotation of the wheel (see diagram).

But, the moment the rotor speed exceeds the speed at which the fluid is leaving the turbine, that same fluid starts to go backwards,

even though it's moving forwards! To help explain this, imagine standing in a trailer and throwing an apple out of the back. If the trailer is stationary and you toss the apple out, it will simply fly gracefully away at, say, 20mph and that'll be that.

OUT OF THE BLUE

However, if the trailer is being towed along at 60mph as you prepare to make your throw, things will be very different. Apart from playing havoc with your hair, the forward motion will also mean that both you and the apple are already travelling at 60mph. Throwing the apple out of the back at 20mph will certainly move it away from you, but your effort won't be enough to stop its overall forward motion. So a luckless pedestrian, who happens to be walking along beside the road in the same direction as you and the trailer are travelling, runs the serious risk of a nasty crack on the back of the head from an aggressive Cox's Orange Pippin flying along at 40mph. It's quite a tricky concept to get your head around unless, of course, you're that unfortunate pedestrian, when everything suddenly and painfully becomes very clear – like a bolt from the blue!

The fluid's 'change in direction' means that it starts falling on the

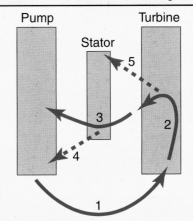

Pump

Turbine

Stator

1. Fluid thrown from pump over to drive turbine rotor.
2. Fluid direction switched by turbine vanes – energy absorbed by turbine.
3. Stator, locked by one-way clutch, redirects fluid towards centre of pump.
4. Without the stator fluid would follow this path and upset the pump.
5. As turbine speed builds, fluid begins to get flung in this direction and starts hitting the back of the stator vanes. This causes stator to freewheel, allowing fluid past with ease.

backs of the stator's vanes, which causes it to begin free-wheeling. It's important that this happens. The stator's vanes can only cope efficiently when fluid strikes them from the correct direction. Any deviation from this causes chaos and has a drastic effect on fluid transfer to the pump. So, to get over this, the stator is allowed to free-wheel in the same direction as the fluid striking it, which minimises the interference as the liquid passes.

MAXIMUM EFFICIENCY

Automatic transmission has traditionally been less economic, from a fuel consumption point of view, than the manual equivalent. At the root of this problem is the fluid link and the inevitable slippage it causes. The fact that the engine-driven pump rotor is always inclined to spin faster than the turbine rotor which drives the gearbox, means that power and therefore, fuel, will always be wasted.

But it's not all doom and gloom thanks to some bright spark who came up with the idea of fitting a lock-up clutch between the torque converter's pump and turbine rotors. This locks the two together once the speeds of the rotors has equalised, and provides what's effectively direct drive, as in a manual car. Of course, this system only cuts in at certain times and so, although it's made the economics of owning an auto 'box much better, there is still a price to be paid at the pump.

Next month, in the final part of this series, we'll be peering into the inner workings of the automatic gearbox – an intricate and complicated world of planetary gears, brake bands and hydraulically-operated clutches.

Next Month
Auto and CVT transmissions

TECHNICAL TOPIC: *Auto maintenance*

As I'm sure you've gathered from what's been discussed in this episode already, automatic transmission is a complicated business. Fault diagnosis on a modern, electronically-controlled 'box is way beyond DIY level, requiring specialist diagnostic equipment and considerable deductive skills. Even the older-style transmissions, on cars from the 1970s and '80s, represent a significant challenge for all but the most experienced technician.

With such thoughts in mind, vehicle designers have worked tirelessly to reduce maintenance requirments and so, nowadays, state-of-the-art auto transmissions are virtually 'fit and forget' items. In many respects this is just as well because the potential for getting things wrong is enormous. Talk about opening up a can or worms! Delving inside even the simplest automatic gearbox has the potential to turn into the sort of job you wish you'd never started. So, in all honestly, the best advice is to leave well alone, and to restrict your interest to external matters only.

On older 'boxes just about all you can hope to do is check and top up the transmission fluid and adjust the kickdown cable. On newer stuff, forget it and call in the professionals! To be honest, most workshops these days will recommend a new or exchange gearbox at the first sign of trouble. It's simply not worth their getting involved in the complicated nuts and bolts of a stripdown and repair.

Unfortunately, costs are likely to be high whichever way the problems are tackled. To illustrate the point I remember a fault I had with a Senator 3.0 24v I ran a few years ago. It developed a strange knocking sound under acceleration and one specialist's opinion pointed towards a problem with the auto 'box. I was quoted about £6,000 as the replacement cost of a new 'box from Germany! I loved the car dearly but, with 160,000+ miles on the clock and a resale value of perhaps just a couple of grand, the maths didn't add up. Fortunately, the problem turned out to be nothing more serious than a dried out wheel bearing (caused by the exhaust pipe), and cost me £125 to put right!

(1) The procedure varies when checking automatic gearbox oil levels. Always refer to the workshop manual for the correct method. In most cases the oil will have to be dipped with the gearbox up to normal operating termperature. Once again, the procedure for achieving this can vary. Often it will be necessary to run the selector lever through each of its positions, pausing in each one to allow the gearbox to engage. Take your time with this.

(2) It may sound ridiculously obvious, but make sure that you are working with the correct dip stick when checking the gearbox oil level. Don't get confused and spend time taking readings from the engine oil dipstick!

(3) Dipstick design varies from car to car. A clear explanation will be contained in the workshop manual so you'll know exactly what you're supposed to be looking for. In some cases you'll find markings for levels taken with the gearbox both hot or cold. Don't get these two muddled. Measurements taken with the gearbox cold can appear falsely high simply because the contents of the torque convertor will have drained back into the 'box itself. The danger then is that the well-intentioned owner may withdraw oil to bring it back to what appears to be the correct level. However, when the engine is next started most of what's left will be sucked straight into the torque convertor, leaving the gearbox itself woefully short. A lot of gearboxes are sealed for life nowadays and so, thankfully, this is becoming less and less of an issue.

(4) Low oil level in the gearbox will affect the way the drive is taken up, usually delaying the point at which the gear is engaged and causing a more violent uptake of power. When cleaning the dipstick make sure that you use a lint-free cloth. The last thing you want is to transfer small pieces of material into the gearbox.

(5) Be careful to specify the correct transmission fluid for the gearbox you are working on. Never simply assume you know which should be used. Always check to be sure. In a lot of cases the fluid will have to be added down through the dipstick tube, which can be both fiddly and slow. If you can't get hold of a convenient 'squeezy'-type bottle like this one (complete with small nozzle), you'll have to make do with a suitably sized plastic funnel. Make sure it's spotlessly clean before use.

(6) On older automatic gearboxes the 'kick-down' mechanism (which drops the 'box to a lower ratio to enhance hard acceleration for overtaking etc.) is controlled by a cable linked to the throttle pedal. The mechanism is activated by pressing the pedal to the floor and so correct adjustment is essential. If kickdown isn't working then cable adjustment should be the first port of call.

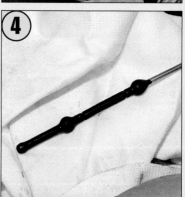

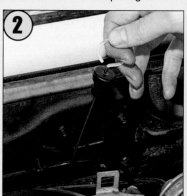

Back to Basics

Part 23:
Chris Graham concludes this series with auto transmission.

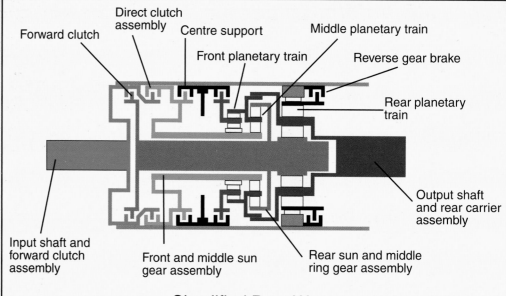

Simplified Borg Warner auto transmission

Direct clutch assembly — *Centre support* — *Middle planetary train* — *Forward clutch* — *Front planetary train* — *Reverse gear brake* — *Rear planetary train* — *Output shaft and rear carrier assembly* — *Rear sun and middle ring gear assembly* — *Front and middle sun gear assembly* — *Input shaft and forward clutch assembly*

I thought we'd end this series on a classical note, with a touch of Greek mythology. Legend has it that Pandora, sent by the Gods as a punishment for mankind, grew painfully curious about a mysterious box she'd been given. Although she'd been warned never to open it, curiosity eventually got the better of her and she peeked inside. The moment the lid was lifted all hell was let loose, literally. Out rushed the ills of humanity – sickness, suffering, hatred, jealousy and greed. Today, of course, Pandora's box is a euphemism commonly used to describe anything that's awkward or difficult to deal with. So how appropriate then to apply it to the automatic gearbox, which must surely be one of the most complicated and technically involved automotive components around.

I set out on this feature intending to present a pithy explanation of how an auto transmission works, but I've rapidly reached the conclusion that that simply isn't possible in the space available. The sheer operational complexity of these units – even old-fashioned examples from the 1960s – precludes any sort of meaningful simplification without the aid of a Disney-style animation, and I'm afraid my iMac just isn't up to the job! But what I can do is run through some of the basic principles to give you an idea about what's going on inside these highly complex devices.

GEARED FOR ACTION

There's a fundamental difference between the contents of a manual gearbox and what you find inside an auto version. As we've seen previously in this series, a manual transmission is based around differently sized gear wheels which are mounted solidly on metal shafts. The shafts slide to and fro in response to movements of the gear lever, and the gears interact together to provide the various ratios. Things work rather differently with an automatic transmission. Take one apart and you'll find it relies on what are called planetary gear trains (see diagram). Instead of gear wheels running on shafts, planetary gears operate in a rotary manner, with a central sun wheel being orbited by a number of planet wheels (held on a carrier) which, in turn, run within an internally-toother ring gear or annulus. These wheels are known collectively as epicyclic gears. If you think back to the hours we all spent playing with that clever drawing toy, the Spirograph, you'll get some idea of the principles involved here.

The key to achieving different gear speeds from a planetary gear train lies in the ability to prevent one or more of the components rotating. The real beauty of the system is that any one of the three main components (sun wheel, planet wheel assembly or ring gear) can be set up to be either the power input or output. The flexibility this creates allows different rotational output speeds to be obtained from the same input and, thus, gears can be selected. Unfortunately, once again, things aren't quite as simple as this. A single planetary gear train isn't enough to create a transmission offering four forward gears and one reverse. To get this desirable combination requires that a pair of gear trains are married up, which is when things start to get really complicated!

Obviously, the success of the whole system rests on the efficient control of the rotational movement within the 'box, and this is achieved using a set of special brakes and clutches which lock the various components at the correct time. Control for this comes from a complex system of hydraulically-operated valves.

FANTASTIC FLUID

The fluid needed to pressurise the hydraulic system is the same fluid which lubricates the rest of the gearbox and is used inside the torque converter. It's a pretty special brew. A single pump, which takes its power from the torque converter, and so runs whenever the engine does, provides the high pressure necessary to operate the system. As you will appreciate,

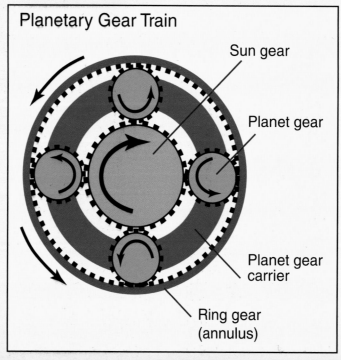

Planetary Gear Train

Sun gear — *Planet gear* — *Planet gear carrier* — *Ring gear (annulus)*

the fluid's role is vital and so it's essential that the correct specification is used. It has to be multifunctional, and resistant to the high temperatures generated, particularly when the car is being driven in heavy, stop/start traffic.

Incidentally, the fact that the hydraulic pump is powered by the torque converter is the reason why automatic cars cannot be bump started. Without the pump running there is no fluid pressure generated and so none of the brake or clutch systems within the gearbox operate. Without these the 'box simply runs in neutral.

A typical automatic gearbox will be fitted with a number of multi-disc clutches and brake bands. The clutches (with various types of friction coating) are used to provide the adjustable link between the main input shaft (transmitting rotational power from the engine) and the gear trains. Whereas the brake bands are employed to act on the gear trains themselves, holding whichever part is necessary at the time. The brake bands are literally just that – circular strips of spring steel lined with a friction material. The band is pinched tight around the component being braked, and this closing action is governed by a hydraulically-operated servo actuator. They are applied by hydraulic action, and released by a corresponding reduction in pressure.

However, brake bands, by their very nature, are heavy beasts. So, in a bid to save weight and space, some manufacturers have switched away from them in favour of clutches for both roles. The other benefit of this change is that the maintenance requirements for the gearbox are reduced. The friction coatings on the brake bands inevitably wear and the bands have to be adjusted accordingly.

KEEPING CONTROL

The hydraulic system on even the simplest automatic gearbox is a necessarily complicated one. A range of valve types is used, most of which are grouped together in the valve box, which also contains an absolute labyrinth of cast passageways down which the fluid is routed. But there are four valves of particular importance which are worthy of a mention here. The first is called the **manual valve**. This is operated by the gear

selector lever inside the car (controlled by the driver). When the lever is used to select 'N' or 'P', the manual valve shuts off the operating fluid circuits so that no pressure reaches the brakes/clutches. In all other lever positions, the valve directs fluid pressure down the appropriate lines to activate brakes/clutches, and prevents it from flowing down others so that inappropriate gears cannot be selected.

The **primary regulator valve** is included to control the pressure of the fluid being delivered throughout the system. This is another vital role because too much pressure wastes energy and can cause all sorts of operational problems. It is also responsible for sending fluid, at a reduced pressure, to the torque converter, around the lubricating channels and off to the oil cooler (if one is fitted).

Another important player is the **governor valve**, which is actually fitted to the gearbox's output shaft. It receives fluid at full pressure from the system, but then adjusts this before redirecting it off to the various shift valves (which directly control clutch and brake operation). Pressure regulation is determined by the speed at which the valve is being spun by the output shaft, and it rises as vehicle speed increases.

KICKDOWN CONTROL

The last of the quartet is the **throttle valve**, which helps to control system fluid pressure in relation to throttle setting. Under light throttle, or when the engine is at idle, the valve exerts next to no fluid pressure. But, at the other extreme, when the throttle pedal is floored by the driver, the valve acts to send high pressure fluid to operate the 'kickdown' function, which causes the gearbox to change down one gear to enhance acceleration for overtaking.

The shift valves, which directly control brake and clutch operation, have fluid inputs from both the governor and the throttle valves, and it's the pressure difference between these two sources which drives the spring-loaded plunger inside each valve. It's a kind of balancing act where gear changes are determined by the speed of the car and the throttle position. An added subtlety of the system ensures that, under hard acceleration,

1st gear

2nd gear

3rd gear

4th gear

Reverse

| | Input | | Held |
| | Output | | Joined |

the change-up points occur higher up the rev range than under more gentle driving. Individual shift valves are set to work at different pressures, so that they operate one at a time.

Of course, nowadays we're into the age of electronic control, and the shift valves are operated in response to electronic rather than mechanical sensing. An electronic control module (ECM), that's usually a separate unit from the vehicle's engine management ECM, marshals information from an array of sensors around the vehicle. Solenoids are then used to switch the shift valves when

required. The degree of sophistication of these systems is now very impressive, with the best of them able to 'think' about and account for aspects such as vehicle body roll, wheel spin and vehicle skidding. Many also offer different operating modes to the driver, so that performance can be adjusted to suit sporty driving styles or bad weather conditions.

GOOD RELIABILITY?

There is little doubt that automatic transmission is now

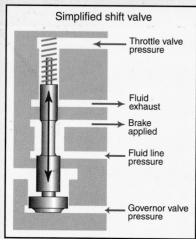

Simplified shift valve

- Throttle valve pressure
- Fluid exhaust
- Brake applied
- Fluid line pressure
- Governor valve pressure

better than it's ever been, in every respect. The levels of operational flexibility, durability and general efficiency offered by a state-of-the-art auto 'box can leave you gasping. Gone, thankfully, are the days of the power-sapping, gas-guzzling, harsh-changing units which used to delight in switching gears at the most inopportune moments. Now we have crisp, efficient performers which, thanks to electronic control, are able to work effortlessly and almost unnoticed under all driving conditions.

There is a downside, though. The very electronics which offer such advantages in operational performance are, at the same time, an ever-present Achilles' heal for most systems. There remain question marks over long-term durability, particularly considering the harsh environment in which most gearboxes are forced to exist. Water ingress, dirt or oil contamination and electrical interference can all play havoc with the sensitive electronics involved.

There have been instances where something as simple as an engine misfire has been sufficient to register as a gearbox problem. The sensors within the transmission system picked up the electrical jolt caused by the misfire, and misinterpreted it as a problem within the gearbox. Not wishing to take any chances, the gearbox ECM throws the whole system into its self-protecting 'limp-home' mode which dramatically reduces overall performance but allows the car to be driven. Typically this will limit the driver to just one forward gear and reverse.

SILKY SMOOTH

The one snag with the automatic gearbox, or a manual one come to that, is that it's limited to a fixed number of gears. Consequently, however good the driver or the electronic control system, the chances are that the 'box will get caught in the wrong gear every now and again. In an ideal world our cars would have an infinite number of gear ratios so that, whatever the road conditions,

there'd always be a gear to match the requirements. Well, it turns out that this is more or less possible, thanks to a system known as CVT – continuously variable transmission.

It's not a new idea, with some of the first development work into variable transmission being done in America as long ago as the late 1800s. However, it wasn't until the late 1950s that a Dutch doctor, named H van Doorne, brought the idea to life with his Variomatic system. It was used by Daf for a number of years, giving rise to many cruel jokes about elastic bands. But, teasing aside, the basic idea was a good one. Volvo certainly thought so because, back in the 1970s it splashed out to buy Daf so it could get its hands on the technology. Since then Ford and Nissan have both dabbled with the idea, and Audi currently offers versions of its A6 equipped with the latest system, branded Multitronic.

It's now claimed that a good CVT unit will better a conventional automatic transmission in terms of fuel economy, as well as being more comfortable and relaxing to use. But how does it work? Well, yes, you've guessed it, it's another pretty complicated beast! At its heart is a strong belt – these days made of shaped

metal sections – which runs between pairs of pulleys. The basic principle is rather like the gearing on a bicycle, in that the diameter of the gear wheels around which the chain runs alters as different gears are selected. But the crucial difference with CVT is that there are only two fixed ratios – the highest and the lowest. Everything in between is infinitely variable, hence the tremendous operational flexibility.

SLIDING PULLEYS

The really clever bit is the way the gear ratios are altered. It's probably best to explain the idea by looking at the early system used by Volvo. The pairs of pulleys are tapered (see diagram) so that a V-section is formed between them into which the shaped drive belt sits. Then, to alter the circumference around which the belt is forced to run, the space between the pair is altered by a sliding action.

One of the pulley pairs is called the primary unit and this is the one that's connected to the propshaft and takes its drive from the engine, via an automatic clutch. The other pulley pair, known as the secondary unit, is linked to drive shafts via fixed reduction gear wheels and transmits drive to the wheels. The spacing between the primary unit pulleys, and hence the operating circumference, is

controlled by the position [of] centrifugal weights inside t[he] fixed pulley. At rest these weigh[ts] ensure that the two pulleys a[re] at their widest spacing, setti[ng] the circumference at its smalles[t.] This equates to a low gear rat[io] which is ideal for starting the c[ar] from a standstill.

As the speed builds, th[e] increasing centrifugal forc[e] acting on the weights cause[s] them to swing out and thi[s,] thanks to a simple lever actio[n,] slides the outer pulley towar[d] the inner one, closing the ga[p.] This squeezes the drive belt o[ut] further from the centre [of] rotation, effectively increasi[ng] the gear ratio to suit the high[er] vehicle speed.

However, this is only half th[e] story because, as the belt is [of] fixed length and can't b[e] stretched (for obvious reasons[)] compensation for the primar[y] unit's change in 'size' has to b[e] made at the secondary pulle[y] assembly. As the workin[g] circumference of the primar[y] increases so the secondary mus[t] be correspondingly reduced. [A] hefty return spring holds th[e] secondary pulleys together [in] their resting state, but [is] compressed to allow the pulley[s] to be separated as spee[d] increases and the primary pa[ir] closes up. It's a very neat solutio[n] to a tricky problem, and a suitab[le] fitting note on which to draw thi[s] series to a close.

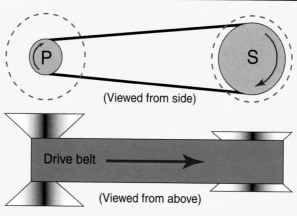

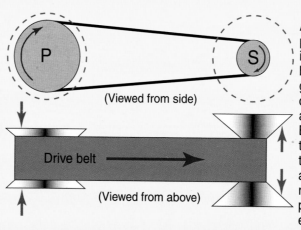

Basic CVT principle

Low speed

When starting from rest the Primary unit (P) is 'open' so that the drive belt sits close to the centre of rotation. The Secondary unit (S) adopts the opposite stance. The return spring holds the pair of pulleys close together so the belt is forced to run around a large circumference. This set-up represents a low gear ratio.

(Viewed from side)

Drive belt →

(Viewed from above)

High speed

At high speed the relative positions are reversed. Weights in the Primary unit are thrown out by the rotation, and cause the gap between the two pulleys to close, forcing the belt to run around a larger diameter. Because the belt cannot stretch, the increased tension overcomes the Secondary unit's return spring and forces the pulleys apart. This represents a high ratio. The positions between these two extremes are infinitely variable.

(Viewed from side)

Drive belt →

(Viewed from above)